REA FR...
O...
ITS WEAPONS
ITS OUTCOME

Spy Satellites
Nuclear Weapons
Ballistic Missiles
Submarine-Launched Ballistic Missiles
Strategic Cruise Missiles
Mega-Artillery
Human Warriors on the Battlefield of Outer Space
Spy Planes
Stealth Aircraft
Airborne Command and Control
Communications
Secret Naval Vessels
Unorthodox Weapons
Nuclear-Powered Vehicles
Star Wars

Secret Weapons of the Cold War

BILL YENNE is the author of more than two dozen books on the military, aviation and space-related topics including *Secret Weapons of WWII*. He lives in San Francisco.

SECRET WEAPONS OF THE COLD WAR

BILL YENNE

BERKLEY BOOKS, NEW YORK

THE BERKLEY PUBLISHING GROUP
Published by the Penguin Group
Penguin Group (USA) Inc.
375 Hudson Street, New York, New York 10014, USA
Penguin Group (Canada), 10 Alcorn Avenue, Toronto, Ontario M4V 3B2, Canada
(a division of Pearson Penguin Canada Inc.)
Penguin Books Ltd., 80 Strand, London WC2R 0RL, England
Penguin Group Ireland, 25 St. Stephen's Green, Dublin 2, Ireland (a division of Penguin Books Ltd.)
Penguin Group (Australia), 250 Camberwell Road, Camberwell, Victoria 3124, Australia
(a division of Pearson Australia Group Pty. Ltd.)
Penguin Books India Pvt. Ltd., 11 Community Centre, Panchsheel Park, New Delhi—110 017, India
Penguin Group (NZ), Cnr. Airborne and Rosedale Roads, Albany, Auckland 1310, New Zealand
(a division of Pearson New Zealand Ltd.)
Penguin Books (South Africa) (Pty.) Ltd., 24 Sturdee Avenue, Rosebank, Johannesburg 2196,
South Africa

Penguin Books Ltd., Registered Offices: 80 Strand, London WC2R 0RL, England

SECRET WEAPONS OF THE COLD WAR

A Berkley Book / published by arrangement with the author

PRINTING HISTORY
Berkley edition / March 2005

Copyright © 2005 by Bill Yenne.
Interior text design by Stacy Irwin.

ISBN: 0-425-20149-X

BERKLEY®
Berkley Books are published by The Berkley Publishing Group,
a division of Penguin Group (USA) Inc.,
375 Hudson Street, New York, New York 10014.
BERKLEY is a registered trademark of Penguin Group (USA) Inc.
The "B" design is a trademark belonging to Penguin Group (USA) Inc.

PRINTED IN THE UNITED STATES OF AMERICA

10 9 8 7 6 5 4 3 2 1

Table of Contents

INTRODUCTION

DURING THE LONG, DARK DECADES OF THE COLD WAR, LIVES would have been risked, taken or lost to learn much of the information that we have brought together in this volume. These weapons include the "silver bullets" and the "aces in the hole" with which one of the two superpowers would have used to checkmate the opposite side if or *when* the Cold War turned hot.

The weapons and hardware described herein were developed behind cloaks of both secrecy and urgency during a time when their creators imagined that total war could, and indeed probably *would*, occur at any moment and without warning.

The end of the Cold War has resulted in the declassification of documents, programs and weapons that would probably have remained secret indefinitely had the Cold War not ended. Many American weapons—and we have no idea how many—were so secret and compartmentalized during the Cold War that they remained unknown even after the Cold War ended. In some cases, secret programs were so secret, and those involved so thoroughly sworn to secrecy, that nearly all traces of these programs have disappeared.

So little was known in the West about Soviet weapons that even the spies had to guess. With Soviet nuclear ballistic missiles, for example, nearly everything that was known was gleaned from the occasional parades in Moscow's Red Square or from tracking the trajectory of their test launches.

Soviet equipment remained so secret that Western intelligence often did not even know the official names and designations of much of it. This led to the practice by the North Atlantic Treaty Organization (NATO) of assigning its own series of code names to Soviet hardware. For example, ballistic missiles were given code names beginning with B, fighters were given names beginning with F, and so on. Submarines were given such class names as November, Golf and Yankee. These code names are mentioned when applicable herein.

The history of the Cold War may have been filled with stories and scandals involving security leaks and disclosed secrets, but it is also filled with amazing instances of secrets that remained secrets for long periods of time and are known now only because they were deliberately disclosed.

Take, for example, the case of the Tacit Blue, which is described in detail in Chapter 10. Tacit Blue is one of many "black" programs that would probably still be secret had it not been deliberately revealed. This large airplane was conceived in 1978 and flown 135 times between 1982 and 1985, yet its existence was never even hinted at by the popular press. Tacit Blue was kept completely under wraps for eighteen years until the U.S. Air Force deliberately decided to unveil it in 1996.

The existence of many other weapons was known to the general public during the Cold War, but the details about them were closely guarded secrets until the decade following the end of the Cold War.

Some of the weapons in this book were, and are, so terrible that their value lay only in the threat of their use. An exchange of thermonuclear weapons, for example, had, and has, the potential to disastrously alter the course of civilization. Others range from the hellishly destructive to the extraordinarily innovative to the truly bizarre. Most of the weapons included are from the military arsenals of the superpowers, but a number of them were designed for high-tech espionage.

Here, then, is an overview of many of the Cold War's most closely guarded weapons. These are the weapons for whose secrets men and women from both sides of the Iron Curtain once risked their lives.

CHAPTER 1

What Was the Cold War?

WEAPONS OF ANY ERA MUST BE UNDERSTOOD AGAINST THE backdrop of the times in which they were developed and/or deployed. To understand the weaponry and hardware of a war or conflict, it is useful, even necessary, to understand the history and the character of the war itself.

WHAT WAS THE COLD WAR?

Recently, some have taken to referring to the Cold War as "World War III." In fact, it was exactly the opposite of World War III. It was what occurred between the "superpowers"—the Soviet Union and the United States—in lieu of World War III.

Webster's dictionary defines a *cold war* as "a state of political tension that stops short of actual full-scale war." The element of tension inherent in cold wars flows from the fear that they might turn hot at any moment. In the case of this twentieth century Cold War, the fear and tension were underscored by the presence of immense arsenals of nuclear weapons.

There have been many other examples of cold wars throughout history. From the end of the Hundred Years' War in 1453 until Waterloo in 1815, the relationship between England and France can be described as an almost perpetual cold war, one that occasionally boiled over into brief and bloody battles and geographically limited hot wars of a few years' duration. So too was the Cold War between the Soviet Union and the United States punctuated by a series of smaller "brushfire" wars and larger conflicts in Korea, Vietnam and Afghanistan. In each of these, the forces of one superpower battled forces that had received supplies and advice from the opposite superpower.

WHEN WAS THE COLD WAR?

In hot wars, there are usually clearly defined attacks and defeats, declarations and armistices, as well as beginnings and ends. Because the Cold War was a "state of political tension," there is no convenient start and conclusion. The first signs of that tension could be seen as early as 1945, even before the end of World War II. However, the date from which the battle lines were clearly defined is probably best pegged to June 24, 1948, the date that the Soviet Union initiated the Berlin Blockade.

A specific date for the end of the Cold War can be placed as early as November 9, 1989, when East Germans began crossing the Berlin Wall and destroying large segments of it without any interference from East German border guards. Certainly the Cold War was officially over two years later on Christmas Eve in 1991, when the red, hammer-and-sickle flag of the Soviet Union was hauled down from above the Kremlin in Moscow for the last time.

The Comintern and the Godfather of the Cold War

To understand the Cold War, it is necessary to understand the motives of those who created it.

Just as Adolf Hitler was the man most responsible for lighting the bonfire that became World War II, the godfather of the Cold War was the man born Josef Vissarionovich Djugashvill.

This man, accountable for the violent deaths of more human beings than any other person in modern—and possibly all—history, was born at Gori in Georgia—the Georgia that was then part of the Russian Empire—on December 21,

1879, the son of a failed shoemaker who physically abused him. After his father's death in 1890, Josef's mother forced him into a seminary, but he quit in 1901 to join the underground opposition to Russia's Tsar Nicholas II. In 1903, the young revolutionary joined the Bolshevik Party of Vladimir Ilyich Ulyanov—a one-time attorney who called himself "Lenin." Josef spent the next dozen years organizing strikes, clubbing opponents, staging robberies and fomenting antigovernment violence in Georgia as well as in Russia. In 1912, at the time Lenin made him a member of their Bolshevik Central Committee, Josef took the name Stalin, meaning "man of steel."

As Josef Stalin, he took part in the 1917 Russian Revolution, in which the Bolsheviks overthrew the tsar, and he eventually became general secretary of the Central Committee. Stalin's position in the new scheme of things gave him the control of the apparatus of the Bolshevik Party— soon to become the Communist Party—that would ultimately give him the total power he so craved.

The Communist Party was not yet that great monolithic organization that it would later become. At the time, it was just one of many socialist organizations that existed around the world. Lenin, Stalin and their compatriots were nevertheless determined that their Communist Party would be the leading voice of what was characterized as the world socialist movement. They could envision their monolith arising from the myriad squabbling socialist groups.

In 1919, Lenin, Stalin and their fellow travelers had formed the Communist International (Comintern) to claim the leadership of the global socialist movement and to establish Moscow as its center. The policy of Comintern was to create Communist parties around the world, and to use them to foment the overthrow of all noncommunist governments. In turn, all of the global communist governments would be rigidly controlled from the center—Moscow. The Soviet Communist Party was no longer intended to be the leading voice, but the only voice.

Though the Comintern was advertised and disguised as an international organization, it would be unyieldingly controlled by the Soviet Union. All power would flow from the monolith at the center.

Communism proclaimed an end to private property, in which all property would be taken from its owners and given not to the masses (as often preached) but to the state. Centralized control was an essential component of Communist Party doctrine and of the Comintern.

In 1922, Lenin and Stalin formally created the Union of Soviet Socialist Republics, or Soviet Union, by transforming the tsar's former Russian Empire into a new Communist empire. The tsar's former colonies all remained—as de facto colonies of the Soviet Union. Instead of freeing the nations of Central Asia that had been part of the tsar's empire, the Communist Party merely incorporated Armenia, Azerbaijan, Georgia, Kazakhstan, Kyrgyzstan, Moldavia, Tajikistan, Turkmenistan, Ukraine and Uzbekistan into the Soviet Union. Along with Russia and Byelorussia (White Russia), they all became Soviet Socialist Republics.

What was done with these nations served as a template for what the Comintern intended to perpetuate around the world.

When Lenin died in 1924, Stalin became the supreme leader of the party and of the Soviet Union. During the 1920s and 1930s, he ruled with an iron fist, using his feared secret police, the NKVD (Narodny Kommisariat Vnuternnikh Del, or People's Commissariat for Internal Affairs), to enforce his will. Staunchly refusing to tolerate any internal opposition within the Soviet Union, he arrested, tried and executed well over half of the party's Central Committee and Party Congress. Mass arrests and internal exile—to Siberia—became a dreaded part of life in Stalin's Soviet Union. During the 1930s, he jailed and/or executed as many as 20 million people, mostly Russians.

Meanwhile, under the Comintern, Stalin actively recruited agents and party loyalists for the goal of toppling governments around the world, from the capitalist United States to the colonial powers of Europe.

Stalin derided all forms of noncommunist government, but he held a special animosity for Hitler and Nazism. Nevertheless, in August 1939, Stalin signed a nonaggression pact with Hitler. Much to the surprise of socialists around the world, Hitler and Stalin were in bed together. Less than two weeks later, Hitler invaded Poland and World War II began. Under the pact, Stalin agreed not to intervene to stop Hitler's aggression. In return, Hitler permitted Stalin to incorporate about a third of Polish territory into the Soviet Union. A secret corollary to the Hitler-Stalin pact allowed for the independent Baltic nations of Estonia, Latvia, and Lithuania to be absorbed into the Soviet Union as Soviet Socialist Republics. They would remain as such for a half century. Ironically, it was a pact with the Nazis that had allowed the Comintern to have its way with three nations that had not been part of the Soviet empire when it was created in 1922.

In June 1941, when Hitler turned on Stalin and Germany invaded the Soviet Union, the "man of steel" was caught by surprise. The Germans enjoyed immediate military success, and it was only the severe Russian winter that blunted their drive on Moscow in December 1941. Stalin rallied his people, built the world's largest army and, with the aid of Britain and the United States, defeated Nazi Germany in 1945.

To not offend Britain and the United States, Stalin pragmatically downplayed the Comintern. He had advocated the overthrow of capitalism and the British monarchy for two decades, but now Stalin bit his lip and begged them to help him. As Stalin had crawled into bed with Hitler in 1939, he now put the Comintern aside and happily posed for smiling group portraits with British and American leaders.

As for his own people, who had been brutalized by his secret police throughout the 1930s, Stalin put on a smile, posed for pictures with small children and packaged the war as being on behalf not of the Communist International, but of Mother Russia.

Setting the Stage for the Cold War

By 1944, as the tide of World War II changed, the Soviet armies pushed German forces out of Mother Russia and across the nations of Eastern Europe. Following the Comintern template, the Soviet Union took control of each of the nations from which it had ejected the Germans. Each was occupied by Soviet troops during the last year of the war. With these troops came the NKVD and the Communist Party commissars. Initially, there was some pretense of establishing a multiparty government, but the Communist Party quickly dealt with the opposition by eliminating it.

Within a few years of the end of World War II in 1945, Stalin solidified his grip on all of Eastern Europe. States that emerged from Nazi domination with multiparty governments soon became one-party states. The one party was always the Communist Party. As soon as a communist government loyal to Stalin was installed, all industry was nationalized and the farms were collectivized.

In both Bulgaria and Romania, the monarchies were abolished and one-party rule was established by the end of 1947. In Hungary, the Communist Party received less than 20 percent of the vote in 1945 elections, but eventually controlled the interior ministry and the police. Early in 1948, the communist police arrested leading political figures and forced the prime minister to resign. Hungary became a one-party state in 1949. Like Hungary, Czechoslovakia emerged from World War II with a multiparty government. By February 1948, after Jan Masaryk, the noncommunist foreign minister, died under dubious circumstances, Czechoslovakia became a one-party state.

In Poland, where the German attack had been the catalyst that started World War II, Stalin's campaign for control began even earlier than 1945. During his great purges of the 1930s, Stalin had learned that absolute political control flows from the total elimination of any opposition. In the Soviet Union, Stalin had consolidated his power by literally massacring the upper echelons of the Soviet military's officer corps during the 1930s. He would do the same with the Polish officer corps. In 1943, a mass grave of some 10,000 Polish officers was discovered in the Katyn Forest. The evidence indicated that they had been murdered by the Soviets. Stalin, naturally, blamed the Germans. In 1990, the Russian government finally admitted that the Soviets had murdered the officers.

Throughout World War II, the prewar Polish government continued to do business in exile in London. They expected to go back to Warsaw when the Germans were chased out. In July 1944, however, the Soviet Union established a provisional Polish government loyal to Stalin, and in March 1945, they began arresting Polish leaders loyal to the prewar government. By 1947, Poland was a one-party state, and in 1949, Soviet Marshal Konstantin Rokossovsky was made minister of defense and commander in chief of the Polish army.

Though the consolidation of Soviet power in Eastern Europe would take place mainly during 1947 and 1948, it was clear within a year after World War II where Stalin was headed in his goal to draw an Iron Curtain across the recently liberated continent.

The term Iron Curtain, coined on March 5, 1946, by Britain's wartime Prime Minister Winston Spencer Churchill during a speech in Fulton, Missouri, quickly came into common usage to describe the new political reality that had descended upon Europe in the wake of the war. It was a reality that would shape global politics for the next forty-five years.

"A shadow has fallen upon the scenes so lately lighted by the Allied victory," said Churchill.

> Nobody knows what Soviet Russia and its Communist international organization intends to do in the immediate future, or what are the limits, if any, to their expansive and proselytizing tendencies. . . . From Stettin in the Baltic to Trieste in the Adriatic, an iron curtain has descended across the Continent. Behind that line lie all the capitals of the ancient states of Central and Eastern Europe. Warsaw,

Berlin, Prague, Vienna, Budapest, Belgrade, Bucharest and Sofia, all these famous cities and the populations around them lie in what I must call the Soviet sphere, and all are subject in one form or another, not only to Soviet influence but to a very high and, in many cases, increasing measure of control from Moscow. . . . The Communist parties, which were very small in all these Eastern States of Europe, have been raised to pre-eminence and power far beyond their numbers and are seeking everywhere to obtain totalitarian control.

In June 1947, the United States launched the Marshall Plan, named for Secretary of State George Marshall. This historic effort was designed to feed the starving victims of World War II, and to revive and jump start the economy of war-torn Europe. All of Western Europe, including western Germany, would benefit from the Marshall Plan. The United States offered to extend the Plan to Eastern Europe, but Stalin wouldn't hear of it. He certainly did not want his new puppet states beholden to the United States.

Under a plan adopted at the Yalta Conference in February 1945, Germany was occupied by the victorious Allies that summer. About a quarter of Germany's prewar land area, including Silesia and Pomerania, was cut off and made part of postwar Poland. The rest of Germany was turned into four occupation zones. The United States zone of occupation was in the south, the British zone in the northwest and the French-occupied territory adjacent to the Franco-German border. The Soviet zone was the north-central part of prewar Germany, including Berlin, the capital. The Yalta plan also called for American, British, French and Soviet occupation zones within Berlin. All of these Berlin zones would be surrounded by the Soviet zone of Germany.

The American, British, and French occupiers set about cleaning up vestiges of Naziism and grooming the Western parts of Germany to become a unified, economically viable, democratic nation. Stalin had a completely different idea in mind. He imagined that he would eventually establish a Communist Party–led government in all of Germany. As a start, he set about constructing one in the Soviet zone.

The Cold War Begins

In his consolidation of power in eastern Germany, Stalin was nagged by the presence within his zone of the American, British, and French sectors of Berlin known as West Berlin. The Yalta agreement guaranteed free access by all four powers to Berlin, but Stalin's wartime allies had to travel through his zone to get to West Berlin. Stalin didn't like this, and he insisted that all of Berlin be turned over to Soviet control. The others refused his demand, so Stalin decided to force the issue.

On June 24, 1948, Soviet forces sealed the borders of their zone to road, rail and barge traffic. West Berlin was suddenly isolated. The Cold War had begun.

In Washington, President Harry Truman studied his options. Sending a convoy escorted by troops and tanks was considered and rejected. Truman feared that such a move would lead to a shootout that could escalate into World War III. Furthermore, there were simply not enough American troops left in Europe to support military action. The millions of United States soldiers and the five great American field armies that had defeated Germany three years earlier were gone, replaced by a minuscule constabulary force.

Stalin's position was clear—nothing went in or out of West Berlin until the Allies withdrew and the whole city was his. This included food and fuel for the millions of civilians for which the Allies were responsible. Starvation was imminent. Stalin knew it and expected the outnumbered Allies to back down and pull out.

During World War II, while the United States had built the world's largest navy and air force, the Soviet Union had built the largest land army that the world had ever seen.

With the defeat of the Axis and the end of the war, the United States responded to social and political pressures to "get the boys home" and to return the citizen soldiers to civilian life as fast as they had been mobilized to fight the Axis. The United States demobilized its 16-million-man military, including not just the army but the navy and air force as well. This demobilization, which seemed right and necessary in 1945 and 1946, was not met with a reciprocal demobilization by the Soviet Union. Stalin kept the 25-million-man Red Army largely intact, thus putting any potential opposition to Comintern at a distinct numeric disadvantage.

The solution to the Berlin Blockade came from U.S. Air Force Major general Curtis Emerson LeMay. The wartime commander of the B-29 force in the Pacific that had helped to cripple Japan, LeMay was now commander of the United States Air Forces in Europe (USAFE). His idea was to beat the Blockade by flying over it. He bet that even Stalin would not start shooting down unarmed transports carrying food to starving children. LeMay was right—Stalin would blink first. This would not be the last Cold War confrontation in which the crusty LeMay would keep the Soviet Union at bay.

Using the C-47 transport aircraft at his disposal, LeMay began the Berlin Airlift on June 26 with thirty-two flights carrying mainly 80 tons of medicine and dehydrated foodstuffs. Deliveries on Day 2 jumped up to 295 tons. Gradually, the C-47s were augmented and eventually replaced by a mix of larger C-54s, U.S. Navy R5Ds and British transports. Over the ensuing fifteen months, American and British pilots made 277,000 flights into Berlin from four primary airfields in the western sectors of Germany, carrying almost 2.3 million tons of supplies, including coal, on an around-the-clock basis.

Finally, the Soviet Union admitted defeat, agreeing to lift the blockade on May 12, 1949. The Berlin Airlift operations continued until September 30 while the surface routes gradually reopened and were brought up to capacity.

The Soviet Union had backed down in round one, but Berlin would remain the focal point of Cold War tensions for the next four decades.

War Plans for World War III

Even before the Berlin Blockade had begun, the United States and the United Kingdom had recognized the consequences of a potential conflict in which their drastically demobilized armies would face a full-strength Soviet army in central Europe. Against this backdrop, the United States and United Kingdom decided that it would be prudent to develop contingency plans to wage a defensive war against the Soviet Union, using the resources that were available to gradually prepare for likely combat scenarios.

By the time of Churchill's Iron Curtain speech, the United States government was coming to recognize the potential threat, and contingency plans were being drafted. The first General War Plan for defending Western Europe from a Soviet ground invasion was code-named Pincher, and it was completed in June 1946, three months after Churchill spoke in Fulton, Missouri.

Meanwhile, there was a growing fear that Europe was merely the most obvious of several potential battlegrounds in World War III. Several Operation Pincher corollary plans, completed in 1946, dealt with defending against Soviet offensive action in other possible theaters. War Plan Griddle called for action to secure Turkey against a Soviet invasion because a loss of Turkey would put Soviet armies at the threshold of the Middle East. This was further elaborated upon in War Plan Caldron, which considered military operations to counter a direct Soviet invasion of the Middle East. A related strategy, War Plan Cockspur of December 1946, covered the counterattack against a possible Soviet invasion of Italy. War Plan Broadview dealt with defense of North America against a Soviet invasion.

As they had with Broadview in 1946, Pentagon war planners would continue to seriously study fighting a land war against the Soviet Union in North America. For example, War Plan Deerland, issued in September 1947, laid out plans for the defense against a Soviet invasion of New York and New England by way of Canada.

Just how pessimistic American planners were during the

late 1940s is illustrated in Joint War Plan JWPC-474.1 of May 1947, which discussed a major Soviet invasion of Western Europe and concluded that there could be no realistic defense using the ground troops that were then available. Joint Strategic Plan JSPC-496.1, code-named Broiler, which was completed by the Joint Chiefs of Staff on November 8, 1947, considered the same issue and determined that the only way that the United States could defeat the Soviet Union was through the use of nuclear weapons.

Equally dismal prospects were projected when War Plan Moonrise of August 1947 considered an American reaction to a direct Soviet intervention in the Chinese Civil War.

The general inadequacies of the United States conventional arsenal were apparent, and planners hoped that the contingency plans would not have to be implemented. Gradually, the Joint Chiefs of Staff began preparations of a long-term plan. War Plan JSPG-500 of March 1948, code-named Bushwacker, was the general plan for fighting World War III in or after 1952. Until Bushwacker was fully implemented, a massive nuclear air offensive by the American Strategic Air Command was considered to be the only way to hold the Soviet forces down while the United States undertook the slow process of mobilizing for conventional warfare.

The U.S. Air Force planning for Bushwacker continued to evolve into 1949 via War Plans Fleetwood and Trojan, which set a goal of stockpiling 400 nuclear weapons by January 1953. Much of the evolution of the Strategic Air Command that actually did take place in the 1950s, including the huge build up of B-47 bombers and the development of the B-52, can be understood more clearly in the context of these plans.

Bushwacker was succeeded by War Plan Dropshot (JCS-1920.1) in 1949, which outlined the strategy for a global nuclear and conventional war to be conducted in or after 1957. Dropshot was accompanied by Offtackle, a near-term emergency war plan designed to be activated immediately with the limited resources available in 1949.

All of these plans were developed against the backdrop of a Cold War that nobody assumed would stay cold for long.

The Nature of the Cold War

The Cold War was like a chess game. Moves by one side drew countermoves from the other. The history of the Cold War is told in these moves. As in chess, Stalin won in some moves and lost in others. During 1945–1948, he succeeded in assembling a large portfolio of puppet states in Eastern Europe through a mix of subversion and heavy-handed coercion. At the same time, he also reached toward Greece, Italy and France, but failed.

Though Stalin had been disappointed in Berlin during the winter of 1948–1949, he had also backed a successful communist revolution in China. By October 1949, the communist Chinese had captured all of China—except Taiwan. That island would remain under the control of the former Chinese Nationalist government. Both sides claimed Taiwan, as well as all of the rest of China. This would remain a source of tension throughout the Cold War and beyond.

The United States and the United Kingdom had been caught by surprise with the Berlin Blockade. It was a rude wake-up call. They looked across the Iron Curtain, saw the vast Soviet army, still intact four years after World War II, and compared this to their own paltry constabulary. Had Stalin wanted to launch a military invasion of Western Europe, nothing could have stood in his way.

The countermove to the Soviet threat in Europe was twofold. The United States and United Kingdom would build up their own ground and air forces to defend Western Europe, but at the same time, the nations of Western Europe would also be part of the defense. The umbrella organization for the defense of Western Europe would be a single unified military command. In April 1949, even as the Berlin Airlift was going strong, NATO was established. Though the centerpiece would be the forces of the United States, Canada and the United Kingdom, NATO would also include the armed forces of Belgium, Denmark, France, Iceland, Italy, Luxembourg, the Netherlands, Norway and Portugal. Greece and Turkey joined in 1952, and West Germany (Bundesrepublik Deutschland [BRD]) was added in 1955.

In turn, the Soviet Union countered NATO with an alliance of its own. Created in 1955 by Soviet Premier Nikita Khrushchev—Stalin's successor—it was an agreement by which the signatories agreed to militarily defend the communist empire created by the Soviet Union in the late 1940s. Known as the Warsaw Pact, this coalition included Albania, Bulgaria, Romania, Hungary, Poland, and Czechoslovakia, as well as the Soviet Union and East Germany (Deutsche Demokratische Republik [DDR]).

The Cold War and the Iron Curtain had divided the world. Commentators would come to classify the globe into "Worlds." The First World included the NATO countries and those aligned with them. The Second World was the Soviet Union, China and the Warsaw Pact nations behind the Iron Curtain. There was also a Third World. This was the so-called underdeveloped world, including much of Latin America as well as the nations of Africa and Asia that had once been European colonies but would gradually become independent nations in the two decades after World War II.

Though Europe would remain as the nexus of high anxiety throughout the Cold War, the determined resistance promised by NATO effectively curtailed Soviet mischief along the Iron Curtain for the duration. Stalin had to look elsewhere. Mainly, he and his successors would turn to the Third World.

In January 1950, Stalin was offered an amazing opportunity. United States Secretary of State Dean Acheson made a serious blunder when he announced that he considered Korea to be "outside our defense perimeter." Like Germany, Korea had been divided into occupation zones after World War II. The Soviet Union occupied the north, the United States the south. As with Germany, the United

States had only a handful of troops on the ground. Stalin sensed a golden opportunity.

On June 25, 1950, Soviet-backed North Korean troops invaded the South. They captured nearly all of Korea before the United States managed to turn the tide. The United States led a multinational force under United Nations auspices in a bloody three-year war against North Korean and Communist Chinese troops that ended on a ceasefire line that lay within a few miles of where the war had begun. The direct Soviet involvement in terms of men and materials was far more extensive than was known at the time.

The Korean War was the most intense conventional war that was fought during the Cold War period. The communists would discover that more subtle actions would bear better results. Returning to the old Comintern playbook, they provoked and/or supported insurrections throughout the world—principally the Third World. Through the years, they successfully co-opted revolutions from Cuba to Angola. In Indochina, the revolution against French rule was packaged as nationalism, but executed under the red banner of communism. In 1954, an exhausted France pulled out of Indochina, leaving a divided Vietnam and a communist desire to unite the country under communist rule. They got their way twenty-one years later—but only after the United States invested a decade and 47,355 American lives to stop them.

In most cases, neither the Soviet Union nor the United States used its own personnel in these brushfire battles, but rather, they sent advisors to train, equip and sometimes lead indigenous proxy forces in Third World brushfire wars. In two notable instances, the superpowers used their own regular forces to fight the proxies of the opposite superpower. The United States intervened in Vietnam, and the Soviet Union invaded Afghanistan. Both of these wars lasted a decade, and both were demoralizing failures.

In their own Second World, however, the Soviet Union had used massive conventional invasions to a successful end. Ironically, while it was inciting communist revolutions in the Third World, the Soviet Union was brutally crushing noncommunist revolutions within its own empire. The first came in October 1956, when a noncommunist government declared Hungary neutral and withdrew it from the Warsaw Pact. The Soviet Union launched a massive invasion, spearheaded by tanks, that ruthlessly overpowered the Hungarians and restored Soviet rule.

A dozen years later, Czechoslovakia tried the same approach. In March 1968, under Alexander Dubcek, the nation experienced the so-called Prague Spring, an extensive effort at restoring democracy and personal freedoms. In August, the Soviet armor once again poured into the capital of a puppet state to unmercifully put down a threat to communist rule. Dubcek was arrested and taken to Moscow.

These conflicts aside, the overarching characteristic of the Cold War was the perpetual sense that World War III could occur at any moment. Both superpowers prepared for it and both prepared to defend against it. As their respective nuclear arsenals grew exponentially, the fear of the consequences of World War III grew as well.

When the Cold War Almost Turned Hot

Direct overt confrontation between the superpowers during the Cold War was rare, probably because both sides dreaded that such an action would quickly devolve into World War III and a nuclear Armageddon.

Two of the most notable showdowns occurred during the brief presidency of John F. Kennedy (1961–1963). In both cases, it was a matter of Khrushchev pushing Kennedy to the limit.

The first of these incidents occurred in Berlin, the symbolic centerpoint of the Cold War. East Berlin was hemorrhaging people. Citizens of communist East Germany were using West Berlin as a means to escape to a better life in West Germany. This was a major embarrassment to the Soviet Union.

In August 1961, East Germany and the Soviet Union began sealing the border between the two sectors of Berlin with barbed wire and barricades. A torrent of East Berliners raced to flee, evading checkpoints, jumping barbed wire and escaping into West Berlin in droves. East German and Soviet guards shot as many as they could, but this did not stop the Easterners. Work began immediately on a solid wall 12 feet high and 100 miles long.

As in the case of the Berlin Blockade, the Soviet Union failed to drive NATO out of West Berlin. However, the failure of the United States to do anything to stop construction of the Berlin Wall served to encourage Khrushchev to press forward toward other mischief.

By 1961, Cuba was one of the crown jewels of Khrushchev's empire. Not only was it the Western Hemisphere's first communist state, it successfully survived a counterrevolution at the Bay of Pigs in April 1961. It was far away and hard to supply, but it was just 90 miles from the United States. Having Cuba was, for Khrushchev, like thumbing his nose at the United States. In 1962, he upped the ante, deciding to secretly situate offensive nuclear weapons in Cuba. The arsenal installed in Cuba included RS-12 ballistic missiles (see chapter 4) with sufficient range to target all of the southeastern United States, reaching as far north as Washington, D.C. The reaction by the Kennedy administration to initial reports was one of disbelief, but further reconnaissance led to the irrefutable confirmation.

By mid-October 1962, almost continuous surveillance flights showed that several offensive missile sites were already operational in Cuba. In a televised address on October 22, Kennedy demanded that the weapons be removed, and announced a naval blockade and a quarantine zone around Cuba to prevent further missiles from arriving. Publicly, he threatened a full nuclear retaliation against the Soviet Union itself if any missiles were launched. Privately, he sweetened the deal by offering to withdraw U.S. Army Jupiter missiles then deployed to Turkey.

As with the Berlin Blockade, the Soviet Union backed down. The offensive weapons were removed from Cuba. A

most fearsome catastrophe had been averted, more nar-
rowly than most people at the time could have imagined.

Speaking on the fortieth anniversary of the Cuban Missile Crisis, historian and former Kennedy aide Arthur
Schlesinger said, "This was not only the most dangerous
moment of the Cold War, it was the most dangerous moment in human history. Never before had two contending
powers possessed between them the technical capacity to
blow up the world."

Mutual Assured Destruction

The doctrine of Mutual Assured Destruction, with its appropriate acronym, MAD, was first articulated by Secretary of Defense Robert McNamara during the Kennedy
administration. It implied simply that if it came to the use
of nuclear weapons to fight a World War III between the
Soviet Union and the United States, the side that started it
could be assured that it, too, would be destroyed. MAD
would remain as the guiding principal of American and Soviet strategy under the presidential administrations of Lyndon Johnson, Richard Nixon, Gerald Ford and Jimmy
Carter—as well as under the Soviet premierships of Leonid
Brezhnev, Yuri Andropov and Konstantin Chernenko.

It was not until 1983 that an American president would
articulate a policy that would break the horrible stalemate
of MAD. Ronald Reagan's notion was that the Cold War
should end. He was not alone in observing that the Soviet
Union would not demobilize the threat designed two gen-
erations earlier by Josef Stalin without a demonstration of
strength designed to exhibit that perpetual confrontation
was pointless, and that MAD was *mad*.

On March 23, 1983, when Reagan addressed the United
States on the future of national defense, there had been the
usual calls for cutting back the defense budget. He opened
his remarks by saying that this was "the same kind of talk
that led the democracies to neglect their defenses in the
1930s and invite the tragedy of World War II."

He was referring to the accommodations made with

Hitler in 1938 and 1939 regarding Czechoslovakia that had encouraged the Nazi dictator to launch the offensive that developed into World War II.

Having said that "We must not let that grim chapter of history repeat itself through apathy or neglect," Reagan recalled that his predecessors in the Oval Office had "appeared before you on other occasions to describe the threat posed by Soviet power and have proposed steps to address that threat. But since the advent of nuclear weapons, those steps have been increasingly directed toward deterrence of aggression through the promise of retaliation. This approach to stability through offensive threat has worked. We and our allies have succeeded in preventing nuclear war for more than three decades. In recent months, however, my advisers, including in particular the Joint Chiefs of Staff, have underscored the necessity to break out of a future that relies solely on offensive retaliation for our security."

Reagan then went on to say that he had "become more and more deeply convinced that the human spirit must be capable of rising above dealing with other nations and human beings by threatening their existence. Feeling this way, I believe we must thoroughly examine every opportunity for reducing tensions and for introducing greater stability into the strategic calculus on both sides. One of the most important contributions we can make is, of course, to lower the level of all arms, and particularly nuclear arms."

The president explained that the United States and the Soviet Union were then engaged in negotiations to bring about a mutual reduction of nuclear weapons, and that he was personally committed to this course. However, he added that even with reductions, the superpowers would still have to rely on the specter of retaliation and mutual threat. He then denounced MAD by asking rhetorically, "Wouldn't it be better to save lives than to avenge them? Are we not capable of demonstrating our peaceful intentions by applying all our abilities and our ingenuity to achieving a truly lasting stability?"

To this, he answered, "I think we are. Indeed, we must."

Then, he asked, "What if free people could live secure in the knowledge that their security did not rest upon the threat of instant United States retaliation to deter a Soviet attack, that we could intercept and destroy strategic ballistic missiles before they reached our own soil or that of our allies?"

His answer to this question sent reverberations throughout the world. Reagan proposed the Strategic Defense Initiative (SDI), a United States reliance on MAD, and possibly even end the Cold War itself.

The Beginning of the End

For decades, the overarching weapons-related issue of the Cold War had been nuclear weapons. Beginning in 1983, the principal weapons-related issue became the defense against them through the SDI that is discussed in chapter 16 of this volume.

While the United States officially embraced the SDI, there were many in the world who feared it. In part, this fear flowed from a widespread public misunderstanding of the SDI. The media had used the unfortunate buzz words, Star Wars, to describe it, and this colored it as an offensive, rather than defensive, program.

There was no misunderstanding on the part of the Soviet military. Their fear of the SDI came with an all-too-clear understanding of a system that could potentially negate their nuclear striking power. They did, however, take some comfort from the fact that the international opposition to the SDI denounced the United States for threatening to upset the balance of power inherent in the doctrine of MAD.

The opponents of SDI also ignored the fact that the Soviet Union was, in 1983, the only superpower that actually had a defensive antiballistic missile system in place, and that this system relied on the use of nuclear weapons.

Little did those who opposed the SDI realize that the Soviet Union itself was working on some Star Wars programs of its own, such as the Polyus Skif "battle star."

When Gorbachev assumed the Soviet premiership in 1985, the Soviet Union was in shambles. After nearly seven decades of Five Year Plans, and of trying to make communism work as an economic doctrine, it was clear that it wouldn't work. Gorbachev initiated the doctrine of Perestroika, a decentralization of the Soviet economy. Still, this was not enough. The Soviet Union and the Soviet war machine were crumbling from within. The Soviet economy desperately needed to get out from beneath the crushing demands of a military bound by the requirements of MAD.

The turning point came in October 1986, when Gorbachev and Reagan met face to face at an historic summit conference in Reykjavik, Iceland. To save his economy, Gorbachev proposed extreme mutual cuts in all types of nuclear weapons. Reagan readily agreed.

An historic moment had been reached. However, Gorbachev, trying to appease the Cold Warriors at home, wouldn't leave it at that. He demanded that Reagan and the United States promise never to deploy the national missile defense envisioned by the SDI. Both Gorbachev and his general staff knew that their own missile defense programs lagged far behind the technological capabilities of the United States. If the SDI was successful, it would be a geopolitical checkmate.

Reagan did the last thing that Gorbachev expected. He called the Soviet leader's bluff at Reykjavik, stood up and left the room. The international media interpreted this as Reagan having snatched failure from the jaws of success. However, both Reagan and Gorbachev saw this for what it was—the beginning of the end.

Back to Where It All Started

June 12, 1987, found Ronald Reagan back in the place where the Cold War had started. He stood before the Brandenburg Gate in the western part of the still-divided city of Berlin and glared at the Berlin Wall. His speech was delivered to the people of West Berlin, yet it was also audible by way of loudspeakers to listeners on the east side of the Berlin Wall.

He recalled President John F. Kennedy's visit to this spot in 1963, observing that "We come to Berlin, we American presidents, because it's our duty to speak, in this place, of freedom."

"Behind me stands a wall that encircles the free sectors of this city," Reagan said, paraphrasing Churchill's Iron Curtain speech. "[It is] part of a vast system of barriers that divides the entire continent of Europe. From the Baltic, south, those barriers cut across Germany in a gash of barbed wire, concrete, dog runs, and guard towers. Farther south, there may be no visible, no obvious wall. But there remain armed guards and checkpoints all the same—still a restriction on the right to travel, still an instrument to impose upon ordinary men and women the will of a totalitarian state. Yet it is here in Berlin where the wall emerges most clearly; here, cutting across your city, where the news photo and the television screen have imprinted this brutal division of a continent upon the mind of the world. Standing before the Brandenburg Gate, every man is a German, separated from his fellow men. Every man is a Berliner, forced to look upon a scar."

Just as German President Richard von Weizsacker had said, "The German question is open as long as the Brandenburg Gate is closed," Reagan said that "As long as the gate is closed, as long as this scar of a wall is permitted to stand, it is not the German question alone that remains open, but the question of freedom for all mankind. Yet I do not come here to lament. For I find in Berlin a message of hope, even in the shadow of this wall, a message of triumph."

Reagan went on to recall that in the 1950s, Soviet Premier Khrushchev had predicted, "We will bury you," adding that "In the West today, we see a free world that has achieved a level of prosperity and well-being unprecedented in all human history. In the Communist world, we see failure, technological backwardness, declining standards of health, even want of the most basic kind—too little food. Even today, the Soviet Union still cannot feed itself. After these four decades, then, there stands before the entire world one great and inescapable conclusion: Freedom leads to prosperity. Freedom replaces the ancient hatreds among the nations with comity and peace. Freedom is the victor."

Speaking of Gorbachev, and the tentative steps that he had taken since Reykjavik to reform the Soviet empire, Reagan noted, "We hear much from Moscow about a new policy of reform and openness. Some political prisoners have been released. . . . Some economic enterprises have been permitted to operate with greater freedom from state control. Are these the beginnings of profound changes in the Soviet state? Or are they token gestures, intended to raise false hopes in the West, or to strengthen the Soviet system without changing it?"

Then Reagan redirected his remarks as though he was speaking directly to Gorbachev. "There is one sign the Soviets can make that would be unmistakable, that would advance dramatically the cause of freedom and peace," Reagan explained. "General Secretary Gorbachev, if you seek peace, if you seek prosperity for the Soviet Union and Eastern Europe, if you seek liberalization: Come here to this gate! Mr. Gorbachev, open this gate! *Mr. Gorbachev, tear down this Wall*!"

The End of the Cold War

The Cold War died a strange death.

A little more than two years after Reagan had called for Gorbachev to tear it down, the Berlin Wall did come down. It was torn down, however, not by Gorbachev, nor by force of arms, but by the people whom it had imprisoned for more than a generation.

When the Berlin Wall came down in 1989, and the Soviet Union gradually unraveled through the end of 1991, the world breathed a sigh of relief. Having hung over the heads of the world's population for four decades, the Cold War was over.

From the end of World War II—but especially from the time of the Berlin Blockade of 1948–1949, through the Cuban Missile Crisis of 1962—the threat of a third world war had constantly been the Sword of Damocles of civilization.

The Soviet Union had ended more with a whimper than the terrible bang of the long feared World War III. Within this book are the swords that would have been the agents of that "bang."

Thankfully, cool heads prevailed and Damocles's Sword was finally beaten into a plowshare.

Though new threats were even then crawling from their dank, dark holes in Southwest Asia, the world breathed easier—at least for a moment.

CHAPTER 2

Spy Satellites

INTELLIGENCE GATHERING HAS BEEN A VITAL ASPECT OF waging war since the dawn of human conflict. Just as the level of sophistication of battlefield weapons evolved and improved through time, so too did the technology of military surveillance. During the Cold War, as the utility of other weapons may have been more in the threat of their use than in their actual use, intelligence technology emerged as the cornerstone of the respective arsenals.

As with other weapons in this book, the general public knew that spy satellites existed, but it was not until the end of the Cold War that details emerged. Indeed, the following pages detail data that were so secret during the Cold War that the publication of such pages would have been impossible. People would potentially have killed others to know these data—or to protect them.

Corona

During the Cold War, not even the code name—much less the nuances—of Corona was known outside rarified clandestine circles. It was not until Corona came in from the cold in 1995 that we began to understand how truly vast and far-reaching the United States satellite intelligence program had been.

In 1957, the same year that they launched Sputnik, the

world's first earth-orbiting spacecraft, the Soviets also began Intercontinental Ballistic Missile (ICBM) tests. Monitoring the Soviet ICBMs became "job one" for both the Lockheed U-2 spy plane and Corona project. The program observed and kept tabs on both Soviet and Chinese Medium Range Ballistic Missiles (MRBM), Intermediate Range Ballistic Missile (IRBM) and ICBM bases. However, Corona would accomplish much more.

The Corona program returned detailed images of Soviet aircraft and submarines at their bases, atomic weapon storage installations, command and control installations and air defense missile batteries. Corona monitored the construction and deployment of the Soviet surface and submarine fleet. Corona discovered the Soviet antiballistic missile program and Soviet missile bases outside the Soviet Union, such as in Egypt. Corona was also vital in monitoring Soviet compliance with the Strategic Arms Limitation (SALT) Treaties.

Authorized in February 1958 by President Dwight Eisenhower, Corona was the first operational space-based photo-reconnaissance program. After several failed missions in 1959, the first successful Corona mission was flown in August 1960.

Photo-reconnaissance aircraft had been taking pictures using negative film since World War I. The film was flown back to the base, where it was processed, printed and the prints evaluated. By the mid-1950s, U-2 aircraft were conducting routine photo-reconnaissance overflights of the Soviet Union, but there was a constant fear that a U-2 would be shot down. On May 1, 1960, this happened, touching off an international incident of immense proportions. Even before the loss of this U-2 piloted by Francis Gary Powers, the Corona project was envisioned as a satellite that performed the same mission as the U-2, but it would fly too high to be shot down by conventional antiaircraft artillery.

Like the U-2 program, Corona and its successors would be managed by the Central Intelligence Agency (CIA) and

U.S. Air Force through the technical expertise of the joint
National Reconnaissance Office. President Eisenhower explicitly directed that the former should handle the intelligence aspects of Corona, including evaluation of the
photographs, while the Air Force handled operational aspects such as launch and recovery of the film containers.

As with photo-reconnaissance aircraft, Corona would
take pictures using negative film, and that film would be
processed and printed. Satellites would drop film canisters
into the atmosphere, where they would be snatched in
midair by specially configured transport aircraft operated
by the U.S. Air Force's 6593rd Test Squadron, which was
based at Hickam AFB in Hawaii, located across the runway from Honolulu International Airport. Initially, this
squadron used Fairchild C-119Js, but in 1962, they
switched to Lockheed JC-130Bs. The C-119Js could handle the smaller 200-pound capsules, but the JC-130Bs
could recover the capsules that weighed as much as 3,000
pounds used in the later Corona missions.

This unheralded squadron had begun training for its
mission in 1955 and had served in Europe with Project
Genetrix, which is discussed in chapter 9 of this volume.
By 1958, when the squadron began supporting the Corona
mission, they operated nine aircraft, several of which were
deployed simultaneously on a typical recovery mission.

The recovery mission involved two 34-foot poles and a
20-foot nylon cable suspended beneath the rear cargo door
of the aircraft. The parachutes carrying the film capsules
would be snatched on this trapeze-like contraption, a task
that required incredible precision, impeccable timing and
hours of practice. If the recovery attempt missed—which
was almost never—the aircraft would mark the location for
a helicopter. The capsules were designed to float in the
ocean for a couple of hours.

Corona evolved into a number of other programs, including Argon, Lanyard and Crystal. Details of the latter of
these were still top secret after the Cold War ended.

Most of the spacecraft used within Corona and the subsequent programs were code-named Keyhole, although the Department of Defense used the cover name Discoverer to obscure the Corona program until 1962.

Like the later Keyholes, most of the Corona Keyholes were built by Lockheed Space Systems near San Francisco, California. Initially, they were assembled at Menlo Park, California, but in the 1960s, the whole operation was moved to a new Lockheed facility at nearby Sunnyvale. The remarkable Hubble Space Telescope, which was built by Lockheed at Sunnyvale for NASA in the mid-1980s and launched in 1990, is similar to, and a sister ship of, the later Keyhole satellites.

The operational hardware within the Corona Keyholes included Itek panoramic cameras containing 16,000 feet of Eastman Kodak 70mm strip film that offered resolution down to 35 feet during missions in the 1950s, and 5 feet by 1967.

Thor Agena launch vehicles were used to place the Keyhole spacecraft into orbit during the Corona program. The missions each lasted about ten days, covering 8 million square miles each.

Corona was virtually unknown until after the end of the Cold War. It was officially declassified by President Bill Clinton in a February 1995 executive order, under which nearly a million pieces of intelligence imagery acquired in 145 missions by the Corona program through 1972 were made public. The release specifically did not include imagery taken by the Project Gambit spacecraft and their successors.

Weapons System 117L

The grandfather of Corona, and indeed of all United States Cold War spy satellites, was a supersecret U.S. Air Force program known simply as Weapons System (WS) 117L.

This obscure and seemingly innocuous project was directed at developing orbiting espionage platforms when the first launch of an orbiting satellite was still a half decade in the future. During its critical development phase in the late 1950s, the WS-117L program was managed by Colonel Frederic Oder.

First undertaken in 1953 around the time that the first thermonuclear weapons were exploded, WS-117L evolved out of a desire to solve the technical problems related to space-based reconnaissance for high-priority subjects. It was undertaken against the backdrop of a very real fear that the United States was vulnerable to a surprise attack by the Soviet Union—a thermonuclear Pearl Harbor.

Corona was one of the first spinoffs of WS-117L, but there was much more to it. In fact, WS-117L was not one weapons system, but at least three. These included Corona, as well as Sentry (later known as Satellite and Missile Observation System [SAMOS]) and the Missile Detection Alarm System (MIDAS). The latter were added as the mandate of WS-117L grew beyond photo reconnaissance to include missile detection and early warning. MIDAS, with its infrared sensor systems, was a precursor of the later Defense Support Program (DSP) satellites.

Keyhole/Corona

The supersecret development of the Keyhole satellites used by the Corona program began as part of U.S. Air Force Weapon System 117L. In March 1956, Lockheed Space Systems was awarded the contract to build the actual first Keyhole a year before the world's first satellite had been orbited. When that satellite turned out to be the Soviet Sputnik 1, the urgency of Keyhole was clearly underscored. Of course, when the U-2 flown by Francis Gary Powers was shot down in 1960, Corona and Keyhole went from highly desirable to vitally essential.

In the wake of Sputnik, the United States Department of Defense ordered that WS-117L be expedited. Because of the number of people who would necessarily have to be involved in such a complex project, it was decided that a cover story would be developed. It was decided that the Air Force would announce a "scientific satellite" program called Discoverer. Indeed, while large numbers of Lockheed personnel were building the Keyhole satellites at Menlo Park, each worked on just a small part of the program. Fewer than a half dozen Lockheed employees had the whole overview of the project.

The first Keyhole satellites weighed 1,650 pounds, including their Itek panoramic cameras and their 80 pounds of Kodak 70mm film. They would be launched from Vandenberg AFB in California by the U.S. Air Force using a Thor launch vehicle topped with an Agena upper stage.

The first thirty-eight Corona launches were covered with Discoverer designations. Beginning in 1962, the Corona launches were kept secret and no longer given Discoverer numbers.

After a scrubbed launch attempt in January 1959, the first test launch, designated as Discoverer 1, occurred on February 28. Discoverer 2, launched in April, was the first to carry a film capsule, but the capsule was ejected at the wrong place and lost.

Problems with the Corona system, mainly due to Thor rather than Keyhole, very nearly resulted in the program being cancelled before it really got started. Launched between June 1959 and February 1960, Discover Missions 3 through 10 all suffered launch vehicle malfunctions. Mission 11 in April had a successful launch, but another faulty film capsule ejection. Mission 12, which came sixty days after Powers's U-2 was shot down, saw yet another launch vehicle failure.

A cloud of tension hung over the preparations for Discoverer 13. With U-2 flights now suspended, the Corona program had to work. It was, however, "lucky 13" for Corona. The launch on August 10, 1960, was perfect, and the Keyhole's test capsule—which was not carrying film—was successfully ejected two days later. In keeping with the official cover story, the recovery was publicized as an important scientific accomplishment. In terms of the science of recovering small objects dropped into the Earth's atmosphere from outer space, it really was an important scientific accomplishment.

A week later, on August 18, Discoverer 14 was also a quiet success. It was the first of the Corona missions to successfully return a capsule containing film, and the first in which the film canister was snatched in midair by a C-119. The 16,000 feet of film contained clear images with higher-than-expected resolution that amazed and delighted the CIA analysts.

The second-generation Keyholes were the KH-2s, with their film capsules specially configured to facilitate midair recovery. Weighing 2,500 pounds, the KH-2 series made its debut in an October 1960 launch, and was used in three successful missions. The KH-2 was succeeded by the similar KH-3 series, which flew five successful missions between August 1961 and January 1962.

By the end of 1961, the Corona program had quietly confirmed that the Soviet Union had deployed only about two dozen ICBMs, rather than the nearly 200 that were a subject of concern during the 1960 presidential election campaign. At that time it was perceived that the Soviet Union had the advantage over the United States in terms of ICBM quantity, and this advantage was referred to in the media as the "Missile Gap."

Whereas the first three Keyhole satellite types were fitted with a single camera, the KH-4 series had two: one looking forward, the other aft. The spacecraft were also much larger than earlier Keyholes, ranging from 2,600 pounds in the basic KH-4 to 4,400 pounds in the KH-4A and 6,600 for the KH-4B.

The basic KH-4 was used on twenty successful missions between February 1962 and December 1963, exposing more than 239,000 feet of film. This period of service coincided with the Cuban Missile Crisis of October 1962 and its aftermath. The mission in February 1962, announced as Discoverer 38, was the first Corona mission to provide stereoscopic imagery.

The extensively used KH-4A was the first Keyhole to carry two film capsules. These Keyholes were used in forty-nine successful missions designated with a series numbered in sequence from 1001 through 1052. They took a reported 517,688 useful images, exposing 1.3 million feet of film between August 1963 and October 1969. The KH-4B spacecraft were in service between September 1967 and May 1972, averaging 32,000 feet of film over sixteen successful missions.

Zenit

Though some details of American spy satellites were known before the end of the Cold War, little was known of Soviet spy satellites until very recently. The first such program was the Zenit (Zenith), which was developed at the same time as the Vostok manned spacecraft and with which it shared many features.

The Zenit spacecraft was designed by Sergei Korolev, who had designed Sputnik, the Soviet Union's first successful Earth-orbiting satellite. He began theoretical work on a photo-reconnaissance satellite project in 1956, a year before Sputnik's historic first launch, but it was after Sputnik that Zenit moved into full swing. Because the spacecraft would be roughly similar to Vostok, the two were literally on parallel tracks. They would each have a service module, or mechanical section, and a detachable reentry capsule. The latter would carry an SA-10 film camera in Zenit, a person in Vostok.

Vostok carried its first cosmonaut—Yuri Gagarin—into space more than a year ahead of the first successful Zenit launch. Gagarin's flight came on April 12, 1961, and the first successful Zenit launch came in July 1962 after three failed attempts beginning in December 1961. Nearly two years had passed since the United States had made its first fully operational Keyhole/Corona satellite launch.

With a launch weight of nearly 10,000 pounds, the operational Zenit 2 satellite dwarfed the first Keyhole satellites, which weighed 1,650 pounds. Operationally, however, they were similar. Both exposed and returned photographic film to be recovered on Earth—Keyhole's was snatched out of the air, Zenit parachuted its capsules into Central Asia.

As the Keyhole program was masked as the Discoverer program, the Zenit program used the newly created generic name Kosmos to obscure its real purpose. The Soviet Union knew that the United States was monitoring its launches, so each launch was announced as a Kosmos satellite with a scientific payload. The Kosmos designation was used to cover not only Zenit but literally thousands of various types of spacecraft whose true purpose the Soviets wanted kept secret from the outside world. The United States only used the Discoverer cover designation through 1962. Thereafter, secret missions were simply not announced and the Soviet Union had to guess.

The first successful Zenit 2 deployment was covered as Kosmos 7. Kosmos 9 through 12 were additional launches of Zenit 2 spacecraft in 1962. This was followed by seven launches in 1963, eight apparently successful missions each in 1964 and 1965 and an average of twelve such flights annually between 1966 and 1968. Nearly all of the Zenit 2 missions lasted eight days.

After nine flights in 1969 and three in 1970, the Zenit 2 program was phased out in favor of the improved Zenit 2M satellites. Weighing 7 tons, the Zenit 2Ms were designed to operate for twelve days. In addition to cameras, they carried radiation monitoring equipment that was described as being for "cosmic ray" experiments. The first mission, designated as Kosmos 208, was launched in March 1968, one of three flown by Zenit 2M satellites that year. There were also three in 1969, followed by either nine or ten annually through 1978, except 1975, when eleven were launched. Beginning in 1972, there were at least five missions in which the Zenit 2Ms deployed the smaller Mauka autonomous subsatellites. These then went into an orbit separate from the larger mothership.

While Zenit 2 was on a parallel track with Vostok, it was also on a parallel track with Zenit 4. The two Zenits were essentially identical, but Zenit 2 carried a wide-field camera and Zenit 4 an FTOR-4 high-resolution camera.

The first Zenit 4 launch in November 1963 was designated as Kosmos 22. After three launches in 1964, the Zenit 4 program would average eleven missions annually through 1970, except in 1969, when seventeen Zenit 4s turned their lenses on American targets.

After seven flights in 1979, the Zenit 2M program was terminated in favor of the Zenit 4M family, which was apparently seen as being more versatile.

As had been the case with Zenit 2 and Zenit 4, the Zenit 4M was essentially a Zenit 2M with a high-resolution camera. In this case, the earlier FTOR-4 was succeeded by the improved FTOR-6. The Zenit 4M was also maneuverable, meaning that it could move about to train its camera on a specific target.

Zenit 4M operations began in October 1968 with a mission designated as Kosmos 251. It was clear that the Soviet Union quickly came to depend on the high-resolution imagery provided by the Zenit 4M. After two flights in 1969 and a half dozen in 1970, there were twenty in 1971 and fifteen each in 1972 and 1973.

Gradually, the Zenit 4M was being replaced by an updated sister ship, the Zenit 4MK. The type was first launched in December 1969 as Kosmos 317, but not believed to be fully operational until 1972. Nevertheless, there were three launches in 1970, two in 1971 and three in 1972. The fifteen Zenit 4M launches in 1973 were accompanied by ten of the Zenit 4MK. There were only two Zenit 4M missions in 1974, but fifteen of the Zenit 4MK. By this time, existing stocks of the Zenit 4M hardware had been used or put into mothballs. Meanwhile, the Zenit 4MK averaged more than fifteen launches annually through 1977. It is not known exactly how many can be described as successful.

The Zenit 4M family continued to be improved through the mid- to late 1970s, with the Zenit 4MK gradually superseded by the Zenit 4MKM. First tested in July 1977 as

Kosmos 927, Zenit 4MKM became operational in 1978 after eight test launches in 1977. There were seventeen launches during 1978 and ten in 1979 as it took over from the Zenit 4MK. There were only two launches in 1980 as the program abruptly ended.

As Zenit 4MKM replaced the Zenit 4MK, its development was paralleled by that of the Zenit 4MT. Its hardware was centered around the SA106 topographical camera used for map making. The first test launch in December 1971 was covered as Kosmos 470. After eight test missions through 1975, the program averaged two operational missions annually between 1976 and 1982.

Another member of the Zenit family that evolved during the 1970s was the 4MKT. Described as having an "Earth resources" mission similar to NASA's unclassified Landsat series, the Zenit 4MKT was equipped with the multispectral Priroda 3 camera. Given the fact that launches continued well after the termination of Zenit 4MKM suggests that it had more than Earth resources in its viewfinder.

The Zenit 4MKT was first test launched as Kosmos 771 in September 1975. Two missions were flown annually between 1976 and 1978, and five in 1979. The following year, as Zenit 4MKM flew two missions, Zenit 4MKT flew four. There were three launches annually in 1981 and 1982, but only five total from 1983 through 1985.

The final Zenit satellite was the Zenit 6U. It was similar in size and appearance to the Zenit 4 family, but it was much more maneuverable and versatile. It was also designed to operate for a full two weeks, whereas the Zenit 4 family averaged about twelve days. The first test launch of the Zenit 6U came in November 1976 as Kosmos 867. After three tests in 1977, it became operational with a single mission in 1978. During the early 1980s, Zenit 6U became the true workhorse of the Soviet photo-reconnaissance fleet. The program had nine launches in 1979, but averaged eighteen flights between 1980 and 1983. There were eight Zenit 6U missions in 1984, with the last being launched in June as Kosmos 1573.

By the mid-1980s, however, the digital imaging capabilities of the Yantar satellite series would render Soviet photoreconnaissance satellites using film cameras obsolete.

SAMOS

Like Corona, the Satellite And Missile Observation System, (SAMOS) was a family of United States photoreconnaissance satellites that evolved out of the U.S. Air Force Weapons System 117L program in the late 1950s. With an average weight of more than 4,000 pounds, SAMOS was more than twice as heavy as the early model Keyholes. Because of its weight, SAMOS was launched by the U.S. Air Force's big ICBM-based Atlas launch vehicle.

Unlike Corona, which was declassified in 1995, SAMOS remained top secret past the turn of the century. As such, much less is known about the program. The first six missions, which were flown between October 1960 and March 1962, used a recoverable film capsule system like the Keyholes. Of these, at least one is believed to have gone down within the Soviet Union and to have been recovered.

A second-generation SAMOS, which used a radio relay system to return digital imagery, was used for four missions between April and November 1962. The quality of the imagery was so disappointing, especially in comparison to the outstanding success of Corona, that the SAMOS program was cancelled. Film cameras that had been built for SAMOS, but not yet flown, were diverted for use in Keyholes.

MIDAS

The Missile Detection Alarm System (MIDAS) was one of the three principal spinoff programs from the U.S. Air Force Weapons System 117L project of the 1950s. As the name implies, the primary mission was to provide early warning of Soviet missile launches. The idea was to use the W-17, and later the W-37, infrared sensor to detect the flash from a missile being launched.

MIDAS was undertaken by the Air Force in 1958, and the first successful launch of a MIDAS spacecraft came in May 1960, the same month that the Soviets shot down Francis Gary Powers's U-2 over the Soviet Union. However, this satellite failed shortly after reaching orbit. The MIDAS 3, launched in July 1961, was said to be the first operational MIDAS, but it reportedly had trouble distinguishing solar reflections from missiles.

Though the MIDAS program remains veiled in secrecy, it is known that at least seven MIDAS satellites were orbited between October 1961 and October 1966. The MIDAS spacecraft weighed between 2,300 and 4,400 pounds, and many carried at least one small Environmental Research Satellite (ERS) weighing up to 100 pounds each. The ERS craft were "hitchhiker" satellites built by Thompson Ramo Woolridge (TRW) that were designed to carry a variety of payload types and to deploy from larger satellites after reaching orbit.

The performance of the MIDAS craft reportedly left a great deal to be desired and the program was canceled in favor of going back to the drawing board. Eventually, the MIDAS early warning mission was taken over by the much more successful Defense Support Program (DSP) satellites.

Vela

Just as MIDAS was an early attempt to build a missile early warning satellite, Vela, which means "guardian," was the first United States nuclear explosion detection system. A U.S. Air Force program, the Vela project originated in 1960 with input from NASA, the Atomic Energy Commission (AEC) and the Defense Advanced Research Projects Agency (DARPA), as well as the Air Force's Ballistic Missile Division. Originally code named Vela Hotel, the satellite was merely part of a broader nuclear detection system.

The sensors for the satellite would be built by the AEC's Sandia and Los Alamos Laboratories in New Mexico, while the satellite itself would be built by TRW in Southern California. The Velas were essentially a pair of twenty-sided polyhedrons with sensors on most faces. The satellites stood 4 feet 7 inches tall and weighed between 300 and 500 pounds.

In contrast with the Keyholes and MIDAS, which operated in relatively low orbit, the Vela satellites were in orbit generally between 60,000 and 70,000 miles above the Earth's surface.

Operationally, the Vela satellites were launched in pairs, with the first two sent aloft in October 1963 in time to monitor the 1963 Nuclear Test Ban Treaty. Subsequent Vela dual launches occurred in July 1964 and July 1965. An advanced Vela development program superseded the original Vela series in 1965, and these were first launched in April 1967. Again, it was a pair of satellites launched together on the same day using a pair of Titan 3C boosters.

Additional dual launches occurred May 1969 and April 1970. Composed of a pair of polyhedrons, the peanut-shaped advanced Velas weighed 700 pounds and stood 5 feet tall on the factory floor. The newer craft were capable of detecting both subterranean and atmospheric nuclear explosions. They also took on the secondary task of monitoring solar radiation in conjunction with United States— manned Apollo space missions.

In contrast to the disappointing MIDAS program, Vela worked extremely well. The original Velas operated for more than five years, and the later models all had useful lives of more than a decade. Indeed, they were all still functioning in 1984 when the Vela system was deliberately powered down, and its mission assumed by the DSP.

IMEWS

The Integrated Missile Early Warning Satellites (IMEWS) were a nuclear testing warning satellite that the United States deployed after the successful Vela series, but which operated concurrently with Vela for much of its life. Like Vela, they operated in high orbit, generally between 20,000 and 22,000 miles above the Earth.

Though IMEWS was superseded by the DSP in the 1980s, many of the details of the program were still secret at the turn of the century. The satellites themselves weighed about 1,800 pounds, but little is known about their operational systems. Built by TRW, IMEWS was launched and managed by the U.S. Air Force. The first successful IMEWS deployment came in May 1971, and was followed by launches in March 1972, June 1973 and December 1975.

Keyhole/Argon

The Argon program was essentially a subsidiary to the United States Corona program that flew seven successful missions between February 1961 and August 1964. Argon used the 2,800-pound KH-5 satellite, which was similar to the earlier Keyholes, but which used a single-frame camera rather than a panoramic camera. The KH-5s reportedly exposed 22,503 feet of film, acquiring 38,578 single-frame images of specific targets.

Keyhole/Lanyard

Like the KH-5 Argon, the KH-6 Lanyard project was a spinoff of the successful United States Corona program. As with Argon, the 3,300-pound spacecraft bus was based in the familiar Keyhole configuration, but the KH-6 was fitted with a pair of panoramic cameras that shifted back and forth, each photographing the same subject in order to create stereoscopic, three-dimensional panoramas. The KH-6 Lanyards were fitted with a powerful 66-inch focal-length camera and film canisters containing film that was 4.5 inches wide, twice the 70mm of earlier Keyholes.

One successful mission is known to have been flown in July 1963 with the objective of photographing a Strategic Rocket Forces site in Soviet-occupied Estonia. More than 900 stereoscopic images were taken, but their quality is reported to have been disappointing.

The KH-6 program was terminated after 1963 for reasons that have never been fully explained. The most logical explanation is that the incoming KH-7 Gambit program promised photography with higher resolution.

Keyhole/Gambit

Project Gambit encompassed two Keyhole spacecraft types, both produced for the United States National Reconnaissance Office, and both developed under the technical auspices of the U.S. Air Force Office of Special Projects. Lockheed was the prime contractor for the program, with General Electric constructing the spacecraft "bus" and Eastman Kodak responsible for the film and camera systems.

Still secret a decade past the end of the Cold War, the satellites of Project Gambit carried cameras with a resolution of eighteen inches for early KH-7s and six inches for the "close look" KH-8.

The KH-7's Kodak strip cameras photographed swaths of ground 14 miles wide and nearly 500 miles long. First orbited on July 12, 1963—less than three weeks before the last KH-6 mission—the KH-7 was used for a total of thirty-eight missions, with all but four reported to have been successful. They were tasked principally with photographing Soviet ICBM fields, but in April 1966, they were used to capture images of the Tu-95 bomber base at Dolon in Siberia, as well as the Semipalitinsk nuclear weapons test site. In May 1967, they returned photographs of the secret Soviet missile test areas at Sary Shagan and Kapustin Yar, as well as the big experimental aircraft test center at Ramenskoye near Moscow. Meanwhile, a KH-7 was used to photograph Lop Nur as China was preparing for its first nuclear weapons test there in 1964. For the mid-1960s, these were extraordinary accomplishments for a photo-reconnaissance platform.

The KH-7 Gambits weighed about 4,500 pounds and had an operational life of about a week. The KH-8 Gambits weighed 3.3 tons and were designed to have a life of two months in which to return film in the two independent film capsules with which they were equipped. In practice, some stayed aloft much longer. Both the KH-7 and KH-8 are reported to have flown in very low orbits, with perigees between 75 and 100 miles above the Earth.

The first KH-7 mission was flown in July 1963, followed by four more before the end of the year. There were ten KH-7 missions in 1964, followed by nine in 1965, twelve in 1966 and three in 1967, culminating in a mission launched on June 4 on the eve of the Arab-Israeli Six-Day War.

The KH-8 satellite made its debut in July 1966 and flew three missions that year. There were seven KH-8 flights in 1967, eight in 1968, six in 1969, five in 1970, six in 1971, at least three annually from 1972 through 1974, two annually from 1975 through 1977, one in 1979, possibly none in 1978 and 1980, and one annually between 1981 and 1984. The KH-8s would typically be launched in the early spring and operate through the summer. Operationally, they complemented the larger, higher flying KH-9s, which would go up a few weeks later and operate through the end of the year. The last KH-8 mission is believed to have been launched in April 1984.

In service for nearly two decades, the KH-8s were the longest-serving class of film return photo-reconnaissance satellites used by the United States. They were retired in favor of the decision to switch from film to high-resolution digital photography.

Keyhole/Hexagon (Big Bird)
Project Hexagon came on line while Project Gambit was still operational, and the two operated concurrently and probably cooperatively for more than a decade. Best known by the nickname Big Bird, the KH-9 satellites of Project Hexagon were more than twice the size of the earlier Keyhole satellites. They each weighed 12.5 tons and were launched by the Titan 3C heavy-lift launch vehicle.

Whereas earlier Keyholes carried one or two film capsules, the Big Birds had four. Whereas the life of earlier Keyholes was measured in days or weeks, the KH-9s were designed to serve for nine months or more. This allowed more than one to be on station at all times to provide continuous photo-reconnaissance coverage of areas of interest within the Soviet Union and elsewhere.

Like the Gambit Keyholes, the Hexagon Big Birds carried cameras with a ground resolution measured in inches, and some carried large mapping cameras. Like their predecessors, the Big Birds were built by the Lockheed Missiles & Space Company in Sunnyvale, California.

The first Project Hexagon launch came in June 1971, and there were at least three in 1972 in 1974, four in 1973, two in 1975 and one annually from 1976 though 1984, except 1981, when no KH-9s are known to have been launched. Operationally, the KH-9s complemented the smaller KH-8s that operated at lower altitudes. Both would usually be launched in the spring, with the KH-8 going first. By the beginning of the 1980s, the Big Birds were being complemented by even bigger birds, the digital-imaging KH-11s.

The last KH-9 was launched on April 18, 1986. It is perhaps a coincidence that this mission took place on the 211th anniversary of the first United States early warning mission, the famous midnight ride of Paul Revere.

Defense Support Program

The Defense Support Program (DSP) evolved directly from the IMEWS program and the first five launches of DSP hardware between 1976 and 1982 carried IMEWS series designations. Like IMEWS, they operated in high Earth orbit, usually between 20,000 and 25,000 miles, roughly in the same environment as geosynchronous weather satellites.

Using infrared sensors, DSP combined the nuclear detection mission that had begun with the Vela project with the missile early warning mission that had begun with the trouble-plagued MIDAS project. Weighing about 3,700 pounds and standing 9 feet, 6 inches tall, the DSP satellites (known as DSPS) were each fitted with nuclear detection sensors and a 3.6-meter Schmidt telescope that had a 2,000-element infrared sensing system.

Designed to have a service life of three to five years, the first DSPS was launched as IMEWS 6 in June 1976. Additional launches under IMEWS designators occurred in February 1977, June 1979, March 1981 and March 1982. Later known DSPS launches followed in April and December 1984, with the latter being considered as a backup satellite. The last Cold War launch of the DSP came in November 1987. The DSPS were on station during the 1991 Gulf War and were used to monitor Iraq's launches of Scud missiles against Israel and Saudi Arabia.

Keyhole/Dorian

The numbering sequence of the Keyhole series of United States photo-reconnaissance satellites leads from the photographic film KH-9 to the digital imaging KH-11, passing the KH-10 designator. In fact, the Project Dorian KH-10 is unique among the Keyhole series in that it was the only one not built by Lockheed and the only one that was to have carried a human crew. Built by the Douglas Aircraft Company, the Project Dorian KH-10 is better known as the Manned Orbiting Laboratory (MOL), and it is discussed in chapter 8 of this book.

White Cloud

The White Cloud spacecraft were a series of supersecret ocean-surveillance satellites used by the U.S. Navy to monitor the movement of Soviet ships and submarines. Developed for the Naval Research Laboratory by Martin Marietta Corporation, they were part of the Naval Ocean Surveillance System (NOSS), which monitored radio traffic and radar transmissions using triangulation.

First launched in April 1976, the White Cloud satellites operated in orbits 700 miles above the Earth. As with MIDAS satellites, White Clouds carried small hitchhiker satellites that were deployed after reaching orbit. The White Clouds and their hitchhikers operated in "clouds," or clusters. The last two are believed to have been launched in February 1986 and May 1987.

The White Cloud project was so secret that Naval Research Laboratory personnel were not even permitted to use the word in telephone conversations, that is, until souvenir postal covers with pictures of a White Cloud satellite and Vandenberg AFB postage cancellations showed up for sale at the tourist gift shop in the cafeteria at NASA's Johnson Space Center in October 1984!

Yantar

Before the end of the Cold War, Yantar (Amber) was one of the most heavily guarded secrets in the world. Virtually nothing was known about it outside the Soviet Union.

The Yantar project was the successor program to the Soviet Union's immensely prolific Zenit series of photo-reconnaissance satellites. Yantar operated from the late 1970s through the end of the Cold War—and beyond. These craft would have the mission of conducting photo-reconnaissance flights over the United States and Western Europe, and the secondary mission of providing the Soviet Union with early warning of American ICBM launches. The Minuteman fields of Montana and the Dakotas were Yantar's watchful eye for decades.

While Zenit was based on the Vostok manned spacecraft, Yantar was based on the Soyuz manned capsule. Soyuz spacecraft first carried Soviet cosmonauts into orbit in 1967, and they would still be the principal means by which Russian cosmonauts reached orbit in the twenty-first century. The basic Soyuz "bus" has also been adapted as the uncrewed Progress supply craft that was first used in the 1980s to resupply the Soviet space station Mir.

Like Soyuz, Yantar consisted of a large service module with deployable solar panels and a recoverable reentry capsule. Instead of a two- or three-cosmonaut crew, the capsule contained camera equipment and returnable film capsules. The Yantar spacecraft were over twenty feet long and each had a launch weight of about 7.5 tons. Yantar's operational orbital altitude was generally between 120 and 200 miles.

Zenit was originally designed with a service life of about a week, and late variants extended that to two weeks. On the other hand, Yantar 2K was designed from the outset to operate for a month, and Yantar 1KFT for six to eight weeks. In addition to a longer service life, Yantar was designed to carry twice the film as Zenit, as well as multiple film return capsules. The Zhemchug-4 film camera and the primary computer could also be returned and reused. As with Zenit, the Yantar launches would be announced as Kosmos launches.

The design work on the Yantar project began as early as 1964, and the formal authorization from the Soviet government to go ahead with construction of the system came in 1967. By this time, the Soyuz program had matured to the point where its bus could be adapted for Yantar. The Soyuz flight-control system and on-board computers were also adapted for Yantar, although many components were developed explicitly for Yantar and eventually the two appeared as distinctly different spacecraft.

It was originally hoped that Yantar would be operational by 1969, but numerous hardware and software problems would plague the program, delaying various development milestones. Flight testing of systems intended for the Yantar 2K aboard Zenit satellites began in 1973. The first test launch, designated as Kosmos 697, came in December 1974 after a launch failure in May of that year. After three further tests in 1975 and 1976, the first fully configured Yantar 2K was launched as Kosmos 905 in April 1977, and it successfully returned a film capsule.

After two further evaluation flights in 1977, the Yantar 2K flew is first fully operational mission as Kosmos 1028 in August 1978. Three missions annually followed in 1979 and 1980, and there were nine in 1981 as the Reagan Administration came into office with the intention of expanding United States defensive capabilities. The Soviets wanted to keep an eye on a revitalized American defense establishment.

Four Yantar-2K missions followed in 1982, and there

were three in 1983 as the Yantar 2K was phased out in favor of the Yantar 4K.

The Yantar 2K's secondary mission of providing early warning of American ICBM launches had not worked as planned, so in 1977, the Soviet Union initiated the effort to develop a more capable system to supersede it. The Yantar 4K program was born. There would be two spokes to the program, the Yantar 4K1, code-named Oktan, and the Yantar 4K2, which was code-named Kobalt. The two would be distinguished by the type of booster rocket for which they were designed.

Externally, the new Yantar was similar to the earlier Yantar, but internally it carried much-updated systems, including the Zhemchug-18 camera with a better lens and greater film capacity. The mission duration capability for the Yantar 4K spacecraft was also expanded from four weeks to six weeks, although a number of missions would last as long as eight weeks.

In contrast with the troublesome glitches that had delayed the Yantar 2K, the Yantar 4K program went amazingly well, achieving its development milestones on or ahead of schedule. It took seven years to develop the Yantar 2K, but just two for the Yantar 4K.

The first flight test of the Yantar 4K spacecraft came in April 1979 as Kosmos 1097. Two further test flights in 1980 and 1981 led to the system becoming operational in 1982. After five missions in 1982, the new Yantar began replacing the Yantar 2K. There were seven Yantar 4K flights in 1983, the last year that the Yantar 2K was used. Yantar 4K satellites would be launched eight times a year from 1984 though 1987, and there would be seven missions annually in 1988 and 1989.

Seven Yantar 4K launches in 1990 did not all lead to successful missions, and there were only five in 1991. The last Soviet launch was in November of that year. The Russians continued the Yantar 4K program with six in 1992 and an average of three annually through 1996. After that, the program was reduced to one a year, but it continued past the turn of the century.

In addition to the photo-reconnaissance and early warning Yantars, the Soviet Union developed a Yantar follow-on to the Zenit 4MT, which had been designed for the precision mapping mission. The initial design studies for this program began in 1967. The next, and more advanced, Yantar variant went through a series of design studies over the next decade, but was not ready for deployment until 1981. Designated as the Yantar 1KFT, it carried a KVR-1000 camera with a 1000mm telephoto lens, a Yakhont-1 TK-350 topographic camera and/or an APO-Oktan 8 camera system, which had a resolution of about thirty-three feet.

The first Yantar 1KFT flight, masked as Kosmos 1246, was launched in February 1981. The second launch, as Kosmos 1370, did not occur until May 1982. Between 1983 and 1986, Yantar 1KFT launches occurred annually in the latter half of the year. In 1987, there were two missions, one in July and one in November. The same was true in 1988, with the launches occurring in May and December. After one launch annually in 1989 and 1990, there were two in 1991. The first was in February, the second in December, just a week before the Soviet flag was hauled down from the Kremlin for the last time.

The Russian government continued the annual Yantar 1KFY missions through 1994, after which they turned to launching one every two years. The last Yantar 1KFY mission of the twentieth century was Kosmos 2349 in February 1998; the first of the twenty-first century was Kosmos 2373 in September 2000.

Digital Yantar/Terilen

Any study of Soviet military hardware reveals one overriding policy, and that is that when the Soviet Union developed a piece of equipment that worked, they stayed with that design for a long time—probably much longer than their counterparts in the West would have. This was true with everything from AK-47 automatic rifles to Soyuz spacecraft. So it was with photo-reconnaissance satellites.

The United States gravitated away from film in the 1980s, embracing digital imaging for its versatility and its ease of operation. On the other side, the Yantar series continued to use the same film return method as the earliest Soviet Zenits and American Keyholes—and the Russians were still using it after the Soviet Union ceased to exist.

The Soviets were not so much cautious in their approach to digital imaging as they were technologically behind the West. With the help of a vigorous espionage effort in this direction, they were able to initiate their first study of a digital spy satellite in 1977.

This program led to the craft designated as the Yantar 4KS and code-named Terilen. Originally, there was to have been a Yantar 4KS1 that was to have been followed by a more sophisticated Yantar 4KS2 and was intended to match America's mysterious and obviously very potent KH-11. However, the Yantar 4KS2 did not measure up to expectations and the project was cancelled in 1983 in favor of improving the Yantar 4KS1 and embarking on the all-new Arkon program.

As the name suggests, the Yantar 4SK1 was similar in size and external appearance to the previous members of the Yantar 4 family. In addition to the camera hardware, a major difference was to be the duration for which the new craft was designed. Because they had only so much film, photo-reconnaissance Yantars were designed to remain on station for a month or two. Because they never ran out of film, the first generation Yantar 4SK1 was designed for thirty weeks, and later variants for nearly forty weeks.

The first test launch came in December 1982, masked as Kosmos 1426. Single launches occurred in both 1984 and 1985, with the Yantar 4SK1 probably operational in the three missions launched in 1986. Two missions were launched in 1987, and there was at least one successful launch in 1988. A two-mission annual schedule, with one launch in the spring and one in the autumn, was maintained between 1989 and 1992, except in 1991, when there was a single launch in July.

With the collapse of the Soviet Union, Russia kept the Yantar 4SK1 in service, albeit with fewer missions. Only five missions were flown between 1993 and the turn of the century. All of these, however, remained in orbit for more than a year.

Keyhole/Kennan (Crystal)

The KH-11 was the first Keyhole to provide the United States with high-resolution electro-optical digital imaging. The resolution of its digital cameras was at least as fine as the resolution of the KH-9 Big Bird's film cameras. The digital imagery was also much better operationally because it could be transmitted electronically. Thus, it was available whenever it was needed, and it did not require a complicated recovery process. The KH-11s also had a much longer useful life. When an earlier Keyhole was out of film, it was done. The KH-11 could continue to return digital images indefinitely. The KH-11 returned digital images via a United States military communications satellite, such as Milstar, Tracking and Data Relay System (TDRS) or Satellite Data System (SDS).

The KH-11s were an order of magnitude better than their predecessors, and an order of magnitude larger. They weighed about 29,000 pounds and were approximately 60 feet long. They were slightly larger than the similar Hubble Space Telescope, which was also built by Lockhead in Sunnyvale. The Hubble weighed 24,000 pounds at launch and was 43.5 feet long. The big KH-11s were typically launched with Titan 34 series heavy-lift boosters. The Hubble was launched from the Space Shuttle's payload bay.

The KH-11 program initially operated under the code name Kennan, but the advanced KH-11 spacecraft were code named Crystal and equipped with the Improved Crystal Metric System (ICMS) for marking and coding digital imagery for map making. The Crystal code name and the

ICMS have continued into the program known under the designation KH-12.

This family of Keyholes operated at higher altitudes than the KH-8 and KH-9, having a perigee of about 150 miles and an apogee of roughly 600 miles.

The later KH-11s and the KH-12s also have infrared imaging capability in addition to their digital optical systems. This permits image gathering at night. The infrared system reportedly allows the KH-11 to "photograph" events that have taken place in the recent past via extremely sensitive sensors that detect minute amounts of residual heat.

From the late 1970s through the end of the Cold War, the United States kept at least two KH-11s in orbit and operational at all times. Each KH-11 was designed with an estimated service life of three years. Since there was no film canister to run empty, the limiting factor was the amount of fuel that was on board for the satellite's maneuvering engines. One KH-11, specifically the sixth one launched (December 1984), was in orbit for eleven years, although it may not have been functioning toward the end of its time in space.

The first KH-11 launch occurred on December 19, 1976, with a second launch in 1978 and annual launches of a single KH-11 between 1980 and 1983.

The seventh and eighth successful launches of the KH-11 program came in October 1987 and November 1988. These launches placed their KH-11s in sun-synchronous orbits, in which their respective ground tracks would be repeated every ninety-six hours, overlapping one another for forty-eight hours.

As the Cold War came to a close, the KH-11s were superseded by the more advanced KH-12 family, which is occasionally listed as KH-11B. With the end of the Cold War came new challenges for the Keyhole system. KH-11s provided the United States with the first detailed imagery of the 1990 Iraqi invasion of Kuwait, and were invaluable during the 1991 Gulf War.

Arkon

While most Cold War spy satellites were among the deepest and darkest secrets of their time, the most advanced digital spy satellite developed by the Soviet Union became well publicized and far from secret. The reason was that it was not actually flown until after the Soviet Union had ceased to exist.

The program began at the height of the Cold War, when the capabilities of the American KH-11 were providing Soviet planners with a rude wake-up call. Originally, the idea was to build upon the capabilities of the Yantar 4SK program that was under way in the early 1980s. However, in 1983, as President Ronald Reagan announced the Strategic Defense Initiative, this notion was abandoned in favor of starting over from scratch and building an all-new digital reconnaissance platform from the ground up. Several design bureaus submitted proposals, with Lavockhin finally selected to build the satellite to be known as Arkon. Like the KH-11, it was to be designed around a reflector telescope system with a long focal length.

The ambitious project called for clusters of ten or more of the new Arkon satellites with full coverage of the Earth's entire surface and to get the first Arkon into space as early as 1986. The process of designing such a groundbreaking satellite as the Soviet Union was collapsing around them proved too much for Soviet technicians. The flight-test program was postponed to 1991, but the Soviet Union ended with Arkon still a work in progress.

If there was any doubt of the collapse of communism and the notion of Russian antagonism for capitalism, it would certainly have been dashed by the circumstances of Arkon's debut. The first Arkon test launch finally got off the ground in June 1997, timed to coincide with the Russian commercial space exhibition at the Paris Air Show!

This would be the only Arkon launch of the twentieth century, but a second launch followed in July 2002.

Keyhole/Improved Crystal (Ikon)

The Lockheed KH-12 surveillance satellite can be considered to be essentially a bigger and better version of the KH-11. Indeed, some references to this supersecret spysat call it the KH-11B. The KH-12 was the first Keyhole to be capable of providing the United States with high-resolution, electro-optical digital imaging in real time, rather than relaying all of its data via a communications satellite. The KH-12 has an improved infrared imaging system, and also adds signals intelligence gathering to its portfolio. It not only looks, it listens.

Much heavier than the KH-11s, the KH-12s weigh 43,000 pounds at launch, although they are said to have had roughly the same exterior dimensions. They were originally designed to be accommodated in the 60-foot payload bay of the Space Shuttle, but they have been operationally launched with Titan 4 series heavy-lift expendable boosters.

The KH-12s are designed to be the most maneuverable Keyholes yet, and the increased weight is primarily for the propellant that makes the maneuverability possible. This also extended the design life of the KH-12 to about eight years.

Like the later KH-11 satellites, the KH-12 is equipped with the Improved Crystal Metric System (ICMS) for marking and coding digital imagery. The KH-12 is listed alternately as operating under the code name Crystal, or under the new code name Ikon. A post–Cold War system, the KH-12 was first launched in November 1992 and subsequent launches occurred throughout the 1990s and beyond.

Misty/Zirconic

A deeper Cold War secret than Keyhole was (and still is) Air Force Program 731, code-named Misty. The idea behind AFP-731 was to create a shadow to the Keyhole program that embodied low-observable or "stealth" technology to prevent a photo-reconnaissance satellite from being detected by radar. The program originated during the Reagan

Administration at a time when stealth aircraft such as the
F-117 and B-2 were under development. Operationally, the
AFP-731 satellite would shadow the Keyhole and move into
position over a target after the Keyhole satellite had moved
on. Just when the Soviets tracking the Keyhole thought it
was safe, Misty would be on station and watching them.

An AFP-731 satellite is known to have been launched in
February 1990 by the Space Shuttle *Discovery* during
STS-36, one of the series of classified Department of De-
fense missions that occurred during the Cold War. This
AFP-731 was placed into an orbit roughly 500 miles above
the Earth's surface.

The AFP-731 project is shrouded within a family of
top-secret stealthy satellite programs that are said to be under the code name Zirconic and which continue into the
twenty-first century.

CHAPTER 3

Nuclear Weapons

NUCLEAR WEAPONS WERE THE CENTERPIECE OF THE COLD war. The existence and potential use of nuclear weapons defined the Cold War as would no other weapons system. The weapon that had helped to end World War II became the signature Sword of Damocles of the decades that followed. They were hardly secret weapons insofar as everyone knew they were there, but they were certainly secret in the sense that little aside from their horrible destructive potential was widely known.

The secrecy was in the details. Though both sides knew the other had "the bomb," precise data were so sketchy that the most massive espionage offensive in history was launched to learn those elusive details about the opposing force.

It was only after the end of the Cold War that we started to learn all the facts, beginning with how much the Soviet Union had relied on espionage to learn the secrets that helped them build their first bomb. The efforts of such legendary spies as Klaus Fuchs and Julius and Ethel Rosenberg, who'd had access to the inner workings of the wartime United States Manhattan Project, were vital, but nobody in the West knew how vital until the Cold War was over. In fact, until the 1990s, with the disclosure of transcripts from the Venona counterspy program, the Rosenbergs actually had a small band of supporters who insisted that the sinister spies had been framed.

For four years after World War II, nuclear weapons were a United States monopoly, but soon that would change. The best intelligence available to United States military planners at the time of the Berlin Blockade estimated that the Soviet Union would not have a nuclear weapons capability until 1952 at the earliest and probably not until 1955. Nevertheless, the United States was cautiously conducting atmospheric sampling, watching and waiting.

On August 29, 1949, at a place called Semipalatinsk in Siberia, the Soviet Union secretly exploded its first nuclear fission device. No announcement was made. The test remained a secret for four days, when a U.S. Air Force RB-29 of the 375th Air Weather Reconnaissance Squadron based at Eielson AFB in Alaska detected the first radioactive evidence in the atmosphere. Additional missions were ordered, samples were collected and analysis was done. On September 23, President Harry Truman went public, telling the world that the Soviet Union was a nuclear power.

The Hydrogen Bomb

Suddenly faced with a nuclear arms race, both sides independently moved to the next step, a nuclear fusion weapon with much greater destructive power. Because a fusion weapon uses hydrogen to trigger a thermonuclear blast, the new weapon would come to be known in popular parlance as a hydrogen bomb.

The idea for a fusion weapon had been discussed in scientific circles well before the first fission bombs were exploded in 1945. Physicists Enrico Fermi and Edward Teller had studied the possibility of a fusion weapon during World War II, and in April 1946, Teller undertook a topsecret theoretical study at the Atomic Energy Commission's (AEC's) Los Alamos National Laboratory in New Mexico.

Within weeks of the first Soviet fission test, the AEC

proposed that a secret program to develop a hydrogen bomb be initiated. Amid a great deal of debate behind closed doors, President Truman finally signed off on the project on January 31, 1950. Teller's team went to work, but they were not alone.

Across the globe at a secret location near Sarov, in the Volga River country of central Russia, a hydrogen bomb project was already under way. In fact, the Soviet Union had not one but two hydrogen bomb programs underway since 1948. Just as the United States Manhattan Project had built two different types of fission devices in 1945, the Soviets followed a dual track toward thermonuclear weapons in case one didn't work. One program was code-named Sloyka, after a type of pastry, and was headed by Andrei Sakharov. The other, headed by Yakov Zeldovich, was code-named Truba (Tube), a deliberate reference to the secret British involvement in the Manhattan Project, which was code-named Tube Alloy. The Soviet hydrogen bomb projects were the most closely guarded secrets in Josef Stalin's secretive empire. The West had no idea.

Teller's project bore fruit first. Late in 1952, the AEC undertook Operation Ivy, the first hydrogen bomb live fire test program. The first explosion, code-named Mike, occurred on November 1 at the Eniwetok Proving Ground in the Marshall Islands of the South Pacific.

Less than a year later, on August 13, 1953, Sakharov's Sloyka was detonated in the first test of a Soviet hydrogen bomb.

The most destructive weapons on Earth were now in the hands of two superpowers engaged in a global struggle for primacy. Over the ensuing years, the two sides would compete to build more and more, and to refine the delivery systems to deploy them in the unthinkable World War III that many people imagined was inevitable.

The Cold War and the Spread of Nuclear Weapons
The Cold War ended four decades after the nuclear arms race began—without having boiled over into World War

III. After 1945, no nuclear weapons were used in combat during the twentieth century. However, in a harbinger of the dark fears that would haunt the twenty-first century, more and more nations would be added to the roster of nuclear powers.

Having shared in the early American efforts, the United Kingdom decided to join the club officially, testing its first nuclear device in 1952. France, nominally allied with Britain and the United States, chose to pursue an independent nuclear program and tested its first nuclear weapon in 1960.

The People's Republic of China, like France, wished to have an independent nuclear capability for the sake of national prestige and joined the roster in 1964. This, in turn, led to China's leading antagonist becoming a nuclear power. In 1974, India became the first nation in the so-called Third World to explode a nuclear weapon. After India became a nuclear power, its arch-rival Pakistan raced to join the club. Pakistan would be the last nation to join the nuclear club in the twentieth century in 1998.

Israel, meanwhile, is thought to have secretly developed a nuclear capability without having conducted a test. There are unconfirmed reports that South Africa may have conducted an unannounced nuclear test in 1979. This may or may not have been in cooperation with Israel.

While no nuclear weapons were used in wartime during the Cold War, there were more than 2,000 nuclear test explosions, reaching a peak of 178 in 1962, the year of the Cuban Missile Crisis. Between 1946 and 1992, the United States conducted 215 atmospheric tests and 815 underground tests. Between 1949 and 1990, the Soviet Union conducted 219 tests in the atmosphere and 496 underground. Neither side conducted any atmospheric tests after they signed the Nuclear Test Ban Treaty of 1963.

Through 1991, Britain had conducted a total of 45 tests. Both France and China continued testing through 1996, reaching twentieth-century totals of 210 and 45, respectively. India went more than two decades after its first nuclear test in 1974, but tested three in a row in May 1998, prompting a pair of tests by Pakistan before the end of the month.

After the end of the Cold War, both the United States and the nations of the former Soviet Union took steps to lock down the nuclear arsenals that had been on hair-trigger alert for four decades. Among the new nations that emerged from the collapse of the Soviet Union, only Russia is thought to still be armed with nuclear weapons. The others, especially Ukraine, which inherited huge nuclear stockpiles, deliberately chose to suspend their membership in the nuclear club.

However, not all of the weapons-grade material that existed in the Soviet Union at the end of the Cold War is accounted for. Just as the nuclear genie that slipped from its bottle at the end of World War II had set the tone for the Cold War, the material that slipped from the genie's bottle at the end of the Cold War may set the stage for dark events in the twenty-first century.

The Strategic Triad
The delivery systems for both the United States and Soviet nuclear arsenals were built on three-legged stools that were known in the United States as the Strategic Triad. This would have involved the use in wartime of three distinctly different weapons systems, each with its own characteristics of effectiveness and survivability.

Each weapons system in the two Triads had its own strengths. The Intercontinental Ballistic Missiles (ICBMs) have the advantages of immediate readiness, quick reaction time and the ability to penetrate all known enemy defenses. The Submarine Launched Ballistic Missiles (SLBMs) had the same readiness and reaction advantages, as well as the protection of mobility. ICBMs missiles were in hardened silos impervious to all but direct or near-direct hits, but the opposite side did know exactly where all the silos were located and had almost certainly targeted each of them.

The SLBMs, by contrast, were never in the same place, and a moving target is always harder to hit than a stationary one. Because of their nuclear power plants, the subs could stay submerged at sea for months at a time. Although their mobility made them harder to hit, it also reduced the SLBM's accuracy. Because the missiles were enclosed in a submarine, they were a bit smaller and had a shorter range than the land-based ICBMs.

Manned bombers lacked the immediate readiness and speed of the missiles, but offered a higher degree of flexibility. Bombers could be placed on airborne alert during time of crisis and could be recalled to their base when the crisis abated. Missiles could not be recalled. Once fired, they would have gone all the way. Bombers, once launched, could also be diverted to other targets.

In the United States, two of the three legs of the Triad (manned bombers and ICBMs) were under the command and control of the U.S. Air Force Strategic Air Command (SAC), and the third leg (SLBMs) was controlled by the U.S. Navy.

The Soviet Union's triad was under the operational control of the Soviet navy and not one, but two, strategic air commands. The Soviet air force, unlike its American counterpart, was actually three services rather than one. There were the Strategic Rocket Forces, the Troops of Air Defense (Protivo Vozdoshnaya Oborona Strany, or PVO Strany), and the Soviet Air Force (Voenno Vozdushnye Sily, or VVS). Within this command structure, the parallel to the SAC mission was performed by the Strategic Rocket Forces and VVS's Long-Range Aviation (Dal'naya Aviatsiya, or DA).

The Strategic Air Command

Two legs of the United States Strategic Triad resided within the SAC of the U.S. Air Force. During the nine years (1948–1957) that it was under the command of General Curtis Emerson LeMay, the command was transformed from a collection of World War II bombers into the most formidable aerial strike force that the world has ever seen. The almost incalculable striking power that SAC wielded made it the weapon most feared by Josef Stalin and his successors when they were at their most aggressive. It can be said that the power of SAC was the secret weapon that prevented World War III.

SAC's primary role was to act as the U.S. Air Force's long-range strategic strike force, maintaining and controlling strategic bombers and missiles for immediate reaction in time of nuclear war.

The manned bomber was the oldest and central element of strategic airpower and of SAC's arsenal. For more than four decades, the Boeing B-52 Stratofortress was the mainstay of the SAC bomber fleet. SAC also maintained two fleets of aircraft for ancillary functions. First, there was the fleet of over 600 aerial refueling tankers that serve the aerial refueling needs of the entire U.S. Air Force. Second was a fleet of highly secret high-performance reconnaissance aircraft, such as the U-2 and the SR-71.

In March 1946, the combat assets of the wartime U.S. Army Air Forces were divided into three component commands, which would be the centerpiece of the separate and independent U.S. Air Force, which would be created in September 1947. In addition to SAC, these were the Tactical Air Command (TAC) and the Air Defense Command (ADC).

In 1948, SAC headquarters was moved from Andrews AFB in suburban Washington, D.C., to Offutt AFB in Nebraska, where it would remain. Having presided over the defeat of Japan in World War II as commander of the XXI Bomber Command, General LeMay had later organized the Berlin Airlift as commander of U.S. Air Forces in Europe.

LeMay was a determined professional airman, a rising star in the new elite of Air Force officers who had received their baptism of fire in the skies over Germany and Japan. One of his first steps was to initiate exhausting but realistic drills, including maximum-effort, simulated-bombing missions against targets throughout the United States. Having reorganized training, he reorganized and streamlined everything about SAC, turning it into the most elite command within the United States armed forces. When LeMay took over, SAC had only 70 strategic bombers that were not war surplus. When he departed, he left his successor with a total of 2,711 aircraft, including 243 B-52s and 1,285 B-47s.

Through the years, the SAC would add more than a thousand ICBMs to its arsenal and carry the responsibility for the lion's share of the American nuclear deterrent force. Itself a victim of the Cold War, SAC was disbanded in 1992. Its aircraft were merged with those of TAC into the newly formed Air Combat Command (ACC). The remaining ICBM force was assigned to the Air Force Space Command (AFSPC). The latter answered to the unified multiservice Strategic Command (STRATCOM). The latter was a unified command that also now had command and control of the U.S. Navy's submarine-based ballistic missiles.

The Other Strategic Air Commands

During the years of the Cold War, the SAC was not an isolated entity. It existed in a world inhabited by other nations with strategic ambitions, strategic nuclear weapons, and strategic air commands. During World War II, the only nations capable of carrying out a sustained, integrated strategic air offensive were Britain, the United States, and to a certain extent, Germany, although they lacked a strategic bomber. Both the Japanese and the Soviets concentrated almost entirely on tactical aircraft for tactical air warfare. After the war, both the Americans and the British set about developing a new generation of strategic jet bombers, from the American B-47 and B-52 to the British "V bombers," the Valiant, Victor and Vulcan.

The Soviet Union became a convert to the idea of strategic airpower when it occupied Germany after the war and witnessed firsthand the effectiveness of the Anglo-American strategic air offensive. Their first venture into the realm of strategic aircraft took place by way of several American B-29 Superfortress strategic bombers that had made forced landings at Vladivostok after raids on Japan toward the end of the war. Recognizing the importance of the B-29s, the Soviets interned the big bombers rather than turning them back to the Americans. They were turned over to the Tupolev design bureau, which disassembled them and duplicated their every detail, producing several hundred Soviet "B-29s" under the Tupolev designation Tu-4. With this, Tupolev became the Soviet design bureau responsible for the nearly all the Soviet strategic bombers of the coming four decades.

The third nation to achieve nuclear weapons, Britain briefly maintained a small Triad of nuclear forces. Land-based ballistic missiles served only briefly in the 1960s, and the last long-range strategic bombers were retired by the Royal Air Force in the early 1980s. With this, Britain's strategic nuclear strike force consisted only of four Resolution Class nuclear submarines, each armed with sixteen Polaris three-MIRV missiles.

France was the fourth nation to acquire nuclear weapons and was the only nation other than the two superpowers, and perhaps China, to have developed and maintained a Triad during most of the Cold War. France withdrew from the military command of NATO in 1966, determined to develop its own independent strategic forces. France had six nuclear submarines, each equipped with sixteen M-20 missiles and an experimental diesel with four missile tubes. The land-based leg of the French Triad consisted of eighteen silo-based S-3 intermediate-range missiles and six strategic bomber squadrons equipped with Dassault-Breguet Mirage IV bombers. With aerial refueling, this aircraft gave the French Armee de l'air Commandement des Forces Aeriennes Strategique (Strategic Air Command) more than sufficient range to reach targets in the Soviet Union.

As noted above, the Soviet Union's Triad was under the operational control of the Soviet navy and, the Strategic Rocket Forces and the Dal'naya Aviatsiya of the Soviet Air Force (Voenno Vozdushnye Sily, or VVS). Within this command structure, the Strategic Rocket Forces maintained a peak inventory of nearly 1,400 ICBMs, including more than 300 of the huge SS-18 Satans (Soviet designa-

tion R-36M). In addition to the ICBMs, the Strategic
Rocket Forces had operational control of over 600 IRBMs
and MRBMs, 500 of them deployed in the western USSR
within striking range of Western Europe and the rest deployed within range of China.

The Dal'naya Aviatsiya had a peak operating capacity
of more than 600 strategic bombers organized into three
bomber corps or air armies—two opposite NATO and one
in the Far East opposite China. The most well known of the
heavy bombers was the Tupolev Tu-95 (NATO code name
Bear). In service since 1955, the Bear had proven to be one
of the most successful warplanes designed in the Soviet
Union. The huge bomber uniquely combined a swept-wing
configuration with turboprop power plants to achieve a
speed and performance level comparable to many jets
(transports included) of its size and weight class, even jets
of much more modern design. Because of its maximum
range of over 10,000 miles, the Bear had been adapted for
a maritime reconnaissance role and was frequently encountered off the coast of the southeastern United States
on its regular reconnaisance runs between the Soviet
Union and Cuba.

Soviet jet bombers (code-named by NATO with words
beginning with B) included the M-4 Bison and Tu-16 Bad-
ger of the 1950s, the Tu-22 Blinder of the 1960s, the Tu-
22M Backfire and the Tu-160 Blackjack. The latter two
were both operational during the 1980s and still in service
at the end of the Cold War.

Strategic Nuclear Planning

To be used effectively, the three separate parts of the Triads
were designed to work together. The weapons systems
were the hardware of the strategic deterrent, but the complex planning for their deployment was the software. Scenarios had to be diagramed, targets selected and
uninterrupted communications assured so that plans and
data could be transmitted.

In the United States, it was the Joint Strategic Target

Planning Staff (JSTPS) who wrote the program. This program included the Single Integrated Operational Plan (SIOP) and National Strategic Target List (NSTL). The JSTPS was established in August 1960 by the Eisenhower administration's Secretary of Defense Thomas Gates in reaction to a need to coordinate the strategic nuclear weapons policies of the various services. The JSTPS was to report to the Joint Chiefs of Staff (JCS) through its Director of Strategic Target Planning (DSTP), who was also the commander in chief of SAC.

The JSTPS was composed of a number of SAC personnel who, like their commander, served a double role. JSTPS also included representation from the Army, Navy, and Marine Corps. The JSTPS was, in turn, divided into two directorates, one of them composed of targeting specialists whose job it was to continually review the NSTL; the other composed of operations specialists whose job was to come up with the best SIOP to successfully attack and destroy the targets on the NSTL if SAC and/or the Navy were called upon to did so.

In addition to representatives from the various United States military services on the JSTPS, there were also representatives of various United States unified military theater commands—Atlantic, Pacific, and European. To ensure as broad a spectrum as possible, a group of Allied officers from the NATO high command also served on the JSTPS.

The targets on the NSTL were always classified as secret, though they were not always the same from month to month or year to year. Originally they included primarily cities and population centers in the Soviet Union, but in the 1970s, the emphasis had shifted to industrial and military targets, including the Soviet ICBM fields.

The primary targets—the nuclear forces—included not only the missile bases (IRBM as well as ICBM) but nuclear weapons storage sites, strategic command-and-control centers and strategic bomber and submarine bases as well. The secondary targets included other command-and-control centers, and the tertiary targets included conventional military bases and supply depots as well as military logistics and transportation systems. The fourth and fifth categories include war and other industries, respectively. The former included munitions and weapons factories, refineries and rail yards, and the latter, such industries as cement, coal, steel and electric power.

Although it was no secret that the majority of the targets on this constantly updated list were in the Soviet Union, targets in other countries were probably added from time to time. For example, it was known that one of the retaliatory options discussed in the wake of the seizure of the United States embassy in Tehran in 1979–1981 led to contingency plans for nuclear strikes on targets in Iran. It was probably safe to assume that had these strikes taken place, they would have been made by aircraft rather than ICBMs.

The SIOP, like the NSTL, was flexible and always changing to take into account such factors as changes in the level of available weapons technology. The SIOP was a final-option type of plan, the kind to be executed only when deterrence and all other methods for preventing attack had failed. It was in itself a major part of deterrence.

The SIOP directorate used all available intelligence information about Soviet and other nations' intentions and capabilities to create a computer simulation of a variety of potential conflicts. By using a computer model, the directorate could evaluate a variety of scenarios using various combinations of the strategic weapons available—the Triad.

All of the conceivable potential scenarios were wargamed in advance, because, in the event of a real emergency, there would be only six to thirty minutes for the president of the United States to order execution of the SIOP.

The Fractional Orbital Bombardment System

One of the most frightening developments involving nuclear weapons during the Cold War was the Soviet Union's Fractional Orbital Bombardment System (FOBS). It was an orbital nuclear weapons system designed to attack the

continental United States by placing a targetable thermonuclear warhead—or warheads—into the Earth's orbit.
The term *fractional* derived from the fact that the warhead
package could be placed into orbit or it could be brought
down quickly, after a fraction of an orbit. This warhead
package could also, theoretically, be parked in orbit indefinitely and dropped at will.

In August 1961, Premier Nikita Khrushchev observed
that the Soviet Union owned 100-megaton nuclear weapons
and that it was now successfully orbiting cosmonauts—
something that the United States had not yet done with its
astronauts. He then boasted that the Soviet Union could just
as easily replace the cosmonauts "with other loads that can
be directed to any place on Earth."

He would also later brag that FOBS could hit the United
States from any direction. Since the American early-
warning system looked north, watching for an ICBM barrage coming over the North Pole, FOBS could be launched
the other way and strike the United States from the south.

The Soviets hoped to overcome any potential American
antiballistic missile defensive system by separating the
larger, more trackable missile from its warhead. After the
antiballistic missile had hit the ICBM, they'd drop the warhead. This would amount to the nuclear checkmate that
Khrushchev so eagerly wanted to achieve.

Within a year of Khrushchev's boast, there were several
orbital bombing programs on the drawing boards within the
Soviet Union. These studies were looking at the technical
aspects of both the FOBS warheads and the launch vehicles.
The idea was that the Strategic Rocket Forces would be able
to choose the best of three different approaches to this
daunting technological challenge.

Discussed in the ballistic missiles section in chapter 4,
one of the most important of the latter was the GR-1 Global
Rocket. It was being designed by Sergei Korolev, who was
also working on a FOBS warhead. Another project was under
the direction of Korolev's chief rival, Vladimir Chelomei,
who was then also working on the Rakatoplan, the first So-

viet spaceplane. Another launch system, being designed by Mikhail Yangel, was an adaptation of the R-36 ICBM, which was known by the NATO code name SS-9 Scarp. Also discussed in chapter 4, this rocket was ultimately selected to be used with the FOBS under the R-36-O designation.

CHAPTER 4

Ballistic Missiles

IF NUCLEAR WEAPONS WERE THE ULTIMATE WEAPON NOT used in World War III, then the ultimate delivery system for these weapons was the Intercontinental Ballistic Missile (ICBM). In the early days of the Cold War, the strategic forces of the United States and the Soviet Union would have relied upon manned, long-range bombers to carry nuclear weapons into one another's heartland. From the 1960s on, the unstoppable threat of ICBMs became the Cold War's worst nightmare.

As the name implies, ICBMs had intercontinental range, meaning that they were capable of travelling across the globe from the Soviet Union to North America and vice versa. Before the range capability expanded to intercontinental, ballistic missile development evolved in stages of progressively longer ranging missiles. Many shorter range missiles are still in service and classed as follows: Short Range Ballistic Missiles (SRBMs) have a range up to 620 miles, Medium Range Ballistic Missiles (MRBMs) have a range up to 1,860 miles, and Intermediate Range Ballistic Missiles (IRBMs) have a range up to 3,100 miles.

Whereas ICBMs were the weapons with which the Soviet Union and the United States could threaten one another, MRBMs and IRBMs were important for the arsenal of the Soviet Strategic Rocket Forces because they could be—and were—used to intimidate Western Europe.

The technical development of ICBMs began during World War II. As nuclear weapons were taking shape in the United States, the precursors to early ballistic missiles were taking shape in Germany. The mastermind of the German wartime ballistic missile program was a visionary engineer named Wernher Magnus Maximillian von Braun. He had always claimed that his real interest was in space travel, and in the 1960s, he would be the man who spear-headed the successful American effort to put human beings on the surface of the Moon.

The grandfather of all ballistic missiles on both sides of the Iron Curtain was Germany's Vergeltungswaffe (Vengeance Weapon) 2 (V-2), which was technically des-ignated A4. The V-2 missile was 5 feet 6 inches in diame-ter, and 46 feet 1 inch tall when positioned vertically for launch. It had guidance fins at the base, which had a 12-foot diameter. Created by von Braun for the German army, it was later adapted by the Soviet Union in the 1950s as the infamous Scud, which, in turn, became a household word during the 1991 Gulf War.

During the last year of World War II, the Germans launched more than 3,200 V-2s, with about half of these di-rected toward England. The death toll in England from the V-2 attacks exceeded 2,700, but, while the ton of high ex-plosives did considerable damage wherever a V-2 hit, few strategically important targets were struck because of guidance shortcomings.

After the end of World War II, V-2s and personnel who'd been active in their development were captured by both the United States and the Soviet Union. These became the seeds from which all postwar MRBMs, IRBMs and ICBMs would germinate.

Like nuclear weapons, ballistic missiles were secret weapons of the Cold War not because their existence was unknown, but because just about everything else about them was. Exceptions came with the American ballistic missiles that were adapted as space launch vehicles. These included both the Martin Titan and Convair Atlas, as well as the Douglas Thor, which evolved into the popular Douglas Delta launch vehicle.

The Soviet ballistic missiles, however, remained as closely guarded secret weapons. They were generally known from the fuzziest of photographs published from time to time in the state media of the Soviet Union, or seen in the parades in Moscow's Red Square celebrating May Day and the anniversary of the October Revolution in 1917 (November in Western calendars). These parades were useful to observers in that they generally identified which missiles were configured for use with mobile launches and which were designed to operate from fixed sites. The former were usually displayed aboard their launchers, while the latter were towed on trailers behind trucks. Beginning in the mid-1950s, the Moscow festivities also showed the relative size of the missiles, as larger and larger ones were displayed each year.

During the Cold War, most ICBMs on both sides were based in subterranean silos, which were concrete tubes beneath the surface of the ground. Such basing gave the ICBMs more protection from enemy action—or from weather conditions—than if they would have been based on the surface.

Both sides considered basing their ICBMs on mobile launchers, but only the Soviet Union actually did so operationally. The advantage of a mobile launcher was that it was difficult for an enemy to find and destroy it. The disadvantages were that mobile missiles were hard to maintain, harder to aim and launch and that they required a much larger crew of people to manage them.

The silos were located in lonely, remote places all across the Great Plains from Montana to Arkansas and across the Soviet Steppes from Derazhnya and Pevomaysk in the west to Svobiodny and Drovyanaya east of Lake Baikal.

The Strategic Air Command (SAC) silos were actually dozens of self-contained underground warrens of passageways and bunkers clustered around ten-story elevator shafts. Each control site, in turn, managed a network of silos, each of which contained a gleaming white projectile. These cold and deadly stalagmites rested in the climate-controlled stillness of their manmade caverns for several decades, ready and waiting to be called upon for an hour-long flight to the Soviet Union.

On each work shift, for all those thousands of shifts, two SAC airmen went to the control room, ready to launch their machines, only to clock out without having pushed the "button." Across the globe on the steppes, Soviet crews were doing the same. Ironically, the SAC "airmen" and their Soviet counterparts who worked at these sites never flew in the air, and never saw the sky during their duty shift.

In the SAC ICBM control rooms, the "button" of the popular vernacular was not really a button at all, but rather a pair of ignition switches located on a pair of identical consoles at opposite ends of the room. As part of the maze of safety features built into the launch system, the missiles could not be launched without the entire launch procedure being followed precisely and simultaneously by two operators at the two consoles. The consoles were located more than arm's length apart so that one person could not go through the launch sequence by himself.

Had the call to launch come, the sequence would have begun with the pair of keys issued to the two SAC controllers at the start of each shift. They would use the keys unlock the console and begin to start the huge engines of the ICBMs under their control.

Other than their size and other bits of information that seeped out here or there, little was known outside the Soviet Union about the Soviet ICBMs—even in the darkened halls of the Western intelligence services. Often what the spies knew amounted to little more than one could learn by reading British fan magazines.

Even the "R for Rocket" and "RT for solid-fuel rocket" designations for Soviet missiles were largely unknown until nearly the end of the Cold War. To address this shortcoming, NATO had been assigning designations and code names of its own. In addition to a code name beginning with the letter S, the Soviet ballistic missiles were given a designation with the prefix SS, for Surface-to-Surface.

We have listed the Soviet ballistic missiles by their R designations, and have retained the use of their colorful NATO nicknames. What follows is not an exhaustive examination of all the ballistic missiles deployed by the two sides, but an overview of the major systems that were important to the unfolding strategic situation during the Cold War.

SN-62 (B-62) Snark

America's Northrop Snark was the first ballistic missile capable of intercontinental range. It was also the first of the postwar generation of cruise missiles. It was a 75 foot 10 inch unmanned jet aircraft capable of flying nearly at the speed of sound. It was designed to fly under remote control for up to 6,300 miles, then fire a detachable nose cone containing a warhead.

The program was undertaken in 1946 by the USAAF (U.S. Air Force after September 1947) and it moved very slowly due to lack of funding. The first successful flight did not occur until April 1951. In September 1955, the Snark test and evaluation program picked up momentum as President Eisenhower established a high priority for ICBMs.

The first two United States units to become operational with ICBMs, the Strategic Air Command's 556th and 702nd Strategic Missile Squadrons, were activated in December 1957 and January 1959. However, nagging problems with guidance systems that had dogged the Snark through its test program would continue. In 1961, the incoming Kennedy administration cited this and ordered the phaseout of this aging milestone of secret weapons technology in favor of the likes of Thor and Atlas.

Redstone

During World War II, Germany's military aircraft were owned and operated by the German air force—the Luftwaffe. However, the German ballistic missile program, specifically the V-2 and its derivatives, was controlled by the German Army—the Heer. These missiles were under the army rather than the air force, under the theory that ballistic missiles were an extension of the army's artillery function.

After World War II, the U.S. Army assumed that it would control ballistic missiles in the United States under the same theory. In fact, it was the Army's land forces, not the USAAF, to which German ballistic missile kingpin Wernher von Braun surrendered, and it was the Army, not the USAAF, that ran Operation Paperclip, the legendary effort to recruit German rocket scientists. It was to the Army's Redstone Arsenal near Huntsville, Alabama—an artillery facility—that von Braun's group was imported. The Army would retain control of this rocket science program after the U.S. Air Force was officially created in 1947.

It was not until 1955 that Secretary of Defense Charles Wilson gave the Air Force sole responsibility for the development and deployment of missiles with a range greater than 200 miles. Until then, it was a turf war.

The Army never built an ICBM, but America's first generation of postwar vertically launched ballistic missiles were predominantly Army programs. With the exception of the MGM-5 Corporal, these were overseen by von Braun. One of the first projects would take von Braun's new home base as its namesake.

The M-8 (later PGM-11) Redstone missile evolved from the experimental Hermes, von Braun's first missile designed in the United States. Like the wartime V-2, both Hermes and Redstone were liquid fuel rockets. The Redstone program received a high priority after the start of the Korean War in 1950 and the first missile made its debut flight in August 1953. By 1958, it had been introduced into active units in Germany. The operational Redstone stood 69 feet high and had a range of 250 miles—a longer range than was permitted under the 1955 Department of Defense directive. Nevertheless, more than 1,000 were built, with Chrysler being the prime contractor.

They were withdrawn from service as offensive weapons by the early 1960s, but two were adapted for use as space launch vehicles for the NASA Mercury program. America's first two astronauts went into space in 1961 atop Redstones.

SM-78 Jupiter

The Jupiter program originated in 1954 at Wernher von Braun's workshop at the U.S. Army's Redstone Arsenal, and was essentially an evolution of the Redstone project. Like the Redstone and von Braun's wartime V-2, it was liquid fueled. And, as with the Redstone, the prime contractor for the Jupiter would be Chrysler.

When Secretary of Defense Charles Wilson decreed in 1955 that the U.S. Air Force should control all ballistic missiles with a range greater than 200 miles, Jupiter was transferred to that service under the "B for bomber" designation B-78 (later SM-78). It preceded Thor chronologically but received its designation later, hence the higher number.

Like the Douglas Thor, the Jupiter was an Intermediate Range Ballistic Missile (IRBM), although it was slightly smaller than the SM-75. It stood 60 feet tall on its semiportable launch table and had a range of about 2,000 miles. Flight testing of preproduction vehicles began in 1955, and the first flight test of a fully configured Jupiter IRBM occurred in May 1957.

The Jupiters were deployed overseas to put them within range of targets in the Soviet Union. One detachment was placed in Italy, but most went to Turkey, where they were on station beginning in 1960. As part of the secret understanding between President John Kennedy and Soviet Premier Nikita Khrushchev that ended the Cuban Missile Crisis in 1962, the Jupiters and their launch infrastructure were withdrawn from Turkey. By 1965, all of the Jupiters everywhere had been withdrawn from active duty. Advances in ICBM technology had rendered them obsolete.

In the meanwhile, the Jupiter C variant was being developed to launch payloads into space. On January 31, 1958, a

Jupiter C was used to launch Explorer 1, the first American satellite in orbit.

R-1 (SS-1) Scunner and R-2 (SS-2) Sibling

As was the case in the United States, the first Soviet ballistic missiles were based on captured German V-2 components. As with the V-2 and the early American missiles, both the Scunner (Nuisance) and Sibling were experimental systems powered by rocket engines that used liquid oxygen and alcohol. Like the V-2, the R-1 used ethyl alcohol, while the R-2 used methyl alcohol. The R-1 stood 55 feet 9 inches, while the R-2 was 68 feet 10 inches tall.

Tested at the top-secret Soviet base at Kapustin Yar, the R-1 first flew in October 1948, a year after the first Soviet test of a captured V-2. The first R-2 was tested in September 1949, a month after the first Soviet nuclear weapon test.

SM-75 Thor

In the United States, the Douglas Aircraft Company had begun investigating the potential of guided missile technology even before the end of World War II with the Roc series of air-launched, radar-guided cruise missiles. After World War II, captured German hardware, including V-2s, was brought to the United States for testing. The V-2 was combined with the Douglas-built Wac Corporal to create the two-stage Bumper Wac, which was tested in 1948. On February 24, 1949, a Bumper Wac was launched to an altitude of 244 miles, flying at over 5,000 mph. This was higher and faster than any man-made vehicle before it and technically it was the first man-made object ever to reach outer space.

In the meantime, Douglas had been working to develop the Thor, a ballistic missile based on an extension of German V-2 technology. Ordered by the U.S. Air Force in December 1955 under the "B for bomber" designation B-75 (later SM-75), the Thor was a 65-foot, nuclear-armed IRBM that was designed to provide an initial ballistic missile capability until the deployment of the Atlas ICBM.

The first Thor was delivered in October 1956, and the first successful Thor launch came in September 1957. Douglas would build more than thirty-five XSM-75s and more than seventy-five SM-75s, which, in turn, became PGM-17A in 1962. Because the range of the Thor was less than 2,000 miles, the missiles were forward deployed to the United Kingdom, where they became operational with the Royal Air Force Bomber Command in 1959. By the end of 1961, there were 20 three-missile squadrons on alert between Yorkshire and Suffolk. They would remain in service for only four years.

Though Thor was soon replaced by ICBMs, it went on to be adapted by NASA for use as a space launch vehicle. Using the Able upper stage, Thor was used to launch many important spacecraft projects during the 1960s. The Thor project eventually developed into the extremely successful Delta series of space launch vehicles that was still going strong in the twenty-first century.

R-11/R-300 (SS-1B/SS-1C) Scud

Given the same NATO SS number as the R-1 Scunner, the Soviet Scud was a more compact missile that had the distinction of many decades of service while the other SS-1 became a forgotten enigma. Smaller than the V-2, while the R-1 and R-2 were larger, the Scud stood 36 feet 11 inches tall. It was liquid fueled, using kerosene in early versions and unsymmetrical dimethylhydrazine in later models. The Scud family were mobile tactical missiles with a range of generally less than 200 miles. The 500-pound payload capacity could include conventional, chemical or nuclear weapons.

The R-11 (Scud A) was first deployed in 1957, and the dimethylhydrazine-powered Scud B arrived on the scene in the early 1960s. Though largely phased out of service with Soviet forces by the 1980s, Scuds had been widely exported

to Warsaw Pact nations and other Soviet clients, notably
Iraq, which used them as an offensive weapon until 1991.

R-5 (SS-3) Shyster
Designed by the brilliant aerospace engineer Sergei
Pavlovich Korolev, the Shyster was the first Soviet MRBM
and the first Soviet missile designed specifically to carry a
nuclear payload. With a range of more than 700 miles, it
brought much of Western Europe within its radius of devastation. It was just over 68 feet long and had a payload of
more than a ton.

The Shyster was first test-fired in January 1955, and entered service with the Strategic Rocket Forces in June
1956. Like the wartime German V-2 and the short range
Scud, the Shyster was able to utilize a mobile launch system that would make it extremely versatile and hard to hit
in the event of war. It was withdrawn from service after
1967, when the R-12 Sandal came online.

R-12 (SS-4) Sandal and R-14 (SS-5) Skean
The earliest Soviet MRBMs followed the German V-2 paradigm of designing for mobile launchers. By the mid-
1960s, the Soviet Union was moving toward silo basing for
MRBMs as well as ICBMs. Both Sandal and Skean were
characteristic of this generation.

In terms of size and range, Sandal was a step beyond the
Shyster, and Skean a step beyond Sandal. Measuring 73
feet 6 inches and 82 feet, respectively, they were both
liquid-fueled MRBMs, with respective range capabilities
of about 1,100 and 2,000 miles. With this, all of Western
Europe was essentially within the targeting range, although
the nuclear warheads would have been fairly small because
increased weight would decrease range.

The Sandal was the centerpiece of one of the Cold
War's most dangerous moments—the Cuban Missile Crisis. United States aerial surveillance identified more than
thirty Sandals in Cuba, but documents released in 2002 in-

dicate that the Soviet Union had placed forty-two Sandals on the island. Their range brought Washington, D.C., within their radius of nuclear destruction.

The R-12 program began in 1955 and flight tests began at Kapustin Yar in June 1957. The Sandal was reportedly operational by late 1958. The original plan was for it to be surface launched, but tests in 1960 led to deployment of a silo-launched variant. Named Dvina after the river of the same name, the silo-based R-12 became operational in 1963. More than 600 R-12s were deployed in the mid-1960s, but most were phased out between 1972 and 1978.

The R-14 program began in 1958, with Mikhail Yangel in charge of the Yuzhnoye design bureau team. The flight testing began in the summer of 1960, and deployment began the following year. Like the R-12, both surface and silo basing scenarios would be utilized. The former became operational with the Strategic Rocket Forces in January 1962, and the silo sites were active in early 1963. At their peak in the late 1960s, there were fewer than 100 R-14s deployed. Most of these were withdrawn between 1971 and 1983.

The Intermediate-Range and Shorter-Range Nuclear Forces (INF) Treaty that went into effect in 1988 called for elimination of the last R-12s and R-14s. There were nearly 150 of the former, but only a half dozen of the latter remained. They were reportedly all dismantled by May 1990.

Blue Streak

The Cold War's ballistic missile race was predominately a contest between the Soviet Union and the United States. However, during the 1950s, the United Kingdom was proceeding under the assumption that it, too, should develop and maintain an IRBM capability independent of that of the United States. With this in mind, work on the Blue Streak program began in 1955. A liquid-fueled missile similar to the Convair Atlas, the Blue Streak stood 61 feet 6 inches tall and had a launch weight of 100 tons. Its range was in excess of 2,000 miles. The missile itself was developed by DeHavilland, with the primary rocket engines produced by Rolls Royce, but based on a North American Rocketdyne design.

It was envisioned that the Blue Streaks would be based in silos located within the United Kingdom. The flight test program began in April 1960 at the Weapons Research Establishment located at Woomera in Australia. However, before the first flight, the Blue Streak was canceled as a weapons system by the British government. In one of the most controversial backroom deals of the Cold War involving the Anglo-American allies, the United States Department of Defense had convinced the United Kingdom Ministry of Defense to abandon its indigenous Blue Streak in favor of America's air-launched Douglas B-87 (later GAM-87) Skybolt strategic missile.

While the Blue Streak test program went flawlessly, the Skybolt program was beset by a series of failures and fell behind schedule. The program was canceled by the United States Department of Defense in December 1962, leaving the British without the weapon that had been promised when they agreed to abandon the Blue Streak. This resulted in a serious straining of relations between the two nations. The United Kingdom would not again undertake an IRBM or MRBM program.

SM-65 Atlas

America's first widely deployed operational ICBM began with a secret project at the end of World War II. With the German V-2 very much in mind, the USAAF (US Air Force after September 1947) invited industry to submit proposals for research and development of a missile capable of hurling a warhead the unheard-of distance of 5,000 miles. In January 1946, engineers at Convair proposed what would be known cryptically as Project MX-774. By 1953, Project MX-774 had evolved into Project Atlas.

In 1955, as President Eisenhower placed the highest national defense priority on the development of the ICBM, the Air Force created its secret Weapons System 107 development project. The first acquisition under WS-107 was an order for the Atlas missile that would be designated under the "B for Bomber" nomenclature B-65. This later changed to SM-65 for "Strategic Missile."

In 1957, Convair created Convair Astronautics as a separate operating division for production of the Atlas, and a new 250-acre plant was constructed on chaparral-covered Kearny Mesa in San Diego County, California. The first successful Atlas launch came in September 1957.

On February 1, 1958, the Air Force's Strategic Air Command (SAC) activated the first Atlas-equipped unit, the 4320th (later 706th) Strategic Missile Wing at Francis E. Warren AFB in Wyoming. Some of the tightest security in Air Force history surrounded the delivery of the first operational Atlases.

The first SAC launch of an Atlas involved an Atlas D, which was test-fired from Vandenberg AFB in California on September 9, 1959. This shot travelled 4,300 miles downrange in the Pacific in sixteen minutes. The Atlas D had a maximum range of 10,360 miles.

By August 1959, there were four active Atlas D units in SAC, and three Atlas E units were activated in 1960. By the end of 1962, six Atlas F squadrons had also been added. By this time, Convair had delivered thirty Atlas Ds, thirty-two Atlas Es and eighty Atlas Fs to thirteen active SAC squadrons. The later Atlas variants were distinguished by a higher gross weight and a range of 11,500 miles.

The Atlas era was short lived. In 1964, SAC began to implement the 1961 Defense Department plan to replace the Atlas and Titan ICBMs with the newer Minuteman. Atlas was replaced because the cost of maintaining a liquid-fuel rocket in a constant state of readiness was greater than for the solid-fuel Minuteman.

By June 1965, all of the Atlas ICBM fleet had been retired, but the Atlas continued to evolve as a launch vehicle for boosting spacecraft into orbit. This use of the Atlas had paralleled that of the ICBM variant. The first had been the December 1958 launch of the U.S. Army's SCORE (Signal

Communication by Orbiting Relay Equipment), the world's first communications satellite.

Atlas was also used for all of the orbital flights of NASA's Mercury manned spaceflight program, beginning with John Glenn's February 1962 mission in *Friendship 7*. At the turn of the century, later generation Atlas missiles were still being used to launch payloads into orbit.

R-7 (SS-6) Sapwood

As the Shyster was the first Soviet MRBM capable of dropping a nuclear weapon on Western Europe, the Sapwood was the first Soviet ICBM capable of hitting the United States with a nuclear weapon. The Soviet government initiated the quest for a missile with this capability early in 1953. The idea was to develop a system that could travel 5,000 miles with a 6,000-pound payload, the weight of the hydrogen bombs that were then in development. To lift this weight, the Sapwood was boosted with five kerosine-fueled engines, one four-chambered main engine and four similar strap-on boosters. The total thrust of over a million pounds was greater than any American rocket of the era. The Sapwood stood 100 feet tall, but later warhead configurations would make it taller than 110 feet.

First test flown in May 1957, the Sapwood was first deployed as an operational ICBM at the beginning January 1960. Though it was the subject of several improvement programs in the early 1960s, the Sapwood was phased out by 1968.

Meanwhile, the Sapwood was destined for a career as a space launch vehicle as well as an ICBM. On October 4, 1957, a Sapwood became the first rocket to place a satellite—Sputnik 1—into Earth orbit. On April 12, 1961, a Sapwood became the first rocket to place a human being—Yuri Gagarin—into Earth orbit. It would go on to evolve into a widely used series of launch vehicles.

R-16 (SS-7) Saddler

While the Sapwood was to be deployed by the Soviet Strategic Rocket Forces as an ICBM, the R-16 was destined to be the first missile that was *widely deployed* as such in the Soviet Union. The Saddler ICBM was similar to the Sapwood in terms of both size and range, but was designed with an improved and interference-shielded guidance system for improved accuracy and reliability. At least three different warhead configurations were eventually deployed on the Saddler.

The missiles were developed for two launch scenarios. Some would be configured for traditional surface launches, while others would be launched from hardened underground silos.

The program got off to an uncertain start in October 1960 when a Saddler exploded on the test pad at the Baikonur Kosmodrome, killing an estimated 100 persons, including Marshal Mitrofan Nedelin, the commander the Strategic Rocket Forces. The incident was known to Western intelligence services at the time, but the details were not fully unveiled until after the Cold War.

The first successful test launch occurred in April 1961, and the surface-launched missiles were operational by the end of the year. In the meantime, the Soviets were busy constructing the network of underground silos and launch facilities. Each launch center would control a trio of silos that were sunk 150 feet into the ground. The debut silo launch came in January 1962, and the silo-based Saddlers were operationally ready in February 1963. The complete inventory of more than 160 Saddlers was in the field by 1965.

The Saddler stood 104 feet tall and had a range in excess of 6,800 miles with a 3,500-pound warhead. The first stage was powered by three dimethylhydrazine-fueled engines, the second stage by a single, larger engine augmented by a four-chamber control engine. Dedicated retrorockets were used to separate the sustainer stages and the warhead. A novel and more reliable autonomous guidance control system that was protected from radio jamming was designed for this missile.

By the provisions of the SALT I Treaty, signed in May 1972, the Soviet Union agreed to a complete phaseout of the Saddlers, although a few had been decommissioned as early as 1971. The final Saddler is believed to have been taken out of service in 1976.

R-9 (SS-8) Sasin

Designed by Sergei Korolev, the Sasin was a two-stage, liquid-fueled Soviet ICBM that was a contemporary of the larger Saddler. Standing 79 feet 2 inches tall, the Sasin could be, and often was, deployed into hardened shelters that had originally been constructed for the Saddler. Produced in smaller numbers than the Saddler, the Sasin had a comparable range and payload capacity. Two types of warhead systems were deigned for the R-9 and had an explosive output up to two megatons.

The Sasin program was initiated in 1959 as a surface-launched system, but it was later decided to design it for either surface or silo launching. The first test launch occurred in April 1961, and the first units were activated with the surface-launched variant in December 1964, although Western analysts had thought they were operational a year earlier.

As with the Saddler, deactivation of the Sasin took place between 1971 and 1976. Because more capable systems were coming online, this time table would have prevailed with or without the SALT I agreement.

R-26 (SS-8) Sasin

In the annals of Soviet ICBMs, the two-stage R-26 presents an interesting case study. It was so secret a secret weapon that Western intelligence analysts didn't realize that it did not exist as an operational system.

The R-26 was a real weapon, ordered in 1960 and ready for testing at the end of 1961, but it was canceled in July 1962 without having been test fired. Nevertheless, the R-26s that had been built were loaded on trailers and displayed at a parade in Moscow's Red Square. Western analysts, who always attempted to draw conclusions about the Soviet nuclear weapons program, saw the R-26 and interpreted the 80-foot missile as an improved version of the R-9 Sasin.

The Soviets had created—possibly by accident—the illusion that the R-26 was an operational missile rather than the empty hulk of a terminated program. The truth would not come out until the end of the Cold War.

GR-1 (SS-10) Scrag

The GR-1 represented an entirely new and ominous turn in Soviet ICBM development, although the true extent of its technological potential would remain a closely guarded secret until the end of the Cold War. Designed by the brilliant Sergei Korelev, the GR-1 project began in 1961 as an effort by the Soviet Strategic Rocket Forces to develop a missile to utilize the Fractional Orbital Bombardment System (FOBS) to place a targetable warhead into Earth orbit.

The GR-1 (First Global Rocket) was 116 feet long with its warhead, although Western estimates put it at 124 feet. It consisted of three stages with a launch weight of 117 tons. The guidance system would have allowed it to drop a 2.2-megaton warhead into target with an accuracy radius of about a mile.

Like the R-26 obfuscation, the GR-1 represented a failure of American espionage to understand the true nature of a Soviet ICBM system. Having been designed by Korolev, who was the father of Soviet manned spaceflight hardware, the GR-1 was described by the commentator at the 1965 Moscow May Day parade as the "sister" of the Vostok and Vokshod.

Western analysts chuckled. It was obvious that the GR-1 was no sister to these launch vehicles. When they'd heard that the Americans had debunked this notion, it was the Soviets' turn to chuckle. To the West, the GR-1 seemed to be just another ICBM, not the first of the dreadful FOBS family.

The first of eight test flights occurred in October 1964, undetected by the Americans. Four years later, in November 1968, the Soviets canceled the GR-1 without having deployed it operationally. A multiple warhead GR-2 system that was being designed during the 1960s is believed to have been canceled as well.

RT-2 (SS-13) Savage

The Savage was atypical of Soviet ICBMs of the 1960s in that it used solid fuel rather than liquid as a propellant. It was also a three-stage system at a time when most Soviet ICBMs had two.

The solid fuel permitted the crew to launch the weapon in a matter of minutes upon getting their order, compared to several hours for contemporary liquid-fuel missiles. Despite this apparent versatility, the solid-fuel engines proved unreliable and ultimately only about sixty RT-2s were built.

Standing 69 feet 9 inches with its 1,200-pound warhead attached, the Savage was designed to deliver this weapon over a range of 7,500 miles. Because it weighed 40,000 pounds—most of which was its solid fuel—the enormous missile was transported as separate stages and stacked in the silo. Despite the bulkiness of this cumbersome weapon, Soviet planners actually considered developing an alternative mobile launcher!

The RT-2 program got under way in November 1959 under the direction of Sergei Korolev. The flight-test program began in February 1966 at Kapustin Yar, and the Strategic Rocket Forces received their five dozen missiles between 1968 and 1972.

In the meantime, the RT-2P variant was designed with electronic countermeasures to defend it against American antiballistic missiles. Testing began at the end of 1969, and the first operational missiles were deployed three years later.

As with the United States Minutemen, the solid fuel permitted the Savages to remain in place and ready to use for extended periods of time. The first-generation RT-2s were reportedly still functional in 1996 when part of the fleet was replaced with newer single-warhead RT-2UTTH Topol-Ms.

RT-20 (SS-15) Scrooge and RT-21 (SS-16 or RS-14) Sinner

The RT-20 was a unique weapon on two counts. It was a hybrid in terms of its propulsion. Its first stage had a solid-fuel engine, while the second stage was fueled with liquid propellants (asymmetrical dimethylhydrazine and nitrogen tetroxide). It was also the first Soviet missile with ICBM range to be road mobile. The Soviet Union had modeled the basing mode of its shorter range MRBMs after that of the German V-2, but the Scrooge was perhaps the first portable missile that was capable of lobbing a 1.5 megaton warhead 5,000 miles.

As it was being designed in the early 1960s, designers at the Yuzhnoye design bureau toyed with a traditional silo-based scenario and a rail-launched mode. However, they eventually settled on using a launcher based on a heavy tank that would be capable of lugging the 30-ton behemoth. The 58-foot 4-inch missile was packed into a canister and carried on a truck until it was time to fire.

Flight testing began in the autumn of 1967, although a dummy RT-20 had been displayed in a Red Square parade two years earlier. The test program did not go as well as planned, and the project was terminated in October 1969.

The RT-21 Sinner was another ultimately unsuccessful attempt at developing a mobile ICBM. It was a three-stage missile, with all three using solid fuel. It stood 65 feet 7 inches and had a maximum range with its single warhead of 6,500 miles.

The RT-21 project began as an IRBM program in 1966, and it evolved into both IRBM and ICBM programs over the ensuing three years (see below). Two dozen flight tests of the RT-21 ICBM occurred between 1972 and 1974. The Sinner ICBM was initially deployed with the Strategic Rocket Forces in 1976, but under the 1979 SALT II agreement, the Soviet Union agreed not to produce, test or deploy "SS-16 type" ICBMs. Nevertheless, a certain amount of test work continued with the missiles until about 1985.

The importance of the RT-20 and RT-21 projects was that they tested the road mobile basing concept that would be adapted for the second-generation RT-2-series ICBMs.

RT-21M Pioneer (SS-20 Saber)

As noted above, when the RT-21 program began in the early 1960s, it was aimed at developing a mobile IRBM. When the program forked, the IRBM path led to the RT-21M, which the Soviets called Pioneer and NATO called Saber. The RT-21M was a two-stage variation on the three-stage RT-21 ICBM. Solid fueled, it stood within a few inches of 54 feet depending on warhead type, and had a range of up to 3,000 miles. Early versions of the Pioneer had single warheads, but later variants were capable of carrying three.

The RT-21M was designed as an eventual replacement for the liquid-fuel R-5 and R-12 missiles that had been deployed into Eastern Europe to target the NATO capitals of Western Europe. Flight testing at Kapustin Yar began in late 1975, and deployment quickly followed in the summer 1976. The multiple-warhead variant came online in the late 1970s. The RT-21Ms were road portable, but could also be set up to be launched from fixed-surface launch sites enclosed in buildings. By 1986, there were more than 400 Pioneer missiles on alert in Eastern Europe.

When the Intermediate-Range and Shorter-Range Nuclear Forces (INF) Treaty took effect in 1988, the Soviets were required to dismantle all of the RT-21Ms and their launchers. This was accomplished by the summer of 1991.

HGM-25A and LGM-25C Titan

The largest of SAC's arsenal of ICBMs was the aptly named Titan. The Titan I stood 98 feet, and the Titan II was 103 feet tall. Their respective launch weights were 110 and 165 tons.

Titan was the first United States ICBM project that began

after President Eisenhower made ICBM technology the top defense priority in 1955. Originally conceived under the same Weapons System 107 program as Atlas, the Titan ICBM would be developed and built by the Glenn L. Martin Company under the "B for Bomber" designation B-68 (later SM-68). The SM-68A Titan I would be a two-stage, liquid-fueled ICBM utilizing both radio and all-inertial guidance with a range of more than 6,000 miles. Whereas the Atlas ICBMs were designed to be surface launched, the Titan was intended to be a silo-launched weapon.

The first successful Titan I launch occurred in February 1959, and the Strategic Air Command made thirty-one successful long-range test firings on the Pacific Missile Range in 1961. The following year, two squadrons of SAC's 703rd Strategic Missile Wing became operational with the Titan I, now designated HGM-25A. By 1965, the Titan Is were phased out in favor of the larger LGM-25C Titan II ICBM, which had a range of 9,300 miles.

First tested in November 1961, the Titan II became operational in June 1963 with the 570th Strategic Missile Squadron. By year's end, SAC had six squadrons active with nine missile sites each. Eventually, 135 Titan IIs would be produced. The Titan II was liquid fueled with a half-and-half mixture of hydrazine and unsymmetrical dimethylhydrazine, with a nitrogen tetroxide oxidizer.

The 9 megaton W53 thermonuclear warheads were the largest deployed on a United States ICBM during the Cold War, and they represented more than a quarter of SAC megatonnage, even though Titans were outnumbered ten to one by Minutemen.

In 1981, because of maintenance issues, the Department of Defense initiated Operation Rivet Cap, an immediate deactivation of the liquid-fueled Titans. The last Titan II was retired from Little Rock AFB, Arkansas, in August 1987, leaving the solid-fuel Minutemen as the principal American ICBM.

Like the Atlas—and unlike the Minuteman—the Titan

would go on to be adapted for a long life as a space launch vehicle that continued past the turn of the century.

R-36 (SS-9) Scarp

For Western military analysts, the parades that the Soviet Union staged semiannually in Moscow were an opportunity to peek under the metaphorical curtain of secrecy and catch a glimpse of what secret weapons the Soviets had been creating. For the Soviets, the parades were an opportunity to "shock and awe" the West.

At few times during the Cold War was the West more shocked or awed at a Red Square parade than in November 1967, when the R-36 Scarp was first shown to the world. There was yet more shock and awe in store for Western analysts when they began to calculate the Scarp's payload capacity and measure its accuracy from the launch that they were able to observe from a distance.

A two-stage, liquid-fuel ICBM, it stood nearly 105 feet 7 inches with its warhead. The Scarp is seen as a direct evolution of the R-16 Saddler, particularly in the fact that the first stages of the two are alike. It is now known that the R-36 was specifically designed to target the Strategic Air Command Minuteman Launch Control Centers. Each center controlled roughly a dozen ICBMs, so the loss of one center would essentially take a whole ICBM field offline.

The first version of the R-36 carried a single warhead that weighed up to 12,500 pounds, while the second, and most widely deployed variant had a 13,500-pound capacity. Subsequent versions were the R-36-O and the multiple-warhead R-36-M that are discussed below.

The R-36 project began in 1962 at the Yuzhnoye design bureau, and flight tests began in September 1963 at the Baikonur Kosmodrome. The first operational deployment by Strategic Rocket Forces units came at the end of 1966. The R-36-Ms began joining their single-warhead sisters in the field in October 1970.

In service, the R-36s were based in hardened silos that

were 136 feet deep. More than 260 silos were constructed
through 1973, and they remained armed with active R-36s
through 1978 when deactivation of the system began.

R-36-O (Fractional Orbital Bombardment System)

Yet more shock and awe was directed toward the R-36 when
it was finally ascertained that it had been married into the
Fractional Orbital Bombardment System (FOBS) family. It
is now known that the R-36-O variant of the R-36 Scarp was
the launch vehicle for the ominous plan to orbit nuclear
weapons in space. The system was designed by Mikhail Yangel in competition with Sergei Korolev's GR-1 weapon,
which was tested, but which did not become operational.

It utilized the first two stages of the R-36, but added a
third stage to carry the warhead and its guidance and
telemetry package into orbit.

There were twenty-four test launches of the FOBS program between December 1965 and August 1971. The first
successful suborbital launch would be the fourth of the program in May 1966. Knowing that the United States CIA
was observing and tracking the launches, the Soviets then
began officially designating the FOBS launches with the
Kosmos prefix that was assigned generically to the majority
of their launches that reached orbital altitude. For example,
in January 1967, the seventh FOBS mission and the first to
deliver a dummy payload to a target was designated as Kosmos 139.

The majority of the subsequent FOBS tests were successful, with a number of shots delivering dummy payloads to equatorial locations in the Pacific Ocean. There
were ten tests in 1967 on the eve of the Outer Space Treaty
going into effect, four in 1968 and four after that. The last
of the two dozen FOBS flights, in August 1971, was a successful test designated as Kosmos 433.

In the meantime, the Strategic Rocket Forces put the
FOBS system onto operational alert in underground silos
at the Baikonur Kosmodrome complex in what is now Kazakhstan. An estimated eighteen FOBS-equipped R-36-O

ICBMs were under the control of the 98th Missile Brigade from 1969 through 1974, and with the Strategic Rocket Forces Orenburg Rocket Army thereafter.

Between 1982 and 1984, under the SALT II Treaty, the Soviet Union is believed to have deactivated the FOBS system and to have destroyed the basing silos. It is believed that no armed and active FOBS payload was placed into orbit.

Beginning in 1968, Yangel had also adapted the R-36-O third stage for use as a space launch system under the name Tsyklon. This system remained in use until the 1990s.

R-36-M (SS-18 or RS-20) Satan

True to its nickname, Satan was long regarded in the West as the most evil of Soviet weapons. The largest ICBM, it dwarfed anything in the United States arsenal and always made the Soviet Strategic Rocket Forces look especially terrifying in the comparison charts that were published by the American Department of Defense during the Cold War. There were six variants of the Satan, ranging in height (with warheads attached) from 110 feet 3 inches to 122 feet 3 inches. Each was a two-stage weapon, fueled by dimethylhydrazine. The first stage delivered 920,000 pounds of thrust; the second, 154,000 pounds. The total launch weight ranged from 366,000 to 419,000 pounds.

More terrifying than its size was the multiple warhead capability. Originally it was equipped with three warheads that could not be independently targeted, but eventually the Satan system evolved to ICBMs with at least two warheads that could be independently targeted. It was widely believed that a sizable majority if the 1,000 United States Minuteman ICBMs could be taken out in a massed, first-strike launch of Satans. Because of this, the Satans became a subject of intense bickering during the SALT arms control talks.

Satan was designed to be retrofitted into existing Scarp missile silos, and it was equipped with a solid-fueled ejector system to eject it before launch. The program began in 1969 at the Yuzhnoye design bureau in Dnepropetrovsk in what is now Ukraine, and the first successful flight test occurred in February 1973. Operational deployment by the Strategic Rocket Forces began in 1975. The second variant, capable of carrying up to eight independently targeted warheads, began tests in 1973, and more than 130 of these were deployed between 1975 and 1978. By 1983, they had been replaced by later model R-36-Ms.

The third version was seen as an improved variation of the original model. It carried an improved guidance system that allowed designers to reduce the size of the warhead in order to save weight. This, in turn, increased the range to nearly 10,000 miles. Flight tests of this version began in October 1977, and it was deployed operationally soon after.

The fourth Satan variant carried at least ten and possibly as many as fourteen independently targeted warheads. The first of an eventual 120 of this R-36-M type were operationally deployed in September 1979. For the next several years, they were in service alongside earlier models, but, by 1984, the early types had been retired.

In 1988, the Strategic Rocket Forces began to take delivery of the fifth Satan variant, the R-36-M2 Voivode (Warlord). Like its predecessor, the new Warlord carried ten independently targeted warheads, but each had its nuclear yield increased to about a megaton. The increased throw weight of individual missiles allowed the Soviet Union to retain substantial hitting power after it made the cuts in overall numbers that were mandated by SALT II.

Testing of a sixth Satan type, an improved R-36-M2 Voivode with a single 20-megaton warhead, was completed in September 1989. These were fielded by the Strategic Rocket Forces in August 1991, just before the collapse of the Soviet Union. As the Cold War ended, Satan launch sites remained in Russia and Kazakhstan. All of the latter were dismantled by 1996, and Russia committed to removing more than 200 of its remaining Satans by 2003.

LGM-30 Minuteman

The Boeing Minuteman is the longest-serving ICBM, and probably the most important offensive missile system in the history of the United States arsenal. It was also the world's first solid-fuel ICBM. The Minuteman outlived its early contemporaries to remain as a key fixture of the American nuclear deterrent force from the 1960s to beyond the turn of the century.

The Minuteman development program began in 1958 under the bomber designation B-80 (later SM-80). The first-generation Minuteman I had its debut launch in February 1961, under the designation LGM-30A. Armed with a 1.2-megaton W59 warhead, the Minuteman I had a range of more than 6,000 miles. The first operational LGM-30A and LGM-30Bs were deployed in 1963, with the first unit being the Strategic Air Command's 10th Strategic Missile Squadron at Malmstrom AFB in Montana. By year's end, six squadrons were active with the first 372 of an eventual 650 Minuteman I missiles.

The next operational variant was the LGM-30F Minuteman II, first tested in 1964. It stood 57 feet 7 inches high, 20 inches taller than the Minuteman I. Its more powerful second-stage engine extended its range to 7,000 miles. The first unit, the 321st Strategic Missile Wing at Grand Forks AFB, North Dakota, became the first operational unit in 1965. By the spring of 1967, 500 LGM-30Fs were in their silos.

The LGM-30G Minuteman III incorporated a Multiple Independently Targetable Reentry Vehicle (MIRV) capability, meaning that each of a Minuteman III's three 175- to 340-kiloton warheads could be directed to a different target. It stood 59 feet 10 inches tall and had a range of more than 8,000 miles. Work on this ultimate Minuteman began in 1965, and the first test launch occurred in August 1968.

The first operational deployment of the Minuteman II was to the 741st Strategic Missile Squadron at Minot AFB in North Dakota in June 1970. By 1974, all of SAC's Minuteman I missiles had been replaced by either the Minuteman II or Minuteman III, and the total in service had reached 999. The Minuteman III would remain in production until 1977, bringing the total number produced—of all variants—to over 2,400.

SAC reached its peak Minuteman deployment in 1978, with 1,180. These were grouped into nine Minuteman II squadrons and eleven Minuteman III squadrons. The Minutemen were all operationally based in hardened silos, although SAC studied various mobile-basing scenarios, especially railroad basing, through the years. In 1960, under Operation Big Star, a modified test train was sent throughout the western and midwestern United States so that factors from communications to roadbed vibration could be evaluated. The study proved the feasibility of such basing, but in 1961, the Department of Defense decided not to proceed with mobile basing for the Minuteman.

For nearly three decades, Minuteman crews across the United States stood ready, twenty-four hours a day, to immediately initiate their launch sequences, but in 1991, with the Cold War over, President George H. W. Bush officially took the Minuteman force off high alert.

In 1992 and 1993, the United States removed and destroyed all of the Minuteman IIs. Meanwhile, under the START II agreement, the Air Force "de-MIRVed" the Minuteman III fleet, retrofitting them with single warheads. At the turn of the century, the Minuteman force consisted of 500 LGM-30Cs. These were based in vast fields controlled by and surrounding Francis E. Warren AFB, Malmstrom AFB, and Minot AFB.

Ironically, the Minuteman III was earmarked for retention by the U.S. Air Force after the retirement of the LGM-118A Peacekeeper, which had originally been conceived as a Minuteman replacement.

UR-100 (SS-11 or RS-10) Sego

Often described as the Soviet Minuteman, the UR-100 was produced in larger numbers than any other Soviet ICBM during the Cold War. With more than 1,400 produced, the UR-100 was the only ICBM that matched the number of Minutemen that were deployed at a given time. Other similarities between the two included their range and their being based in hardened silos. In both cases, about ten silos were controlled by a single control center. Standing 55 feet 6 inches, the UR-100 was within a few inches of being the same height as the various Minuteman variants.

Differences included propellant. Whereas the three-stage Minutemen were designed with solid fuel, the two-stage UR-100s followed the previous Soviet practice of using liquid fuel. Like the Minuteman, the UR-100 was originally deployed with a single warhead with a yield of .6 to 1.2 megatons.

The UR-100 project got under way early in 1963 under the direction of Vladimir Chelomei and his team, and the first launch was conducted at the Baikonur Kosmodrome in April 1965. An initial test launch from a silo occurred three months later. The first missiles reached the Strategic Rocket Forces in November 1966, and the type was deemed operational in July 1967. An estimated 990 of the basic UR-100 were built, making it the most widely produced single ICBM variant in Strategic Rocket Forces history.

The upgraded UR-100K missile, with improved systems, entered flight test in February 1971. Lengthened to 62 feet 4 inches, it had more volume for propellant. With this, the range was increased to about 7,500 miles. The payload capability also increased by 60 percent to more than 2,000 pounds. It became operational in 1973, although recently released Soviet documents indicate that it may have been ready by the end of 1971.

Entering its test phase in July 1971, the UR-100U was similar to the UR-100K, but it carried three warheads. These were not, however, independently targetable. The UR-100U was deployed by September 1974, and possibly sooner. A later version with six warheads was tested, but it never actually entered service with the Strategic Rocket Forces.

There was an estimated total of 420 UR-100Ks and

UR-100Us, and these were deployed into UR-100 silos as the latter were being retired, so there were probably never more than about 1,000 at any given moment. At the time of the collapse of the Soviet Union, just over 300 remained. In accord with the Strategic Arms Reduction Treaty (START), Russia had disposed of the entire fleet by 1996.

UR-100MR (SS-17) Spanker

As the designation implies, the Soviet UR-100MR was an evolution of the previous missiles in the UR-100 ICBM series. The idea with the UR-100MR was to create the first Soviet ICBM to be MIRV-equipped. In this case, "multiple" meant four. In order that the Spanker could be retrofitted into Sego launch silos, the dimensions were similar. The initial version stood 73 feet 10 inches, and the final UR-100MRs were over 78 feet tall. As with its older sisters, the UR-100MR had two stages fueled with asymmetrical dimethylhydrazine and nitrogen tetroxide.

Work began officially in 1970 at the Yuzhnoye design bureau and three years of flight tests began at the Baikonur Kosmodrome in December 1971. Initial deployments with the Strategic Rocket Forces began over the summer of 1975. Flight tests of the final Spanker variant occurred between 1977 and 1979, and it was deployed at the end of 1980. At their peak in 1983, an estimated 150 UR-100M missiles were deployed, but the Soviet Union agreed in the START I Treaty to dismantle them all.

UR-100N (SS-19) Stiletto

The Stiletto was a two-stage, liquid-fueled ICBM built to the same specifications as the Spanker. It stood 78 feet tall and had a payload capacity of 8,700 pounds, more than double that of the Spanker. While the Spanker was equipped with four MIRVs, two of the three Stiletto variants had six. As with the Spanker, there was a variant designed to carry one very large warhead.

Designed by Vladimir Chelomei, the UR-100N began

more than two years of flight tests at the Baikonur Kosmodrome in April 1973. It was deployed with the Strategic Rocket Forces by the end of 1975, and possibly sooner. Over 400 MIRVed Stilettos were deployed, along with about 60 of the "hard target" single-warhead versions. Of these, 300 were still deployed in 1991 when the START I Treaty came into force and the Cold War ended.

As the Soviet Union collapsed, most UR-100N sites were within Russia, but about a third were in Ukraine. The latter retained ownership of the missiles, but Russia was permitted to disarm the nuclear warheads. At the turn of the century, Russia maintained more than 150 active UR-100N launch sites.

LGM-118 Peacekeeper

Given the overwhelming lead the Soviet Union had taken in the deployment of ICBMs in the 1970s, the U.S. Air Force Strategic Air Command began to consider a successor to the Minuteman that would match the multiple-warhead Soviet UR-100 family. Throughout the decade, studies were conducted that considered various configurations for such a new ICBM, which was given the interim designation MX (missile, experimental).

In 1979, the Department of Defense gave the go-ahead for engineering work on the new missile, which would be officially designated as MGM-118 (later redesignated as LGM-118 or LG-118). In 1982, it would be named Peacekeeper by President Ronald Reagan.

Built by Martin Marietta, the Peacekeeper stood 71 feet tall in three solid-fuel stages plus a liquid-fueled post-boost stage. Whereas the MIRVed Minuteman III had three warheads, the MIRVed Peacekeeper had ten Avco Mark 21 reentry vehicles.

The first successful launch occurred in June 1983 at Vandenberg AFB on the California coast and dropped a test payload 4,190 miles downrange near Kwajalein.

In the meantime, the basing scenario was the subject of great controversy. The Carter administration first proposed the so-called Racetrack System to Congress as a way of basing the Peacekeeper. Under this scheme, an enormous system of tracks would be built under hundreds of acres of Utah and Nevada desert. The missiles would be randomly moved through these subsurface tunnels so that it would never be clear where the missiles were on the track and the Soviets would have had to to expend several hundred warheads in a first strike and still not be quite sure that they had destroyed all the Peacekeeper missiles.

The incredible expense required by this plan, plus opposition from cattlemen, with whom such a system would have to compete for necessary and scarce water, led the administration to examine other basing modes.

Eventually the Department of Defense evolved the notion of building a large number of shelters from which the Peacekeepers could be launched, and then moving the missiles from shelter to shelter, like the peas in a shell game. Soviet surveillance satellites in space and ground observers cruising the back roads of Utah in station wagons would never be quite sure which shelter contained a missile. This idea, called the multiple protective shelter (MPS) basing mode, was not well received by the incoming Reagan administration. By June 1981, Congress prohibited the spending of $357 million that had been earmarked for MPS construction until the Reagan administration decided whether it was going to proceed with MPS or not.

Meanwhile, several other proposals were starting to surface. Among them was the logical and cost-effective suggestion of placing the more modern ten-MIRV Peacekeeper in existing Minuteman silos and developing a smaller, more mobile ICBM. Reagan administration Secretary of Defense Caspar Weinberger concurrently favored development of an airmobile system whereby the Peacekeeper would be carried by giant C-5 transports (whose cargo hold was many times larger than a bomber's bomb bay). The Peacekeeper could be dropped by parachute and ignited in midair. Senator John Tower of Texas (then chairman of the powerful Senate Armed Services Committee) pointed to earlier studies of this type of basing mode that showed it to be not only more expensive than MPS but also very unreliable. Congress accepted Tower's assessment of the airmobile mode and rejected it.

In October 1982, the Reagan administration proposed a plan called Closely Spaced Basing (CSB), which was quickly nicknamed "Dense Pack." Under CSB, all of the Peacekeeper missiles would be based together in one small field at SAC's 5,872-acre Francis E. Warren AFB in Wyoming. The rationale for Dense Pack was that with all the missiles so close together, at least some would survive a direct hit. Nevertheless, survivability under the CSB came into serious question, so it was back to the drawing board once again.

In May 1983, Congress had come back to the idea—which it had earlier rejected—of basing the Peacekeeper in former Minuteman III silos. By this time, it was planned that SAC would acquire 100 Peacekeepers.

In December 1986, the first ten Peacekeepers—loaded into silos at Warren AFB—went on full alert with the 90th Strategic Missile Wing. Two years later, fifty Peacekeepers had been installed at the base. Meanwhile, also in December 1986, the Department of Defense announced that the additional fifty Peacekeepers would be deployed in a mobile scenario that was known as Rail Garrison. By the end of 1992, the missiles would be loaded, two each, on twenty-five trains that would be parked at Warren AFB, as well as at five other bases from Spokane to Shreveport.

In April 1989, however, Congress decided to limit Peacekeeper acquisition to the fifty missiles already delivered. There were plans to pull these missiles out of the silos and put them into the Rail Garrison, but the Cold War ended before this happened. At the turn of the century, all fifty Peacekeepers were still in place at Warren AFB, but all were scheduled to be withdrawn from service.

RT-23 (SS-24) Scalpel

If the UR-100 extended family was created and nurtured by the Soviets to match the capabilities of the United States Minuteman, the RT-23 was designed to match the United States Peacekeeper. It gave the Soviet Strategic Rocket Forces a ten-warhead MIRV capability for the first time. It was a three-stage, solid-fueled ICBM that stood 76 to 78 feet tall depending on warhead configuration, and it had a range of nearly 7,000 miles.

It was designed to be based in silos, but the Soviet interest in mobile ICBMs also led to the creation of a railroad-mobile version. As noted above, the United States had considered and abandoned such a basing scenario for its ICBMs, but kept them in silos.

Under study at the Yuzhnoye design bureau since 1969, the project was officially sanctioned in 1976 as a reaction to the MX Program in the United States. Problems that occurred during initial flight testing in 1982 sent the project back to the drawing board until 1984. The first silo-based missile finally became operational with the Strategic Rocket Forces in 1987. Most of the fifty-six silos were near Pervomaysk in the Ukraine, but ten were at the Tatishchevo field in western Russia.

Tests of the railroad-launched Scalpel were successful in 1985, and thirty-six missiles of this version were operational by the end of 1989. Pulled by several diesel locomotives, the trains carrying the missiles typically had three cars carrying one Scalpel each, plus a control car and several passenger and baggage cars for crews and equipment. They were deployed on railroads in three sections of the Soviet Union: near Kostroma, about 250 miles east of Moscow; near Bershet in central Russia; and near Krasnoyarsk in Siberia.

Scalpel production continued in Ukraine after the breakup of the Soviet Union, but ceased in the mid-1990s. Though the START Treaty called for the Scalpels to be dismantled, trainloads of rail-based missiles still existed at the turn of the century.

RT-2PM Topol (SS-25 Sickle)

While the UR-100 ICBM series can be seen as the Soviet Union's silo-based, liquid-fueled answer to the American Minuteman, the RT-2PM Topol (a.k.a. Poplar) was a mobile, solid-fuel missile in the same class as the Minuteman. It continued the development efforts undertaken in the RT-20 (SS-15) Scrooge and RT-21 (SS-16 or RS-14) Sinner programs that were aimed at a truly practical mobile ICBM.

A three-stage missile, the RT-2PM stood 70 feet 6 inches and it had a range of 6,500 miles with a single half-megaton payload. It was designed as a single-warhead ICBM, but tests with multiple warheads were conducted. The launcher was based on a seven-axle MAZ (Minsk Wheeled-Truck-Tractor) chassis that could cruise the back roads of the Soviet Union waiting for the order to launch. Like the earlier RT-21M Pioneer IRBM, the RT-2PM Topol could also be launched from a fixed-surface launch site inside a building.

The RT-2M program began officially in July 1977, and flight testing occurred at the Plesetsk Kosmodrome between February and December 1985. The Strategic Rocket Forces were operational with the missile in the Soviet Far East by May 1988. Nearly 300 had been deployed by 1991, when the Soviet Union was dissolved, but production would continue into the 1990s. The RT-2Ms that had been based in Belarus in 1991 were said to have been shipped to Russia by 1996.

It was Russia's stated intention to insert the Ukraine-made RT-2Ms into silos, replacing their R-36-M Satans. Meanwhile, under the START II Treaty, 16 feet of concrete had been poured into these silos to make them incapable of holding Satans.

RT-2UTTH (SS-27) Topol M

The last Soviet ICBM—and the first Russian ICBM—the RT-2UTTH evolved from the earlier RT-2PM Topol. In October 1991, the Soviet Union made its eleventh-hour decision not to develop the RSS-40 Kuryer small ICBM (the equivalent of the never-deployed American Midgetman small ICBM), so Topol M was the only game in town.

A solid-fuel, three-stage missile similar to the Minuteman III, the Topol M stands 74 feet 6 inches, weighs 47 tons and has a range of nearly 7,000 miles. Though the program was initiated as a Soviet project, the first test launch occurred in December 1994 with Topol M, a Russian ICBM. The first of a planned 300 or so became operational with the Russian Strategic Rocket Forces in 2003, but budget cuts drastically reduced the number that could be deployed. Reportedly, about thirty Topol Ms were based at Svetly in 2004.

CHAPTER 5

Submarine Launched Ballistic Missiles

LIKE THEIR COUSINS THE ICBMS, SUBMARINE LAUNCHED BAL-
listic Missiles (SLBMs) were doomsday weapons designed during the Cold War to conduct strategic nuclear
strikes on the heartland of the Soviet Union and the
United States. The difference, obviously, is that they
were designed to be launched from submarines. This
meant that their launch sites were extremely mobile and
extremely hard to track and to detect—not to mention
very close to the target. A Soviet ICBM launch would
have given the United States about a half hour in which
to react. A Soviet nuclear submarine in the Atlantic
could have gotten close enough to the eastern seaboard
of the United States to annihilate New York or Washington with just a few minutes' warning—hardly time to do
anything.

The existence of SLBMs necessitated both sides
spending vast resources on tracking and detection, and
even this provided almost no useful cushion in the ridicu-
lously slim margin of warning time. In the darkest of
doomsday scenarios, the SLBMs aboard the submarines
of the two nations had the potential of rendering a nuclear
checkmate at almost any time.

Rigel and Regulus

The idea of submarine-launched guided missiles never really took hold during World War II. The Germans had a number of very sophisticated missiles, but never showed much interest in launching them from U-boats. The U.S. Navy borrowed missiles from the Army that were based on captured German missiles, but showed no interest in launching them from submarines—until after World War II. Part of the reason was that in the 1940s, missiles would have had to be launched from the deck while the submarine was surfaced, and that is when a submarine is at its most vulnerable. It would be more than a decade before practical underwater launching systems would turn SLBMs from novelties to truly potent weapons.

So the first generation of SLBMs were surface launched. The U.S. Navy was converting some of its surface ships to launch missiles, and these missiles were simply adapted for submarine use. After experimenting with borrowed and adapted KUW-1 Loons and other primitive missiles, the U.S. Navy developed its own true first generation.

The first was the 47-foot Grumman Rigel, a supersonic missile that was tested in 1951 and 1952. Considered very sophisticated for its day, the Rigel had a range of nearly 600 miles. A contemporary of the Rigel was the 45-foot Triton, which was tested between 1951 and 1955. Developed by the Applied Physics Laboratory at Johns Hopkins University, it was faster than the Rigel and one of the first missiles developed for the U.S. Navy that was capable of carrying a nuclear warhead. Neither the Rigel nor Triton entered operational service.

The Vought SSM-N-8 (later RGM-6) Regulus was a small, turbojet-powered cruise missile capable of delivering a 3,000-pound nuclear payload up to 600 miles. Flight testing of the 33-foot Regulus began in 1951, and it became operational in 1954. It was soon complemented by the 57.5-foot Vought RGM-15 Regulus II, a supersonic missile with a range of more than 1,000 miles.

The U.S. Navy deployed the Regulus missiles aboard

surface ships, especially cruisers, as well as aboard submarines. The first successful shipboard launch came in November 1952, with the first submarine launch from the deck of the USS *Tunny* (SSG-282) following in July 1953. The first operational deployment was aboard the cruiser USS *Los Angeles* (CA-135) in 1955.

Submarine deployments began the following year aboard the *Tunny* and the USS *Barbero* (SSG-317). Two larger, diesel-powered submarines, the USS *Grayback* (SSG-574) and USS *Growler* (SSG-577), were also retrofitted to carry the Regulus. The nuclear submarine USS *Halibut* (SSGN-587) was specifically built for the Regulus. On March 25, 1960, the USS *Halibut* became the first nuclear submarine to successfully launch a guided missile. In each submarine, the missiles were carried in a large "hangar" that was located on the deck in order to keep them above the wave tops when the vessel was operating on the surface.

Though innovative and forward looking when it was conceived in the 1950s, the Regulus program was soon overtaken by the Polaris program, with its underwater launch capability. The last operational Regulus deployment was aboard the *Halibut* in 1964. Today, the USS *Growler* and a Regulus are on display at the Intrepid Sea-Air-Space Museum in New York City.

Early Soviet SLBM Systems

In the 1950s, the Soviet Union moved to adapt vertical-launch, land-based ballistic missiles for use aboard submarines, and these early weapons preceded the U.S. Navy's development of the Polaris. The 34-foot R-11, NATO code-named Scud, was first launched from a submarine in September 1955 in the White Sea close off the Kola Peninsula. Eleven months later, the submarine B-67 undertook the first long-range patrol armed with R-11s. Based on experience gained from this initial deployment, the R-11 was redesigned to increase its service life when exposed to a maritime environment. Tests of the thus improved R-11 are known to have occurred in 1958. This missile would remain in service until 1967.

The 49-foot R-13 missile, NATO code-named Sark, was initially deployed aboard 629 Class and 658 Class submarines—NATO code-named Golf and Hotel, respectively—in October 1961. These would remain in service for more than a decade, with the phase-out beginning in about 1973.

In retrospect, the deployment of both Scud and Sark aboard submarines was probably more experimental than operational. It was a means of using an off-the-shelf system to evaluate the SLBM concept before moving on to a weapon designed from the ground up as an SLBM.

Polaris

The U.S. Navy initiated the Polaris program in 1956, the same year that the Soviet navy conducted the first submerged launch of the R-21 ballistic missile. Polaris would be a crash program aimed at creating the first ballistic missile capable of both intercontinental range and of being launched underwater.

The Lockheed Missiles & Space Company was charged with this enormous engineering challenge, and the program moved relatively quickly. The first-generation Polaris Al (UGM-27) Fleet Ballistic Missile would acheive its first launch from a submerged submarine in July 1960, and the first Polaris-equipped submarine was on patrol four months after that.

The two-stage, 28.5-foot Polaris Al was fueled with a polyurethane propellant and had ammonium percholorate as the oxidizer. Weighing 28,800 pounds, it had a range in excess of 1,000 miles. The first submerged launch on July 20, 1960, was from the USS *George Washington* (SSBN 598) off Cape Canaveral, Florida. It was followed by a second launch three hours later.

In 1959, Lockheed had already begun work on the Polaris A2, which was first tested on November 10, 1960, and the first submerged launch occurred on October 23, 1961,

from the USS *Ethan Allen* (SSBN-608), the first submarine
designed from the keel up as a nuclear-powered, ballistic
missile submarine. The 31-foot A2 had the same 54-inch
diameter as the A1, so that it could fit the same launch tubes
as the A1. It weighed 32,500 pounds and had a range of
1,500 miles. The A2 became operational in June 1962
aboard the *Ethan Allen*.

The Polaris A3 SLBM was within 2 inches of the same
size as the A2, thus fitting the same tubes as either of its
predecessors. A more capable missile, it had a range of
2,500 miles and weighed 35,700 pounds. Like the U.S. Air
Force land-based Minuteman family, the Polaris family
was now making the transition from a single nuclear warhead to multiple reentry vehicles. Other improvements include those made to propellants, combustion chambers and
velocity control.

The first A3 test launch occurred at Cape Canaveral in
August 1962, and the first submerged launch was from the
USS *Andrew Jackson* (SSBN-619) in October 1963. The
Polaris A3 was first used to equip an operational submarine on patrol with the Atlantic Fleet when the USS *Daniel
Webster* (SSBN-626) was put to sea with 16 A3s in September 1964 from Charleston, South Carolina. Three
months later the USS *Daniel Boone* (SSBN-629) became
the first A3-equipped submarine on patrol in the Pacific.

Beginning in 1962, Lockheed and the U.S. Navy undertook studies of an SLBM that would have a great capacity
to evade the missile defense system—including such
weapons as the mysterious UR-96/A350 Galosh antimissile missile system—that the Soviet Union was known
to be constructing. This led to the Polaris B3 concept,
which involved increasing the missile's gross weight and
expanding the diameter to 74 inches. New systems included
the warm gas reaction attitude control system code-named
Mailman. This system used small jets of compressed gas to
control the position and trajectory when the system was in
outer space.

Both single- and multiple-warhead configurations were

considered for the B3. At the same time, the U.S. Air Force and General Electric were developing the Mark 12 multiple-target reentry vehicle for the Minuteman, and it was decided to incorporate these into the next-generation Polaris. There was considerable discussion over whether to use only the Mark 12, or to also include additional, smaller warheads. The latter configuration was nicknamed Flexible Flyer after the popular sled that many of the engineers had used as children.

By 1964, the design for the U.S. Navy's new SLBM had evolved so far that it was decided to create a new family name to distinguish it from the earlier Polaris family. The Polaris B3 was abandoned in favor of a new missile that would be known as Poseidon C3.

R-21 (SS-N-5) Serb

A contemporary of the U.S. Navy Polaris, the Soviet R-21 was based both on earlier SLBM work done in the Soviet Union and on what could be learned about the Polaris. Because the R-21 designation was unknown in the West, this submarine was given the NATO code name Serb and designated as SS-N-5 by the United States Department of Defense. It would be the first Soviet missile designed to be launched from underwater.

Unlike the two-stage, solid-fuel Polaris, the R-21 was a single-stage, liquid-fuel missile. It was 49 feet long, making it nearly twice the size of the Polaris, but its range of about 870 miles was less than that of even the Polaris A1.

The first submerged launch of the Serb occurred on December 23, 1956, from a modified Whiskey Class submarine. This placed the R-21 program nearly four years ahead of the Polaris program, which was only just then getting under way. By the time of the first submerged Polaris launches in 1960, a number of underwater launches of the R-21 had taken place.

Operational deployment of the R-21 aboard Gold Class submarines began in May 1963, by which time the Polaris program had overtaken the R-21 program with a 1962 de-

ployment of the A2 model. The R-21 was deployed aboard
the Hotel Class submarines in 1964, and Western intelligence agencies estimated that the peak deployment aboard
nineteen submarines occurred in 1971. A long-lived
weapon, the R-21 is known to have still been in the active
inventory of the Soviet in 1989.

R-27 (SS-N-6) Serb

Interpreted by Western intelligence as a close follow-on to
the R-21, the 32-foot R-27 was first observed in a Moscow
Red Square parade in 1967, two years after its first flight
test and given the identification number SS-N-6 and the
same NATO code name as the R-21. Like the R-21, it had a
single stage and it used liquid propellant. It also was a
multiple-warhead SLBM, although these were not independently targetable. The R-27 had a range of 1,500 miles,
matching the range of the Polaris A2.

Operational deployment with the Soviet fleet began in
March 1968. The R-27 was designed to be carried by the
Yankee Class submarines, which were each equipped with
sixteen launch tubes. A series of upgrades through the 1970s
and 1980s would keep the R-27 in service through 1988.

Poseidon C3

The development program for the successor to the Polaris
family of SLBMs was formally initiated by the U.S. Navy
in January 1965. The studies that led to the Poseidon C3
had been ongoing for several years under the Polaris B3
designation, but the new Fleet Ballistic Missile was quite
different from its predecessor. Like Polaris, the Poseidon
was a two-stage, solid fuel missile, but it was 15 tons heavier than the largest Polaris. The 74-inch diameter was 20
inches greater than that of the Polaris A3, the last of that
family that had been deployed, and the Poseidon was 34
feet high, 10 percent taller than the Polaris A3. Nevertheless, naval architects were able to redesign the U.S. Navy's
ballistic missile submarines to accommodate the larger
weapon.

The Poseidon incorporated the large MIRVs that were being developed for the U.S. Air Force Minuteman program, as well as 14 small Mark 3 reentry vehicles.

The first Poseidon test launch occurred at Cape Canaveral in August 1968, and the first successful submerged launch was conducted from the USS *James Madison* (SSBN-627) on July 17, 1970. The latter was closely observed by a Soviet vessel which tried unsuccessfully to pick up some of the closure plate segments that were floating in the ocean after the launch.

The first operational deployment of the Poseidon was aboard the *James Madison*, which departed Charleston on March 31, 1971, with sixteen of the new SLBMs aboard.

R-29 (SS-N-8) Sawfly

The R-29 was the first two-stage SLBM to be operational with the Soviet fleet, although it used liquid propellant like the earlier SLBMs. Work on the R-29 began in 1963, and the first test launch occurred in June 1969. When it became known to Western intelligence, it was given the designation SS-N-8 and the NATO code name Sawfly. The first submerged launch of the 43-foot missile took place in December 1971, and a salvo launch of four R-29s within 30 seconds took place on December 14, 1972.

Operational deployment aboard Delta Class submarines began in March 1974. With a truly intercontinental range of 4,800 miles, the R-29 more than matched the U.S. Navy's Trident I. This meant that it could operate in waters that were relatively safe from the danger presented by U.S Navy attack submarines. Though the R-29 continued to evolve into such distinct new systems as the R-29R and R-29RM, the basic Sawfly would remain with the Soviet fleet until the end of the Cold War.

R-31 (SS-N-17) Snipe

In the early 1970s, as the U.S. Navy was developing the Trident I, its fifth-generation solid-fuel SLBM, the Soviet Union undertook to build its first. Until then, the Soviets had relied on liquid-fueled SLBMs, which have the disadvantage that they cannot be stored reliably for as long as a missile with solid propellant.

The 35-foot solid-fuel R-31 was a two-stage weapon that was designed to be easier to manage and faster to fire than the contemporary R-27 and R-29 SLBMs. When it became known to Western intelligence, it was identified as the SS-N-17 Snipe.

The first ground-launched flight tests began in 1973, and the initial submerged launch came in December 1976 in the White Sea. These tests demonstrated that the R-31 was, in fact, easy to work with and that it matched the range of the R-27. It had been hoped, however, that it would match the range of the intercontinental R-29, but it fell far short of expectations.

Nevertheless, the K-140, a 667A Navaga Class (Yankee II) submarine, was armed with R-31s and deployed in 1980. This single ship operated until 1989, when the R-31 was officially consigned to the scrap heap of failed hardware.

R-29R (SS-N-18) Stingray

Development of the multiple-warhead successor to the R-29 began in 1973 and continued through the decade. The first two stages of the R-29 and R-29R were essentially the same. However, the 46-foot R-29R incorporated a third stage containing up to seven independently targetable reentry vehicles, replacing the simple, single warhead of the R-29. To distinguish the R-29, Western intelligence services referred to it as SS-N-18 and with the especially colorful NATO code name Stingray.

Like the R-29, the R-29R had an extremely long, intercontinental range. The R-29R is able to strike targets from a distance of 3,000 miles with its MIRVed warhead, and 5,000 miles if configured with a single warhead.

Designed for deployment aboard the 667BDR Kalmar Class (Delta III) ballistic missile submarines, the R-29R would equip fourteen such vessels, beginning in 1979. Under the terms of the START I agreement, the Soviet Union agreed not to use more than four MIRVs in each of the R-29s.

R-29RM (SS-N-23) Skif

First flight tested in June 1983 and deployed after 1986, the R-29RM was essentially a higher gross-weight development of the R-29R. It used the same basic three-stage, liquid-propellant format, but was 48.5 feet tall and weighed more than 40 tons, compared to the 35.5 tons of the R-29R. Within this, the payload capacity nearly doubled from 1.8 tons to more than 3 tons. This accommodated up to ten independently targeted reentry vehicles. Additional fuel capacity increased the maximum range to nearly 5,200 miles.

As with the R-29R, a new NATO identification was assigned, and this new variation on the old R-29 became known in Western intelligence circles as the SS-N-23 Skif.

Beginning in 1986, seven 667BDRM Delfin Class (Delta IV) submarines, each with sixteen launch tubes, were armed with R-29M SLBMs. Though the ten-warhead configuration had been tested, it is believed by Western intelligence that—in accordance with the START I agreement—none of the operational R-29RM missiles was equipped with more than four warheads.

In 1988, a modernization effort was undertaken to improve the guidance systems of the R-29RMs. The missiles remained in service with the Russian navy after the collapse of the Soviet Union, and in 1999, Russia disclosed that it would resume production of the weapon.

Trident I C4

The development of the successor to the U.S. Navy's Poseidon SLBM began in November 1971, just eight months after the Poseidon was first deployed. The idea was to create a missile with nearly double the range of the Poseidon, but which would fit the 74-inch by 34-foot launch tubes that had been installed in the ballistic missile submarines to accommodate the Poseidon. The first Trident I test launch occurred at Cape Canaveral in January 1977.

While the Trident I C4 had the same exterior dimensions as the Poseidon C3, it had three, rather than two, solid-fuel stages and it weighed about 73,000 pounds. The Trident's range of 4,600 miles was nearly double that of its predecessor. Both SLBMs were manufactured by Lockheed and both were armed with MIRV. The Trident incorporated electronic stellar-inertial guidance for more accurate control and targeting of the multiple reentry vehicles.

Although the Trident could be accommodated by the existing ballistic missile submarines in the fleet, the U.S. Navy decided to build a new class of submarines that would each carry twenty-four Tridents. This massive shipbuilding program would also effectively modernize the 1960s vintage submarine fleet. The new class was officially known as the Ohio Class—as classes are named after the first vessel in the class—but it would be widely known as the Trident class.

Built by the Electric Boat Division of General Dynamics, the Ohio Class submarines are powered by a single nuclear reactor driving a single shaft. Each is 560 feet long, with a beam of 42 feet and a displacement of more than 18,000 tons when submerged. Each has a top speed of more than 20 knots and a crew of 155.

The first Ohio Class vessel, the USS *Ohio* (SSN-726) was not deployed until November 1981, so the initial Trident I C4 deployment in October 1979 was aboard the older USS *Francis Scott Key* (SSBN 657), which had been upgraded from the Poseidon.

Eventually, there would be eighteen Trident submarines, which would carry roughly half of the total number of United States nuclear warheads. The first eight would be equipped with the Trident I C4, while the remainder, beginning with the USS *Tennessee* (SSBN-734), would be armed from the outset with the new Trident II D5, which is discussed in the following entry.

Trident II D5

In October 1981, President Ronald Reagan called for a modernization of the United States strategic forces that would include the SLBMs with which the U.S. Navy's ballistic missile submarines would be armed. The basic dimentions of the three-stage Trident II D5 would be essentially the same as that of the three-stage C4. Originally, the plan had been to install the D5 on the last six of the eighteen vessels in the new Ohio Class. However, as noted above, the D5 would be available to equip the last ten.

The new missile featured improvements in all of its systems, including guidance and reentry, fire control and navigation. This would lead to a weapon with a heavier payload, additional range and enhanced accuracy.

The initial flight of the Trident II occurred in January 1987, and the fifteen-launch test program continued through September 1988. The first deployment of Trident II was in 1990 aboard the USS *Tennessee* (SSBN-734). As the Cold War came to a close, the Trident II was the standard SLBM in the United States arsenal. In 1996, the Navy began retrofitting its eight Trident I submarines with the Trident II.

R-39 (SS-N-20) Sturgeon

The R-39 was the second major effort by the Soviet Union to develop a solid-fuel SLBM. Development work on the R-39 began in 1973, the same year that flight testing started of the previous solid-fuel SLBM, the R-31. As the R-31 was proving itself to be a disappointment in terms of range, the R-39 program took on a higher sense of importance, especially after flight testing began in 1979.

Like the U.S. Navy's Trident II D5, the R-39 was a three-stage, solid-fuel SLBM with intercontinental range and MIRVs. As with the contemporary R-29RM liquid-fuel missile, "multiple" meant ten. The R-39 was 52.5 feet tall, with a 2.8-ton payload capacity.

As the U.S Navy's Trident SLBM had evolved in conjunction with a new class of ballistic missile submarines—

the Ohio Class—so too did the R-39. The vessels of the 941 Akula Class, originally designated by NATO as the Typhoon Class, were the largest submarines of the Cold War. They were 565 feet long, and double hulled like a catamaran, with a beam of 76 feet. They had a displacement of 48,000 tons, more than double that of the Ohio Class. They were powered by two reactors, compared to the single reactor of the Ohio vessels.

Ordered in 1973, the first of the Typhoons was laid down in 1977 and the six submarines of the class were commissioned between December 1981 and September 1989. All built at the Sevmash state submarine factory in Severodinsk, each was equipped with twenty launch tubes for R-39 missiles. After the fall of the Soviet Union, Russia intended to keep the Typhoons active, but because of maintenance issues, only three of the Typhoons were believed to be in service at the turn of the century.

After extensive testing, the first operational R-39s were deployed in 1984 aboard the first Typhoon Class submarine, the TK-208.

After the fall of the Soviet Union, Russia continued to upgrade the R-39 and plan for yet another class of nuclear ballistic missile submarines. The first of the new Borei Class submarines, the *Yuri Dolgoruki*, was laid down in 1996. The upgraded missile, the R-39M Grom, was first tested in November 1998. However, a series of disastrous explosions at launch during the test program reportedly led to a cancellation of the R-39M in 1999.

CHAPTER 6

Strategic Cruise Missiles

DURING THE LAST DECADE OF THE COLD WAR, CRUISE MIS-
siles achieved the sort of notoriety that had been accorded
to ICBMs in the 1960s, though cruise missiles represented
a much older technology. Indeed, Germany's Fieseler
Fi.103 cruise missile (better known as the Vergeltungswaffe 1 [V-1]) had been one of the most feared secret
weapons of World War II.

By definition, cruise missiles are airplanes that are pur-
posely designed to be flown without a pilot aboard, using
autonomous or remote-control guidance. Tactically, the
idea behind the cruise missile is obvious and straightforward. An armed, but unpiloted, airplane is used to fly to
the target and simply impact it. In situations where a
ground target is so heavily defended that an attacking aircraft has little chance of getting in and out safely, they offer an alternative.

After the second world war, the United States conducted numerous experiments with captured German
cruise missiles and home-grown ones as well. Two early
cruise missiles of note were the Northrop SN-62 (B-62)
Snark that was developed for the U.S. Air Force and the
Vought SSM-N-8 (RGM-6) Regulus that the U.S. Navy developed for use aboard surface ships and submarines.
These are discussed previously in the chapters on ballistic

missiles and submarine launched ballistic missiles, respectively. We've included them in these chapters because, in each case, the idea of developing a very long-range cruise missile was abandoned in favor of vertically launched ballistic missiles.

Other early U.S. Air Force cruise missiles developed during the 1950s included the Martin TM-61 Matador, the Bell GAM-63 Rascal and the North American GAM-77 Hound Dog. Meanwhile, the Soviet Union also developed a number of cruise missiles. These included the air-launched weapons that were identified in NATO nomenclature as AS-1 Kennel, AS-2 Kipper and AS-3 Kangaroo, as well as the surface-launched SSC-2a Salish and SSC-2b Samlet. In all cases, from Snark to Samlet, these missiles resembled—and, in fact, were—pilotless jet aircraft. Each was about the size of a contemporary jet fighter.

During the 1960s and 1970s, cruise missiles were seen as short-range tactical weapons. They were developed to be surface launched for battlefield missions or air launched for such missions as attacking enemy shipping. The United States developed such missiles as the Boeing AGM-69 Short Range Attack Missile (SRAM), which the U.S. Air Force deployed aboard B-52s. The Soviet Union developed a number of similar weapons, including the Raduga KSR-5 (known to NATO as the AS-6 Kingfish) that was used to arm Tupolev Tu-16 and Tupolev Tu-22M bombers.

By the 1970s, McDonnell Douglas Astronautics had developed the RGM/AGM-84 Harpoon, which would be the definitive all-weather antiship missile for the U.S. Navy through the end of the twentieth century. From surface vessels, Harpoons are launched from canister launchers, and from submarines, they are launched through torpedo tubes. From aircraft, they are released from bomb racks. The AGM-84A became operational in the U.S. Navy in 1977. A decade later, they were also ordered by the U.S. Air Force for deployment aboard B-52 bombers.

During the 1980s, the Harpoon was adapted for use against land targets as the AGM-84E Standoff Land Attack

Missile (SLAM). First delivered to the U.S. Navy in 1988, the SLAM combined the airframe, propulsion and control systems of the Harpoon with off-the-shelf guidance components. These include the AGM-65 Maverick imaging infrared seeker, the AGM-62 Walleye data link, and a Global Positioning System (GPS) receiver. In 1998, the U.S. Navy began testing the AGM-84E Standoff Land Attack Missile–Expanded Response (SLAM-ER), which would more than double the range of the SLAM to in excess of 150 miles. SLAM-ER would also have an improved target acquisition system, as well as an enhanced penetration capability and effectiveness against hardened targets.

The Harpoon program evolved against the backdrop of the greatest technological revolution in the field of electronics since the invention of the vacuum tube. The microprocessor revolution of the late 1970s and early 1980s made desktop computers a reality, and in the field of defense electronics, it was now possible to develop the guidance systems that would allow the United States to revisit the use of cruise missiles for the strategic mission. When the Snark had been put on ice a generation earlier, its Achilles heel had been guidance. Now it was time to pick up where things had left off.

The revival of strategic cruise missiles is one of the least understood moments in the history of Cold War weapons. Indeed, it would be a defining moment in the history of the Cold War. Some say that it was the beginning of the end, for it was a point from which the Soviet Union would never be able to come close to matching United States technology.

ALCM and CALCM

The term *cruise missile* entered the vernacular in the early 1980s as the world became aware of the Boeing AGM-86, known officially as the Air Launched Cruise Missile (ALCM).

The ALCM—pronounced *alcum*—traces its roots to a 1968 U.S. Air Force program called SCAD, for Subsonic

Cruise Aircraft Decoy. The idea then had been to develop an air-launched, long-range decoy to lure enemy defense systems away from bombers. SCAD was intended to be an improvement over the McDonnell GAM-72 Quail, which had been tested back in the 1950s. As work continued on the SCAD concept, it gradually occurred to the engineers working on the project that they might as well be developing this new missile as a long-range *attack* missile. In 1973, the Air Force officially scrapped the SCAD concept and reoriented the work already done toward the goal of a strategic cruise missile.

During the 1970s, the revolution in solid-state electronics and guidance systems caught up with the strategic cruise missile. Without this, the ALCM would not have been possible.

The first actual missile in the ALCM family was the 14-foot AGM-86A. Just as the AGM-86A was slated to enter production in 1977, the U.S. Air Force chose to begin full-scale development of the larger AGM-86B with double the range. The evolution of data-processing technology was moving so rapidly that it was possible to improve the ALCM beyond what was previously imagined.

One of the major technological breakthroughs of this period was TERCOM—Terrain Contour Matching (or Mapping). TERCOM was a revolutionary guidance system that could allow a cruise missile to navigate autonomously in three dimensions at low level. With TERCOM, a cruise missile could fly through valleys, avoid hills and fly as close—or closer—to the ground as an airplane flown by a human pilot.

Meanwhile, the U.S. Navy had undertaken development of the General Dynamics BGM-109 Tomahawk sea-launched cruise missile (described later). The Department of Defense wanted to see that the two programs had at least some features in common. This led to the decision to adopt, for both missiles, the Williams F107 turbofan engine of the AGM-86, and the McDonnell Douglas AN/DPW-23 TERCOM of the Tomahawk.

When announced in March 1980, the $4 billion AGM-86B production contract was the largest defense contract issued since the Vietnam War and a tremendous boon to the Boeing Company. Production of the initial batch of 225 AGM-86B ALCMs began in fiscal year 1980, and the first ones became operational in December 1982, with the 416th Bombardment Wing at Griffiss AFB in New York. Production of a total of 1,715 missiles was completed in October 1986.

The AGM-86B was 20 feet 9 inches long, with a wing span of 12 feet, and it weighed 2,900 pounds. It had a range of 1,500 miles and carried a W80 thermonuclear warhead with a yield of up to 150 kilotons. Up to twenty ALCMs could be carried on rotary launchers in the bomb bay of a B-52. Additional ALCMs were carried by B-52s on external underwing pylons.

In June 1986, a small number of AGM-86B missiles were converted to conventional weapons. Their nuclear warheads were replaced by a high-explosive blast/fragmentation warhead, and they were redesignated as the AGM-86C Conventional Air Launched Cruise Missile (CALCM). This modification also replaced the AGM-86B's terrain contour–matching guidance system with an internal GPS capability within the existing inertial navigation computer system.

The CALCM became operational in January 1991 at the onset of Operation Desert Storm. Seven Boeing B-52s from Barksdale AFB launched thirty-five AGM-86Cs at designated high-priority targets in Iraq, marking the beginning of the Desert Storm air campaign. CALCMs were next used against Iraq in September 1996 during Operation Desert Strike.

Through 1997, 200 additional AGM-86Bs were converted to AGM-86C CALCM standard. These would incorporate improvements such as a larger and improved conventional payload capacity and a multichannel GPS receiver.

As the Cold War came to a close, the U.S. Air Force was developing the General Dynamics AGM-129 Advanced ALCM as a successor to the AGM-86B. Like the ALCM, it was designed for a nuclear strike mission, but was adapted for conventional explosives. Both were used in the Gulf Wars of 1991 and 2003.

Granat

The Raduga Kh-55 Granat was the Soviet attempt to build a weapon with the capability of the American AGM-86B ALCM. Known in NATO nomenclature as the AS-15 Kent, the Granat entered development as soon as Soviet bloc intelligence services got wind of the United States intention to build a strategic cruise missile. Given a high priority, the prototype Kh-55 is thought to have been tested as early as 1978, not long after the flight tests of the AGM-86A.

Based on data gleaned from Western sources, the Raduga design bureau modeled the Granat on the AGM-86B very closely. Like the ALCM, it was a small subsonic jet aircraft. It was 19.5 feet long with a wing span of just over 10 feet and it weighed 2,750 pounds. It is reported to have had a range of up to 1,800 miles and it carried a thermonuclear warhead with a yield matching the W80 warhead carried by the AGM-86B. The Granat used inertial guidance and even carried a terrain mapping guidance system modeled after what could be learned of TERCOM.

Designed to be air launched—as was the AGM-86B—the Granat was also adapted for launch from surface ships and submarines, like the Tomahawk. A ground-launched version was also built.

After the fall of the Soviet Union, Russian President Boris Yeltsin announced that Russia would cease production of air- and sea-launched cruise missiles. However, in 1992, Russia followed the U.S. Air Force as it converted ALCMs to CALCMs, and some Kh-55s were retrofitted with high-explosive warheads under the designation Kh-65.

Tomahawk

A nuclear strike weapon fielded during the last decade of the Cold War, the General Dynamics BGM-109 Tomahawk had its baptism of fire as a conventional weapon during Gulf War I in 1991. Armed with a conventional high-explosive warhead, the Tomahawk Land Attack Missile (TLAM) would be used extensively throughout the 1990s, as well as in Gulf War II. Though it had originated in the 1970s as a U.S. Navy weapon, the BGM-109 also served briefly in the 1980s as one of the most important late–Cold War weapons in the U.S. Air Force arsenal.

The original idea was to create a submarine-launched cruise missile that could be fired from the same launch tubes that were used by the Polaris SLBM. In the 1950s, the U.S. Navy had abandoned the Regulus cruise missile in favor of the Polaris. Two decades later, technology had evolved to a point where they were ready to revisit the cruise missile concept. Comparative flight tests of the General Dynamics YBGM-109 and the Ling Temco Vought YBGM-110 (the Y indicates a preproduction flight-test vehicle) led the Navy to select the former for a production contract. The new missile would be used aboard surface ships as well as submarines.

As noted above, the Department of Defense insisted that both the AGM-86B and BGM-109 production-series missiles be powered by the Williams F107 turbofan engine and the McDonnell Douglas AN/DPW-23 TERCOM navigation system. The two missiles were also similar in size. The BGM-109 was 18 feet 3 inches long, with a wing span of 8 feet 9 inches, and it weighed 2,650 pounds. The 550-pound booster used for the submarine launch added 2 feet 3 inches to the length. It had a range of about 700 miles.

The Tomahawk could be armed with a nuclear warhead for an attack against a strategic target ashore (BGM-109A), or with a high-explosive warhead for strikes against ships at sea (BGM-109B) or other targets ashore (BGM-

109C). In addition, a BGM-109D was designed to release a cloud of submunitions—or "bomblets"—over land targets. All U.S. Navy Tomahawks were initially deployed under the BGM-109 designation, but after 1986, submarine-launched Tomahawks were designated as UGM-109, and surface-launched Tomahawks as RGM-109. The AGM-109 designation was set aside for an air-launched version that was never built.

Among the more than 100 ships to be armed with the Tomahawk were the four battleships of the Iowa Class that were recommissioned during the 1980s. Nearly 900 feet long and displacing almost 50,000 tons, these were the only battleships to serve with the U.S. Navy after World War II and the largest non–aircraft carriers in the surface fleet. Their 16-inch guns were the largest such weapons in the world, and the Tomahawk made the four Iowas extremely potent weapons. Each ship was fitted with eight armored box launchers for Tomahawks.

In Gulf War I, Tomahawks from the battleship USS *Wisconsin* (BB-64) launched the initial strikes of Operation Desert Storm. A total of 288 Tomahawk TLAMs were used in Desert Storm, and 330 were used against Iraq in Operation Desert Fox in 1998. During Operation Allied Force in 1999, 160 TLAMs were used against targets in the former Yugoslavia. At the turn of the century, there were about 4,000 Tomahawks in the U.S. Navy arsenal.

Glick-Um

Officially named Gryphon, but best known as "Glick-Um," the BGM-109G Ground Launched Cruise Missile (GLCM) was the U.S. Air Force version of the U.S. Navy's Tomahawk cruise missile. According to the folklore that surrounds the memory of Glick-Um, the weapon ended the Cold War. When large numbers were deployed to continental Europe in the late 1980s, Mikhail Gorbachev and his military commanders are said to have consciously realized that this weapon was impossible to defend against, so they threw in the towel.

Even if this legend about a single-handed victory is mere hyperbole, the GLCM certainly played an important role in the demise of the Cold War.

During the 1950s, the U.S. Air Force had fielded small numbers of ground-launched Martin B-61 (later TM-61) Matador and Martin B-76 (later TM-76 or MGM-13) Mace tactical cruise missiles. Both were withdrawn from service by the mid-1960s, and their replacement was given a low priority and constantly postponed. Finally, in 1977, the Air Force chose to move forward with the BGM-109G GLCM.

The catalyst was the deployment of the Soviet RSD-10 Pioneer, known as the SS-20 Saber in NATO nomenclature. This mobile IRBM had the range to easily deliver a nuclear strike against any target in Western Europe. Both Britain and West Germany were anxious for the United States to do something to counter this threat and to give Western Europe a nuclear deterrent force. The United States answer would be to deploy a combination of the U.S. Army's Martin MGM-31C Pershing II and the Air Force version of the Tomahawk into Europe.

Physically, the BGM-109G Gryphon was the same size and weight as the nuclear-armed Tomahawk. The Gryphon's W84 thermonuclear warhead had the same yield as the Tomahawk's W80. The 1,550-mile range of the GLCM meant that it could be deployed anywhere within Western Europe. The plan was for it also to be as mobile as any of the IRBMs that the Soviets had deployed to Eastern Europe.

For the sake of this mobility, development of the missile moved in conjunction with the parallel development of an enormous transporter-erector-launcher (TEL) vehicle. Manufactured in Germany by Machinenfabrik-Augsburg-Nurnberg (MAN), these huge, 39-ton trucks included an eight-wheel tractor and an eight-wheel trailor with four GLCM missile tubes. Operationally, the missiles would be folded into aluminum tubes that could be stored and transported, then inserted into the launch tubes.

The first GLCM test launch came in May 1980, with test firings from the MAN TEL beginning two years later at Davis-Monthan AFB in Arizona.

Operational deployment began with the activation in July 1982 of the 501st Tactical Missile Wing (TMW) at RAF Greenham Common in the United Kingdom, although the first missiles would not reach the site until the end of 1983. In the meantime, the construction of bunkers and other infrastructure work took place at the base.

The activation of the wing at Greenham Common was followed by activation of the 487th TMW at Comiso AB in Sicily in June 1983, the 485th TMW at Florennes AB in Belgium in August 1984, the 38th TMW at Wueschheim AB in West Germany in April 1985, the 303rd TMW at RAF Molesworth in the United Kingdom in December 1986 and, finally, the 486th TMW at Woensdrecht AB in the Netherlands in August 1987. There would be a total of 464 GLCMs, including 160 in the United Kingdom and 112 in Sicily. West Germany would have 96 GLCMs and 108 Pershing IIs.

Documents recovered from Soviet archives after the end of the Cold War show that the Soviet leadership reacted to the GLCMs with an unusually high level of concern. The TERCOM capability allowed the missiles to fly so low that detecting and intercepting them would have been virtually impossible. It is now known that the Soviet Union greeted the deployment of the GLCMs almost as a strategic checkmate.

In the West, those favoring a continuation of Mutual Assured Destruction through the ongoing Nuclear Freeze Movement also reacted with a singularly elevated degree of distress. A large number of vociferous protesters descended upon the perimeter fence at Greenham Common to establish a semipermanent Peace Camp. Strangely, these individuals launched no similar protest to the widespread deployment of the Soviet RSD-10 IRBMs which were aimed at Britain.

Aside from the noise and a great deal of littering, the protesters did very little to impede operations at Greenham Common. However, things later took a turn to the more sinister. In January 1986, *Jane's Defence Weekly* reported that troops of Spetsnaz (Soviet special forces) controlled by the GRU (Soviet military intelligence) were active among protesters at the Peace Camp. It was also reported that these Spetsnaz personnel were training at full-scale mockups of Greenham Common and other GLCM bases so that they could attack and neutralize them in time of war. In 1992, Vasily Mitrokhin, a former KGB archivist, confirmed that the 1986 report was true.

In the United States, Paul Warnke, who had been director of the Arms Control and Disarmament Agency under the Jimmy Carter administration, insisted in a *Washington Post* op-ed piece that the United States unilaterally halt deployment of the GLCM, regardless of the Soviet deployment of the RSD-10, or else "The United States will face a further deterioration in its relations with the Soviet Union, and Western Europe's confidence in American leadership will decline."

Warnke was right insofar as the fact that the Soviet Union was angry about the GLCM, but the result was just the opposite of what he predicted.

When Warnke complained that the GLCM had "no military justification," he could not have been farther from the mark. The nuclear checkmate afforded by GLCM compelled the Soviet Union to go to the bargaining table for the talks that led to the Intermediate Range and Shorter Range Nuclear Forces (INF) Treaty that went into effect in 1988. The United States agreed to withdrawn the GLCMs only in exchange for parallel demobilization of Soviet weapons in Eastern Europe. The Cold War was one step closer to a conclusion.

After their short-lived, but pivotal, deployment in Europe, the GLCMs were removed from Europe between

1988 and 1991. As for Greenham Common, the U.S. Air
Force turned the base back over to the Royal Air Force in
September 1992. The runways were broken up in 1995 and
the British Ministry of Defence sold the land in 1997.

Two fully configured MAN TELs—with inert GLCMs—
remain. One is at the U.S. Air Force Museum at Wright-
Patterson AFB, Ohio. The other is maintained by the Ground
Launched Cruise Missile Historical Foundation at the Pima
Air & Space Museum in Tucson, Arizona, adjacent to Davis-
Monthan AFB.

CHAPTER 7

Mega-Artillery

ARTILLERY HAS BEEN PART OF THE ARSENAL OF WARFARE since the fifteenth century. Generally, the muzzle-loading guns remained operationally unchanged until the nineteenth century, when newer breach-loading equipment was introduced and the Industrial Revolution improved the art of metalworking and gunsmithing. Dreams of really big artillery that was practical—and safe for the gunners—could now be realized.

In both World War I and World War II, it was the Germans who created and deployed the largest artillery of the day. In 1914, there were the 420mm (16.5-inch) Big Bertha railway guns. Toward the end of World War I, the Germans employed the very long-range Paris Guns, with which they bombarded the French capital from the Forest of Crecy.

In anticipation of World War II, the German arms maker Krupp was called upon to create the mega-artillery of the twentieth century's mega-conflict. Perhaps best known were the 280mm K5 (Kanone 5) cannons, of which the two most famous were Anzio Annie and her sister, The Anzio Express, which proved themselves an unwelcome surprise to Allied forces on the Anzio Beachhead south of Rome early in 1944. The largest gun of World War II was Krupp's monumental 800mm (31.5-inch) cannon that came to be known as Schwere Gustav (heavy Gustav). Designed to at-

tack France's Maginot Line, this gun was eventually used
to annihilate the Soviet city of Sevastopol.

Generally speaking, the artillery used by the major
armies of the world through the Cold War was little
changed from the state of the art reached at the end of
World War II. The 105mm and 155mm guns that were
standard in 1945 were not unlike those in use in 1985.
Naval guns actually got smaller. The U.S. Navy never deployed a gun larger than the 16-inch weapons used on the
Iowa Class battleships of World War II, and there was
never a naval gun larger than the 18.1-inchers with which
Japan's Yamato Class were fitted.

Schwere Gustav was the largest gun fired during the
twentieth century, but during the Cold War, other weapons
and sheer audacity made its immense size and firepower
seem tame.

M65 (T131) Atomic Cannon

Any consideration of the M65 must begin with the rhetorical question: "What were they thinking?" With a maximum
range of 19 miles, or as little as 7 miles with an Mk.9 nuclear shell, this battlefield weapon would have left its crew
dangerously close to a nuclear detonation. It was a weapon
of last resort, a fact that illustrates how dreaded the overwhelming Soviet ground superiority in Central Europe was
in the 1950s.

The M65 was the product of a desire on the part of the
U.S. Army to develop a self-contained nuclear strike capability at a time when the U.S. Air Force managed and controlled most of the United States offensive nuclear arsenal.

During World War II, in response to the very large artillery employed by the Germans, the U.S. Army had studied the feasibility of a mobile 240mm gun. By the late
1940s, these studies had evolved to the point where work
began on the creation of a gun capable of firing a nuclear
shell. The Atomic Cannon program began in 1950 with the
specifications increased to 280mm. The result would be the
largest mobile gun ever deployed by the U.S. Army, and

certainly the most deadly. A total of twenty of the weapons would be manufactured at the Watervliet Arsenal in Watervliet, New York. The first of these was completed in early 1952, and tests were conducted with conventional shells through the first part of 1953.

The M65 test program was then incorporated at the U.S. Army's Operation Upshot Knothole, a series of eleven tests of battlefield nuclear weapons that were conducted between March 17 and June 4, 1953, at the Atomic Energy Commission's Nevada Test Site. The actual nuclear weapons involved were developed by the Los Alamos Nuclear Laboratory. Upshot Knothole was, in turn, conducted in conjunction with Desert Rock V, a readiness exercise designed to train troops to fight on a nuclear battlefield. An estimated 21,000 military personnel were involved in the operation.

The nuclear weapons tests, films of which are still widely shown to illustrate the effects of nuclear blasts, included detonations of weapons mounted on towers or dropped from aircraft. They ranged from the nuclear equivalent of 200 tons of TNT to 43 kilotons. The tenth test, or "shot," was code-named Grable and it was to be the only live firing by the M65.

Test Shot Grable occurred at 8:30 on the morning of May 25, 1953, at Frenchman Flat on the Nevada Test Site. Fired a distance of just 7 miles, the Mk.9 shell delivered a 15 megaton blast. This detonation, with its 500-foot mushroom cloud, was observed from a distance of less than 10 miles by 700 observers—including Secretary of Defense Charles Wilson and Chairman of the Joint Chiefs of Staff Admiral Arthur Radford—as well as 2,600 troops. According to the U.S. Army, some of the soldiers approached to within less than half a mile of ground zero after Grable.

This, the only M65 test, was deemed successful and the guns were ordered into production. Beginning in late 1953, the first of between ten and sixteen Atomic Cannons were deployed overseas to Europe, and one nuclear artillery battalion was formed, the 3rd Battalion of the 82nd Artillery.

Attached to V Corps of the 3rd Armored Division, they were tasked with counterattacking a Soviet armored invasion of West Germany. Annual test firings of the weapons— with conventional rounds, of course—are said to have been conducted at Grafenwohr.

The M65s were mobile guns, transported either by road or rail on a rail chassis constructed by the Baldwin Locomotive Works. The gun itself had a 38.5-foot barrel and weighed 47 tons, while the entire transporter unit weighed in at 83 tons.

In 1955, the lighter Mk.19 round, which offered a range of 15 to 18 miles, was introduced. By 1957, the M65 battalion in Europe was operational with the new shell.

The Atomic Cannon was a relatively short-lived member of the United States nuclear arsenal, however. The 3rd Battalion was disbanded and the M65s were retired from service in 1963.

Today, Atomic Cannons are preserved at the Yuma Proving Ground near Yuma, Arizona; at the Rock Island Arsenal at Rock Island, Illinois; at the Army Ordnance Museum in Aberdeen, Maryland; the Atomic Museum in Albuquerque, New Mexico; at the Fort Sill Museum in Oklahoma; at the Virginia War Memorial Museum in Newport News; and at the Watervliet Arsenal. One is also on public display at a roadside museum in Junction City, Kansas.

Nuclear Field Artillery Shells

As the M65 Atomic Cannon was being developed, the U.S. Army was also working on a parallel project to turn its standard eight-inch (203mm) howitzers into atomic cannons. The idea was that the M65s would, potentially, be high priority targets in time of war and their huge bulk made them slow, sluggish and easy to hit. The lumbering M110 self-propelled 8-inch howitzer, mounted on a tank chassis, was a veritable sports car compared to the M65. A crash program to develop the M422 ensued and full-scale production of the shells began in 1955 and they were stockpiled in Europe by 1957.

Also in 1957, development began on a nuclear shell for the U.S. Army's 155mm guns that would be designated as M454. A reported 1,060 of these were manufactured between 1963 and 1968, and at least some were deployed to Europe. Like the M422, the M454 could be equipped with warheads ranging in yield from one to two kilotons.

In practice, the M422 and M454 presented a significant technical problem. The nuclear shells had a different aerodynamic shape, and hence a different trajectory, than conventional shells. It was deemed necessary in an operational scenario that conventional shells shaped like the M422s and M454s would have to be fired as spotter rounds. One wonders why accuracy would have been important given the large blast radius of a 1- or 2-kiloton nuclear weapon, and the total devastation that would occur within or near that radius. Of course, with just a 9-mile range, any shot would have been a frightening prospect for the gunners.

In 1973, the Army began work on successors to both the M422 and M454 with improved aerodynamic characteristics that would double the 9-mile range of the earlier shells. The respective designations would be M753 and M785.

Aerodynamic testing of the M753 8-inch shell, using dummy rounds, began in 1979, and live nuclear shells were first deployed in 1981. The 155mm shell, on the other hand, underwent repeated program delays and is not believed to have been deployed to field units.

The idea had been to replace all of the M422s with M753s, but production of the latter ended in 1986 before this was accomplished. As the Cold War came to a close, there were still nearly 1,000 M422s in the arsenal, but fewer than 400 M753s. Roughly half of the 155mm M454s were still available for use.

Nuclear Naval Shells

As the U.S. Army developed and deployed nuclear artillery for its field guns to halt a Soviet invasion of Europe, the U.S. Navy was working on similar shells for use in naval bombardment of shore targets. These shells were intended for the Navy's biggest guns—the 16-inch weapons on the four Iowa Class battleships. Each of these World War II–era ships had three triple turrets with the 16-inchers, making them the most formidable surface ships in the world in the decades following World War II.

Work on the Mk.23 naval shell, code-named Katie, began in about 1953 around the time that the U.S. Army was testing its 280mm Atomic Cannon. The Navy, however, kept a much tighter shroud of secrecy draped about Katie than their sister service did with the M65. The Mk.23 shells had a range of over 20 miles, and their 15- to 20-kiloton yield would have made them the most potent nuclear shell ever deployed. They were apparently ready for deployment by 1956, but it is not known whether they were ever placed aboard ship operationally. The U.S. Navy's policy is to never confirm or deny the presence of nuclear weapons aboard its ships.

The Iowa Class ships—USS *Iowa*, USS *New Jersey*, USS *Missouri* and USS *Wisconsin*—were decommissioned between 1955 and 1958, and the Mk.23s are said to have been withdrawn from service in 1962. The USS *New Jersey* was recommissioned during the Vietnam War, and all four were recommissioned from the mid-1980s through the end of the Cold War. During this latter redeployment, the ships were retrofitted to carry Tomahawk cruise missiles, but it is not believed that the Mk.23 nuclear shells were reactivated during this period.

Soviet Nuclear Artillery

The Soviet Atomic Cannon topped its 280mm U.S. Army counterpart with a bore of 406mm that was equivalent to that of the largest American naval guns. Known as the Kondensator 2P, the big gun was based on an existing 406mm artillery piece and developed in the late 1950s in response to the U.S. Army M65. The range was reported to be about the same as the M65. Like the M65, the Soviet Kondensator 2P was road mobile, having been built on a tracked T10 chassis. Also using this chassis was an enormous 420mm breech-loading mortar that was probably designed to accept nuclear ammunition.

Though both the Soviet and American armies developed specialized Atomic Cannons, both concentrated most of their efforts on building nuclear ammunition for existing guns.

Among the first artillery in the Soviet arsenal that was adapted for nuclear weapons was the 203mm B-4 (M1931) howitzer. Originally fielded in the 1930s, it was used during World War II and adapted for a mobile gun carriage early in the Cold War. Introduced in about 1954, the 130mm M-46 Towed Gun was in service for two decades during the Cold War. The high velocity M-46 had a range of more than 17 miles. The Chinese 130mm Type 59 Field Gun is a close copy of the M-46, and, like it, the Type 59 is nuclear capable.

In the middle 1970s, the Soviet Union began to replace the M-46 with 152mm weapons, specifically the 2A36 towed howitzer and the 2S5 Giatsint-S self-propelled gun. The 2S5 reached Soviet forces in Eastern Europe in 1982 and was seen as an important element in a potential invasion of Western Europe during the last decade of the Cold War.

After the Cold War, the Russian forces withdrew the former Soviet assets, including nuclear artillery, from Eastern Europe. However, since 2001, a great deal of concern has been whispered in the back channels of Western intelligence services that terrorist gangs such as al-Qaeda may have gotten their hands on Soviet nuclear artillery shells. Such compact weapons could be adapted for use as "suitcase bombs."

M28 and M29 Davy Crockett

There is perhaps no nuclear weapon of the Cold War that more emphatically begs the rhetorical question, "What were they thinking?" With range capabilities of less than three miles and a nuclear yield varying from 20 to 250 tons, the use of these weapons would have been essentially suicidal.

Named for the legendary nineteenth-century congressman turned soldier of fortune, the Davy Crockett was developed to give U.S. Army infantry units as small as a platoon a nuclear capability. Known informally as the "nuclear bazooka," the two weapons were developed as a means of equalizing the enormous Soviet numeric advantage in terms of troops and tanks.

The M29 was adapted for use with a modified 120mm recoilless rifle, the M29 for the larger 155mm gun. The former weighed just over 100 pounds and could be carried by a jeep. The latter weighed nearly 400 pounds but could be carried by a variety of medium-sized vehicles, including 2.5-ton ("deuce-and-a-half") trucks. More than 6,000 of the M28 and M29 rifles were believed to have been ordered by the U.S. Army, although the number of M388 nuclear rounds is thought to have been closer to 400.

Two live-fire nuclear tests, designated as Little Feller 1 and 2, were conducted in Nevada during July 1962.

The Davy Crocketts were deployed overseas to Germany with the 3rd Armored Division from 1961 through 1971. However, they were withdrawn from service when the U.S. Army became squeamish about having such a weapon under the command of platoon sergeants. The potential for misuse under the fog of battle was considered to outweigh the potential effectiveness of the Davy Crockett. It is not believed that any terrorist group would ever have had access to an armed Davy Crockett.

HARP (High Altitude Research Program)

The idea behind the High Altitude Research Program (HARP) was not new, it was just audacious to the point of being outrageous. On the other hand, it could be argued that HARP was not so terribly impractical, and it was just a case of thinking outside the box. Sir Isaac Newton postulated that an object fired into the sky from a very large gun might go high enough and fast enough to escape the Earth's gravity. Two centuries later, Jules Verne used a very large gun to send a fictional expedition to the moon. Such a scenario was not taken seriously again until 1960, three years into the Space Race between the United States and the Soviet Union.

Today, it is easy to think of Cold War technology in terms of a dual between the United States and the Soviet Union. In the years immediately after World War II, however, many other countries contributed technological footnotes to the Cold War arms race. Like the United States, Canada came out of World War II with its own territory untouched by the ravages of war and anxious to embrace the promising technology of the future. Until the 1960s, Canada had a very robust aerospace industry and a healthy proportion of the hardware reaching the Canadian armed services was designed and built at home.

Into this environment came Ontario-born Gerald Vincent "Gerry" Bull, who graduated in aerospace engineering from the University of Toronto in 1951. He went to work for the Canadian Armament and Research Development Establishment (CARDE), where he became a researcher in supersonic flight. To study the characteristics of aircraft at high speed, it was traditional to put them in a wind tunnel. In the course of his experiments, Bull discovered that time in a wind tunnel is expensive. Realizing that projectiles fired from guns reach supersonic speed, he suggested that firing his test objects from a gun would be much cheaper than renting time in a wind tunnel. It was from this brainstorm that Bull developed the notion of actually launching vehicles with a gun.

While working at CARDE during the 1950s, Bull gradually became an internationally recognized expert in the fields of aerodynamics and ballistics, and a leading theoretician in gun propulsion systems. He was not alone in his studies of the latter. At the same time, Dr. Charles Murphy, at the U.S. Army Ballistic Research Laboratory in Aberdeen, Maryland, was also studying the notion of firing

objects into space. Bull and Murphy got to know one another and eventually the HARP would bring them together.

In 1961, about the time that Bull left CARDE to become a professor at McGill University, he presented his
High Altitude Research Program concept to the Canadian
Department of Defence. With their expression of interest,
Bull convinced the University to fund HARP, and to permit
the use of one of their research stations on the Caribbean
island of Barbados as a launch site.

Charles Murphy expressed an interest in HARP, and the
U.S. Army became involved in supporting the project. The
Americans supplied a 16-inch battleship gun and related
equipment, as well as a radar tracking system. The gun was
bored out to 17 inches and installed in Barbados in April
1962. The projectile was a 200-pound "spacecraft," designed by Bull, that was known as Martlett.

Delayed by the tensions surrounding the Cuban Missile
Crisis in October, the first Martlett test shot did not take
place until January 1963. The series of test firings during
1963 succeeded in lifting Martletts up to 57 miles, which
was significant, but still short of orbital altitude.

At the end of 1963, a second 16-inch HARP gun was relocated to the Highwater test range in Canada and smaller
HARP projects using 5- and 7-inch guns were located at
several other locations, including NASA's little-known
space launch facility at Wallops Island in Virginia.

At Highwater, the length of the 16-inch HARP gun barrel was extended, first to 120 feet, and then to 176 feet.
Creating the longest artillery piece in history increased the
weight to almost 100 tons. This necessitated considerable
reinforcement to the weapon so that the barrel would not
go out of alignment because of its own weight.

In 1966, a third 16-inch HARP gun was located at the
vast U.S. Army proving ground near Yuma, Arizona. It was
this gun that established a world record for the HARP program—and for artillery in general through the turn of the
century—by firing a Martlett 2 projectile to an altitude of
112 miles on November 18.

Ironically, it was also during November 1966 that the Canadian government decided to terminate its share of funding for HARP, effective the following June. With that, the U.S. Army, its own purse string strained by its Vietnam War commitments, opted out as well.

Desperate to see HARP continue, Gerry Bull quickly formed an entity called Space Research Institute (later Space Research Corporation) and succeeded in compelling McGill University to transfer its share of ownership in the HARP project to this enterprise.

Despite Bull's efforts and a wealth of hardware and test data that had been accumulated over four years, HARP was never revived. The guns are believed to have all been scrapped and Gerry Bull himself went on to a career as the archetypical "international man of mystery" (see the following entry).

Babylon Gun

Created during the Cold War by parties not technically engaged in the Cold War, Project Babylon is worth a mention because no discussion of artillery during this period is complete without it. Though it was never test fired or even fully finished, the Babylon Gun holds a place in the record books as the largest artillery piece ever to have been under construction. It had a bore larger than Krupp's Schwere Gustav and a barrel longer than Gerry Bull's HARP. The Babylon Gun was another product of Bull's peculiar genius for imagining big guns, *really* big guns.

In the years following the demise of HARP in 1967, Gerry Bull moved about the globe in the mysterious world of international arms dealers, flaunting his reputation as perhaps the world's foremost freelance ballistics and artillery expert. He handled projects in the Far East and in South America. He created the revolutionary 155mm GC-45 cannon for the South African government that proved itself in the war in Angola.

Along the way, his shady dealings ran him afoul of United States authorities and he did six months of jail time during 1980. When he got out, he relocated to Belgium and began hunting for new customers. Among these was Saddam Hussein, who was seeking large artillery to use in the war then raging between Iraq and Iran. Beginning in 1981, Bull designed new 210mm and 155mm guns for Iraq, that were manufactured in Austria.

As the story goes, Bull had in the back of his mind that Iraq could be induced to spend some of its copious oil revenue on using the HARP concept to launch a space program. By 1988, Gerry Bull had convinced Saddam Hussein to undertake Project Babylon, the creation of Bull's largest guns.

The first Project Babylon weapon was, in effect, a proof-of-concept miniature of the so-called Babylon Gun. Known as the Baby Babylon, it was a formidable weapon. With a bore of 350mm, it was smaller than HARP's battleship gun, but larger than just about anything seen on a land battlefield since World War II. Theoretically capable of orbiting a small object, it was also capable of hitting any target in Israel from within Iraq. The Baby Babylon gun was constructed at a fixed location about an hour north of Baghdad. It was tested in a horizontal position, and later raised to 45 degrees. It is not known to have been used in any offensive actions.

Meanwhile, in March 1988, Bull began work on not one but two full-scale Babylon Guns. They would have an unprecedented bore of 1000mm and a range of more than 600 miles. Based on an extrapolation of the HARP gun's capability, Project Babylon could have placed a 1-ton payload into orbit or have easily bombarded nearly any corner of the Middle East. The 512-foot barrel would be built in twenty-six sections and assembled at a fixed location. These components were manufactured in Britain and disguised for shipment as sections of an oil pipeline.

Though few in the outside world knew about Project Babylon, someone associated with a potential target of the big guns did. On the evening March 22, 1990, as Gerry Bull was nearing the door of his Brussels apartment, an assassin pumped six bullets into the back of his head at close range. Conspiracy theorists suspect that the Israeli Mossad was responsible. Israel certainly would have had the motive. Three weeks later, British customs agents discovered a shipment of barrel sections.

In August 1990, Saddam Hussein went to war without his Babylon Guns. After the end of Gulf War I in the spring of 1991, United Nations inspectors examined and tore down the partially completed first Babylon Gun. It was not rebuilt, although evidence surfaced in 1995 that Iraq was working on a 600mm gun.

CHAPTER 8

Human Warriors on the Battlefield of Outer Space

IN THE DECADE SEPARATING THE 1957 LAUNCH OF SPUTNIK and the enactment of the Outer Space Treaty of 1967, military planners of both superpowers imagined soldiers in outer space, doing battle there as an extension of doing battle on Earth. Just as the terrestrial Cold War was a chess game of moves and countermoves, so too would space become another Cold War chessboard.

Outer space had long been seen as "the final frontier," a place that one day might be explored by humans, just as they had explored the distant and remote frontiers of their home planet. Until World War II, the technology to send man-made objects—much less people—into space did not exist. The whole notion was mere science fiction.

However, the great leaps made by technology during the war put outer space within the technical reach of people for the first time. In February 1949, a U.S. Army Bumper Wac Corporal rocket reached an altitude of about 244 miles to become the first man-made object in outer space. In October 1957, the Soviet Sputnik 1 spacecraft became the first man-made object to enter orbit around the Earth. By the spring of 1961, both superpowers had put people into outer space. The Space Race was on.

In reaction to Sputnik, the United States urgently moved to streamline its space-related activities, especially projects that would involve human space travel. Effective on October 1, the Space Act of 1958 created the National Aeronautics and Space Agency (NASA). This agency superseded the old National Advisory Committee on Aeronautics (NACA) and incorporated all of its functions as well as taking the leading role in space exploration. Though NASA would eventually assume the role of the single United States federal agency to oversee human spaceflight, this was not the case until the mid-1960s.

During this period, independent of NASA, the Air Force did plan its own revolutionary winged spacecraft and its own space *fleet* of manned space stations. The Air Force also planned to purchase a number of examples of the Gemini space capsule that was being developed for NASA.

Today, little is remembered of this amazing and ambitious "other" space program. One of the best-kept secrets about America's pioneering space program during the 1960s is that the true pioneer agency in space technology was not NASA but the U.S. Air Force. With the X-20, the Air Force was more than a decade ahead of NASA in winged, reusable spaceplanes. With the Manned Orbiting Laboratory (MOL), the Air Force was about a half decade ahead of NASA in building space stations.

Dyna-Soar

By the time that NASA was created in 1958, the Air Force had been studying a variety of approaches to human space flight. One of these, the Man In Space Soonest program, with the unfortunate acronym MISS, was created in reaction to the urgency of the Space Race. The mission of the program was exactly what it said. Nobody really expected that it would be any more than that. MISS was transferred to NASA, where it became the Mercury program. The Air Force had set its sights on something a bit more sophisticated. They had in mind a generation of more flexible, reusable, operational spacecraft.

In the late 1950s, before Soviet and American spacemen actually travelled into space, the notion of what shape and configuration their spaceships would take was a clean slate. Nobody had traveled into space and—apart from what we saw in science fiction movies—nobody knew what a spaceship should look like.

Aeronautical engineers naturally imagined that something that flew should have wings, so that it could land safely. Nearly everyone involved in planning for space travel assumed that spaceships, like any other type of ship, would be used again and again. Nobody imaged that such complex machines would be thrown away after a single use!

However, the Space Race caused both the United States and the Soviet Union to adopt the most expedient means of getting human beings in space. Instead of taking the time to develop winged, reusable spacecraft for their human crews, both nations adopted the "man-in-a-can" approach of using less sophisticated but one-time-use ballistic reentry capsules.

Both NASA and its Soviet counterparts would adopt the ballistic reentry capsule rather than developing a sophisticated winged spacecraft. The ballistic reentry capsules would be simpler, cheaper and faster than spacecraft with wings.

In the United States, the manned spacecraft of the 1960s, including Mercury and Gemini, and the three-man Apollo capsule for lunar operations, were all one-time-use spacecraft. At the same time in the Soviet Union, Sergei Korolev was creating Vostok and Vokshod capsules, as well as the three-man Soyuz capsule capable of lunar operations. All were one-time-use spacecraft. While Soyuz never reached the moon, these versatile capsules were still in use in the twenty-first century.

The sophisticated winged spacecraft would have to wait until 1981, but in the late 1950s, we were in a hurry. We had to get into space soonest. We had no time for wings.

Or did we?

Even as NASA was commissioning the McDonnell Aircraft Company of St. Louis to build the first-generation Mercury space capsules, the Boeing Company in Seattle was building a military spacecraft for the Air Force—with wings.

Before Sputnik in 1957—and before the necessity of the MISS concept—the U.S. Air Force's Air Research and Development Command (ARDC) had been working with various contractors on several classified design studies for winged spacecraft, including Project Brass Bell, Project Hywards and Project ROBO (Rocket Bomber). The latter study was based on the theoretical work published in Germany during the 1930s and 1940s by Dr. Eugen Sänger. His theory was that a winged aero-spacecraft could be launched horizontally and achieve sufficient speed to exit the Earth's atmosphere. At this point, the craft could skip across the top of the atmosphere like a flat stone on still water to orbit the Earth or fly into outer space or higher orbit. Finally, it could glide through the Earth's atmosphere on its wings and land like an airplane.

After passing MISS off to NASA, the Air Force merged all the winged spacecraft projects into a single program designated as System 464L.

The Air Force issued a request for 464L proposals to various aerospace firms. In March 1958, the field was narrowed from seven contractors who had submitted proposals to just two—Boeing and a team effort by Bell and Martin—because only these entrants proposed a fully orbital spaceplane.

Boeing won the competition in 1959 by basing its proposal on the Sänger "skip-glide" scenario. The name of the Boeing Spaceplane, Dyna-Soar, was derived from a combination of "dynamic" and "soaring." Ordered by the U.S. Air Force in 1961 under the designation X-20, the Dyna-Soar was to have been a manned spacecraft, a winged vehicle designed for maneuverable reentry through the atmosphere. It would be boosted into space by a Titan III rocket. After entry into space, Dyna-Soar would orbit the Earth, and then reenter when its task had been completed, a concept identical to that of the future Space Shuttle.

As outlined by the Air Force's Dyna-Soar Weapon System Project Office in May 1960, the timetable was ambitious, though not unrealistic. Boeing would complete a full-scale mock-up within a year and have 90 percent of the blueprints on the table by the spring of 1962. The first flight tests for the system would be about a dozen controlled glide tests beginning late in 1963, in which a manned Dyna-Soar would be dropped by a B-52 over Edwards AFB in California. There were ten tail numbers (61-2374 through 61-2383) assigned to the program in 1960, including a first block of three spacecraft for testing.

Through the summer of 1960, the Air Force continued to refine the design of their revolutionary spaceplane. Molybdenum was selected as the overall structural material, with an ablative, heat-shielding material to be added on surfaces that were expected to experience temperatures above 2400 degrees Fahrenheit during reentry. A crew-training procedure was also detailed.

As its configuration was finalized, the X-20 was revealed as a delta-winged vehicle 35 feet 3 inches long, with a wing span of 20 feet 4 inches and a projected gross weight of 11,390 pounds.

In 1960, the Air Force went public with the once-secret X-20 program to give it some public relations spin. General Bernard Schriever, the ARDC Commander, added that, "So far, Dyna-Soar has been programmed solely as an experimental craft for research purposes. However, as the first piloted military space system planned by the United States, Dyna-Soar has important operational potentialities which are now being explored."

There was discussion in the long-range Air Force planning at the time that actually conceived of using Dyna-Soar for roundtrips to the moon!

In the meantime, larger craft were already being planned. In its fiscal year 1962 budget proposals, drafted in 1960, the Air Force would request $20 million to study a 250-ton spacecraft that could fly in the Earth's atmosphere *and* make flights to the moon. Called Space Plane, the new project reflected the optimism borne of the success that the Dyna-Soar seemed to enjoy at the time. Space Plane was identical to the concept that reemerged more than twenty years later as the X-30 National Aerospace Plane (NASP) of the late 1980s—except that NASP couldn't travel to the moon.

The first X-20 flight was projected for the 1965 time frame, but the project was already hitting some political turbulence. When NASA was created, there was an instant rivalry with the Air Force over manned space programs. NASA wanted total control of all programs, but the Air Force wanted to control its own.

Meanwhile, President Eisenhower was on NASA's side. He and his Defense Secretary Thomas Gates had said that unless the Air Force had a specific space vehicle dedicated to a specific military mission, NASA would have responsibility for all space vehicles.

The X-20 could meet that criteria. Though it was initially conceived as a research aircraft that was the prototype for an operational spaceplane, the X-20 clearly could go operational with a military mission. A number of missions come to mind, including that for which there was an obvious need in 1960—reconnaissance. The United States had been conducting top-secret overflights of the Soviet Union using the Lockheed U-2 spy plane (discussed in the following chapter). These had ended abruptly on May 1, 1960, when a U-2 piloted by Francis Gary Powers was shot down near Sverdlovsk. The suspension of reconnaissance flights over the Soviet Union by aircraft had created a void that could be addressed, it seemed, by a manned Air Force spacecraft. Flying in space at orbital speed, the X-20 would be invulnerable to the sort of threat that had been Powers's downfall.

Dyna-Soar was designed to be adapted for operational missions. The primary consideration had been to incorporate lessons that had been learned with military aircraft. The X-20 had a large, flexible payload bay behind the pilot.

For the reconnaissance mission, Dyna-Soar could mount a camera with a Mark V telescope in this payload bay.

Launching satellites was another potential mission. On top of the payload bay was a door similar to what was eventually designed into the Space Shuttle. The Dyna-Soar payload capacity was 1,000 pounds (about 14 pounds per cubic foot). This was immense for an era when spacecraft payloads were measured in a few pounds.

While the Sänger-influenced spaceplanes imagined in the early 1950s had been conceived as bombers, there was never a weapons carrying capability designed into the X-20. The idea of disabling satellites in orbit was discussed as part of the mission but this was not defined as something that the Air Force specifically intended to do. For an anti-satellite mission, the X-20 wouldn't have needed to carry weapons. The pilot could simply touch the satellites and knock them out of orbit, or ruin their capability by breaking up the solar panels or their radio equipment.

In January 1961, John F. Kennedy became the president and with him came an administration with a great deal of enthusiasm for manned space flight. This would help NASA, but not necessarily the Air Force. The festering sore of opposition that Dyna-Soar had felt under Secretary of Defense Thomas Gates was even more pronounced now that Secretary Robert Strange McNamara had taken over the department. McNamara came to government from a brief stint in management at the Ford Motor Company with a mandate to shake up the Defense Department and to make it run more efficiently. One of President Kennedy's "whiz kids," McNamara was an intellectual giant with no practical experience in military affairs who quickly incurred the enmity of the uniformed upper echelons of the military.

McNamara was a technocrat who neither trusted nor understood professional soldiers. In Vietnam, he envisioned an automated battlefield in which our extraordinary technological superiority would allow us to defeat the crude foe with one hand tied behind our back. McNamara succeeded in tying one hand behind the back of the American fighting man, but the enemy—failing to be impressed by American technology—refused to play by McNamara's rules.

McNamara's preference for automation also extended to strategic systems, specifically the manned bomber force of the Air Force Strategic Air Command. With the advent of the ICBM, which became an operational reality at the same time McNamara came into office, the secretary could see no reason to retain manned aircraft in a strategic role. At a time when the United States was at the leading edge of aircraft technology, McNamara played the key role in curtailing several major technological breakthrough programs, such as the Convair B-58 and the North American Aviation XB-70.

The prevailing attitude in McNamara's Defense Department was that any mission that could be performed by manned aircraft could be performed better by unmanned systems. Now he would extend this to manned spacecraft. McNamara was no friend of manned aircraft and, as such, he was far from being an advocate of a radical manned spacecraft that he could scarcely understand. He made one visit to the hangar at Boeing Field in Seattle where the Dyna-Soar was taking shape, but it was fast and perfunctory. He asked few questions. It seemed to those present that his mind was already made up. If President Kennedy's mind was made up, nobody would ever know.

Kennedy would not live to see the demise of Dyna-Soar. The first X-20 vehicle was 90 percent complete at Boeing Field when Kennedy traveled south on November 15, 1963, to tour the rapidly expanding space port at Cape Canaveral in Florida. Project Mercury had ended successfully and all eyes were on the succeeding stages of the growing space effort that Kennedy had promised would put an American on the moon by the end of the decade.

A week later, on November 22, 1963, Kennedy's swing

through the South took him to Dallas, Texas, where he was assassinated.

The assassination was still in the headlines on December 10, when McNamara went before reporters to announce the termination of the program that would have given the United States a manned, winged, reusable spacecraft more than a decade and a half before the eventual debut flight of the Space Shuttle in 1981. Dyna-Soar was dead.

Rakatoplan

The Space Race that pitted the Soviet Union against the United States against the backdrop of the Cold War was like a series of games within a tournament. Each side won its share of games. The Soviet Union successfully beat the United States in the race to get the first unmanned spacecraft into Earth orbit, and the first spacecraft crewed by a man and the first by a woman. The Soviet Union also deployed space stations for a much longer duration. The United States beat the Soviet Union in landing people on the moon and in the routine deployment of winged spacecraft.

In 1969, after the successful Apollo 11 mission, the Soviet Union off-handedly announced that they could have landed a cosmonaut on the moon, but they didn't care to. The Soviet Union also seemed to show no interest in matching the United States in winged, reusable spacecraft.

In fact, in the secret world of the Soviet space program, reality was just the opposite of what was announced. Though not publicly acknowledged until after the end of the Cold War, the Soviet Union had a desperate crash program aimed at beating the NASA Apollo program to the moon. Nearly ready to fly when the United States succeeded in July 1969, the Soviet lunar program was abruptly and silently terminated.

As for winged spacecraft, the Soviet Union had such a program moving in parallel with the United States Dyna-Soar project. Whereas the United States was not shy about revealing the existence of Dyna-Soar, the Soviet Raketo-plan was a deeply secret project whose existence would not be more than whispered for more than a generation after it was terminated.

While Rakatoplan was probably the first manned, winged spacecraft that was to move off the drawing board in the Soviet Union, there had been a number of design studies throughout the 1950s. Among these was one that developed at Myasishchev, the design bureau best remembered for its strategic bombers, especially the M-4 Bison and M-50 Bounder.

The man most responsible for the Rakatoplan was an engineer named Vladimir Nikolaevich Chelomei, whose principal experience had been in cruise missile design dating back to his study of German V-1 cruise missiles immediately after World War II. His work on the manned Rakatoplan spaceplane began in the late 1950s as details about the United States ROBO were seeping out into the mainstream media. His ingenious design included wings that folded into a cone-shaped heat shield. The latter was to be jettisoned after reentry and the wings folded into place to take the vehicle to a runway landing.

The Rakatoplan was to have been a two-place craft to be used to intercept and destroy satellites in orbit. The Dyna-Soar, meanwhile, was originally conceived as a single-seater, but approaching, inspecting and destroying satellites could have been part of its mission as well.

The go-ahead for the Rakatoplan project was given by the Soviet government in 1960, perhaps in response to the progress of the Dyna-Soar program and perhaps because Chelomei had just hired Sergei Khrushchev, the son of Soviet premier Nikita Khrushchev.

The resources of both the Myasishchev and Khrunichev design bureaus were put at Chelomei's disposal for the Raketoplan and other projects. Indeed, Chelomei had also developed a very comprehensive plan for an elaborate network of space stations, but the Soviet government seems to have been most interested in his proposals regarding anti-satellite weapons, of which Rakatoplan was just one.

Chelomei had also proposed his Kosmoplan project, a Mars exploration spacecraft. The latter was cancelled in 1961, when President John F. Kennedy announced the Apollo lunar landing program, and the Soviets undertook a dramatic streamlining of their space program.

In the first test launch of an unmanned Rakatoplan, conducted at Plesetsk in March 1963, the craft reached an altitude of over 600 miles, well into outer space. Nine months later, the Dyna-Soar was canceled and the Soviet Union might have been on the brink of another space first—an operational orbital spaceplane.

However, it was not to be. In May 1964, the Rakatoplan program was ordered terminated in order to devote more resources to space capsules and the Soviet manned lunar landing program. Despite the termination, Chelomei continued to do work on the Rakatoplan until early 1965. His later proposals included a winged version of the Korolev-designed Soyuz spacecraft.

A footnote to the demise of Chelomei's career is that in October 1964, his patron, the man with whom he had too closely associated himself, Nikita Khrushchev, was deposed as Soviet premier and replaced by the less imaginative Leonid Brezhnev.

Blue Gemini

The death of Dyna-Soar was a severe blow to the evolution of spacecraft technology, but it was not the end to the U.S. Air Force's plans for a manned space program that was entirely independent of NASA. The termination of the X-20 marked an end to winged spacecraft, so they turned to an "off-the-shelf" system that was already in development for the only other player in town—NASA.

NASA's Gemini vehicle was a bell-shaped space capsule designed to carry two astronauts. Though of similar overall design and shape, Gemini weighed four times as much as the one-man Mercury capsule that had been used to take the first six American astronauts into space. It stood 19 feet tall, and had a diameter of 10 feet. Like Mercury, it was built by the McDonnell Aircraft Corporation of St. Louis. First ordered in December 1961, Gemini was tested in 1964 and 1965, and carried its first crew, Gus Grissom and John Young, into space in March 1965.

In 1965 and 1966, the NASA Gemini program had chalked up ten successful, almost routine space flights involving twenty astronauts. This number of space travelers was not exceeded in a similar span of time until the middle years of the Space Shuttle program two decades later. In December 1965, Frank Borman and Jim Lovell remained in orbit for what was then a record of 330 hours and 36 minutes—almost two weeks in space. Indeed, it was a longer mission than any of the subsequent Apollo lunar landing operations between 1968 and 1972.

At the same time that NASA's well-publicized ten missions were front page news, the Air Force was quietly laying out plans to acquire Gemini capsules of its own.

Blue Gemini, or Gemini X as the project was known, was part of a much larger effort to maintain a permanent presence in outer space that would have also involved the Manned Orbiting Laboratory (MOL) program, a network of manned space stations (see following entry). The term *blue* was derived from the signature color of the Air Force. Air Force personnel refer to themselves as "blue suiters" (because their uniforms are blue) and use the adjective to describe anything that is associated with their service. Blue Gemini capsules would have been identical to those already being delivered to NASA, except that they would have had U.S. Air Force serial numbers. They would not actually have actually been painted blue.

The idea made perfect economical sense. Blue Gemini capsules would have utilized an extended production run of an already-proven spacecraft. As for pilots, more than half of the men who'd flown in NASA's Gemini program were Air Force pilots on temporary assignment to NASA.

The issue that had led to Dyna-Soar's demise would also end the Blue Gemini program before word of it leaked into the mainstream media.

The issue was the mission. The only defined mission for Blue Gemini was in conjunction with the MOL. As it went, so too did Blue Gemini.

Project Dorian and the Manned Orbiting Laboratory (MOL)

The Air Force had been studying the idea of a semi-permanent manned base in outer space since 1959, and it was formally embraced by the Department of Defense four years later.

Undertaken by the Air Force under the secret code name Project Dorian, the Manned Orbiting Laboratory (MOL) program envisioned a galaxy of relatively inexpensive manned space stations that could be used on an almost continuous basis. When NASA launched its Skylab Space Station in 1973, the agency spoke of space stations in the singular. The Air Force imagined multiple space outposts in Earth's orbit that would be in operation simultaneously.

MOL represented a much-needed improvement over U-2 technology. Instead of braving thousands of miles of hostile airspace and uncertain weather, the MOL astronauts would float high above the range of Soviet countermeasures, snapping the shutters of their Hasselblads for weeks at a time.

Is it any coincidence that the MOL program was officially announced by Secretary of Defense Robert McNamara on December 10, 1963, the same day that he canceled the X-20 Dyna-Soar program? MOL became the trade-off. The Air Force would be compelled to abandon Dyna-Soar in exchange for the support of the Defense Department for an Air Force MOL.

In outlining the virtues of the MOL program, McNamara told the press on December 10 that it would be used for "metallurgical experiments," for supplying information on navigational aids, as well as for "classified projects."

The latter comment brought a general round of knowing laughter from the assembled media.

However, down the road a few miles in Langley, Virginia, there were a few eyebrows being raised at the Central Intelligence Agency. The CIA had held a rather tight operational rein on the U-2 surveillance program and there was now some question as to what role they would now play in the intelligence-gathering potential of the MOLs.

NASA was also out in the cold as far as the MOL program was concerned. Though they would be given the role of providing technical support, the U.S. Air Force would be the lead agency in developing America's first space station. NASA had its hands full with the upcoming Gemini and Apollo programs and did not plan to proceed to development of a space station—then referred to as the Manned Orbiting Research Laboratory (MORL)—until Apollo began to wind down in the early 1970s. They stepped aside to allow the Air Force to move past it. NASA had in mind that it would be going on to something bigger, better and *later*.

In June 1964, Secretary of the Air Force Eugene Zuckert announced that the first MOL research study contracts had been issued to General Electric and to aerospace companies, Douglas and Martin.

Though it was moving slowly through the planning process in 1964, the spark that really got MOL moving came during the NASA Gemini program. In March 1965, as Gemini 3 came over the West coast, astronauts Gus Grissom and John Young looked down in time to see an Air Force missile being fired from Vandenberg AFB. They reported this observation to ground communication and told how well they could see the launch facilities at Vandenberg AFB, as well as those at Cape Canaveral (then Cape Kennedy). The United States was in the doldrums on arms talks with the Soviets and all of a sudden the MOL program moved to the head of the list of priorities within the Department of Defense. Funding, to the tune of $1.5 billion, was authorized in August 1965 and formal contracts were issued.

The launch vehicle for the MOL would be the Martin Titan 3C, a variation on the Titan 2 that served as the launch vehicle for the NASA Gemini spacecraft and as an ICBM. The MOL space station itself would be built by the Douglas Aircraft Company's Missile & Space Systems Division (MSSD) Space Systems Center in Huntington Beach, California. In 1967, when Douglas merged with the McDonnell Aircraft Corporation, makers of the Mercury and Gemini, MSSD would become the McDonnell Douglas Astronautics Company.

The official designation for the MOL would be KH-10, placing it in the same numbering sequence as the Keyhole family of unmanned photo-reconnaissance satellites that are discussed elsewhere in this volume. The KH-10 was the only Keyhole not to be designed by Lockheed, and the only known to have been designed to carry a human crew. The KH-10 space station would be 30 feet 8 inches long, with a diameter of 10 feet. It would weigh 19,000 pounds at launch and have a habitable volume of 400 cubic feet, enough for two astronauts to work in a "shirt sleeves" environment without having to wear space suits. Each crew would serve a 30-day tour of duty aboard a MOL, and would then be replace by another crew on a 30-day rotation. Crews would commute to and from the MOLs in Blue Gemini spacecraft based on NASA's Geminis.

A manned reconnaissance mission in MOL would have involved not just a photographer and cameras but also a photo interpreter and a laboratory to process the film. Such a mission could not only take pictures but develop them as well.

The interpreter would be on board, and if there was something in the picture that wasn't clear, 90 minutes later the mission would be over the same place on the Earth and could take another picture and develop it. This was seen as a clear improvement over existing aerial or satellite reconnaissance that involved getting the film to the ground for processing and interpretation.

The Air Force had already selected a number of experienced military pilots to serve as crew members aboard operational MOLs. There were four Air Force officers, Karol Bobko, Charles Fullerton, Henry Hartsfield, and Donald Peterson, as well as Richard Truly and Robert Crippin of the U.S. Navy and Robert Overmyer, a Marine Corps pilot.

In March 1966, construction work began at the intended MOL launch facility, Space Launch Complex Six (SLC-6, or "Slick Six") at Vandenberg AFB on the California coast.

Through 1966, it was imagined that the first MOL would be built and deployed into Earth orbit by the end of 1968, but in 1967, the schedule slipped, first to 1970 and later to 1972. By early 1968, the MOL mockup was completed, static structural tests of flight representative assemblies were under way and Air Force crews were undergoing training using surplus NASA Gemini capsules.

By the spring of 1969, there were there were several MOLs under construction in Building 45 at the MSSD Space Systems Center in Huntington Beach. Suddenly, on June 10, a month before NASA's historic Apollo 11 lunar landing, the MOL project was terminated by the Nixon administration. The reasons for the cancellation ranged from the usual bugaboo—cost—to a turf war between the Department of Defense and the CIA over who was going to manage intelligence assets.

In any case, America's first space-station program was over. The MOLs were taken out of Building 45 under heavy guard and presumably destroyed. All of the MOL astronauts were transferred to NASA, where they would eventually find themselves in the Space Shuttle program. After two space flights aboard the Shuttle, Richard Truly went on to serve as NASA's administrator from 1986 to 1992.

The Air Force and the Department of Defense never had another space-station program. NASA confidently predicted a 100-man space station by the end of the 1970s, but the only space station that was ever owned and operated by NASA was the three-man Skylab that was inhabited in 1973 and 1974. Attempts by NASA to field a space station in the 1980s and early 1990s never came to fruition, but the agency became a major participant in the International Space Station (ISS) that was first staffed by a crew in 1999.

The Soviet Union, meanwhile, went on to develop a series of successful space stations. These were based, ironically, on information that they had gleaned from the MOL program. The most successful were Salyut 6, in operation from 1977 to 1982, Salyut 7, in service from 1982 to 1986, and finally Mir, which was inhabited continuously from 1986 until it burned up in the Earth's atmosphere in 2000. Several NASA astronauts visited Mir after the Cold War ended and Mir became a Russian—rather than Soviet—outpost.

The nearly finished SLC-6 facility at Vandenberg AFB was mothballed, or sealed up for long-term storage, in 1969. It was refurbished in the 1980s to serve as the West Coast launch facility for the Space Shuttle. Such a launch site was needed to place the Shuttle into a polar orbit because the Cape Canaveral facility was configured for equatorial launches. Polar orbits were necessary for missions which would take the Shuttle over the Soviet Union for the same sort of missions envisioned for the MOL two decades earlier.

After the 1986 *Challenger* disaster, Slick Six was mothballed for a second time without having been used. In the early 1990s, it was renovated again, this time for use in launching satellites using the Titan 4/Centaur launch vehicles, but this program was soon canceled. Revived yet again for use with Boeing Delta IV vehicles, the complex ended the twentieth century having been used for just a single successful launch.

The most trouble-plagued launch facility in the United States, Slick Six is said to have been constructed on a Chumash Indian burial ground that is subject to a curse.

Spiral and the Mikoyan Gurevich MiG-105
By 1964, both of the contestants in the Space Race had each canceled their first-generation spaceplanes, the Dyna-

Soar and the Rakatoplan. In the United States, the Air
Force would not again seriously consider a spaceplane and
NASA would take up their ambitious Space Shuttle project
until the Apollo program had borne fruit. The Soviet air
force, however, was still enamored of the idea of a manned
spaceplane for use as an antisatellite weapon. No sooner
had Rakatoplan faded than the Soviet air force turned to
yet another supersecret spaceplane program. This one would
be undertaken by the Mikoyan-Gurevich design bureau—
best known by the acronym MiG—creators of the leading
Soviet fighter aircraft.

The MiG design bureau had been studying a unique approach to spaceplanes for several years when the spotlight
of official interest was turned their way. The MiG approach
borrowed a page from innovative spaceplane studies undertaken in Germany during World War II by Dr. Eugen
Sänger. While postwar spaceplanes such as Dyna-Soar and
Rakatoplan—and even the Space Shuttle—were designed
for 90-degree vertical launch using a very large rocket or
rockets, Sänger had envisioned launching his spaceplane
with another spaceplane! Sänger's spaceplane would have
been piggybacked on a winged launch vehicle and
launched into space at an angle of 30 degrees.

The MiG spaceplane project, known as Spiral, got
under way early in 1965. The Soviets were watching war-
ily as the U.S. Air Force continued work on the MOL project. MOL was seen as the space-based equivalent of the
U-2s that had been routinely violating Soviet air space a
decade earlier. Just as there was a need then to find a way
to shoot down U-2s, there was a need in the late 1960s to
find a way to shoot down the MOLs. Spiral was the answer.

Initial plans called for a first Spiral test launch by mid-
1967, but it fell behind schedule. The Spiral project continued until June 1969. Within a matter of days of the
cancellation of the MOL program, the Soviets canceled
Spiral.

This, however, would not be the end. During the 1970s,

as the United States was working toward the operational debut of the Space Shuttle, the Soviet Union needed a spaceplane. They turned to MiG, and Spiral was officially resuscitated in 1974. This time, an actual spaceplane would be built, under the designation MiG-105, and it would actually be flight tested.

The MiG-105 was a single-seat vehicle similar in appearance to the X-20 Dyna-Soar, but with a flatter nose. It was 27 feet 8 inches long with folding-tip delta wings that spanned 25 feet when fully deployed.

The United States Dyna-Soar and Space Shuttle were designed with rocket propulsion for take-off, but were designed for unpowered, gliding landings. A great deal of study had gone into adding jet engines to the Space Shuttle for powered flight within the Earth's atmosphere, but this idea was rejected. At the MiG design bureau, however, engineers designed their spaceplane with a Koliesov airbreathing turbojet engine. The American spaceplanes were designed to be capable only of runway landings. They required vertical, rocket-assisted launch. The MiG-105 was capable of taking off from a runway as well.

The first flight of the MiG-105 occurred on October 11, 1976. Although it was entirely within the Earth's atmosphere and it covered a distance of about a dozen miles, this was the first-ever flight of a winged craft theoretically capable of flying in space.

Over the next two years, the MiG-105 prototype made eight flights, all of them within the atmosphere. These flights included several in which the vehicle was air launched from a larger aircraft at high altitude. In these cases, the larger aircraft was a Tu-95 Bear turboprop bomber, rather than the hypersonic winged launch vehicle imagined in the Spiral project. Such a vehicle is not known to have been constructed.

In the eighth flight test, the MiG-105 was damaged beyond repair in a rough landing. While the pilot survived, the spaceplane project did not. The MiG-105 program was canceled and the Soviet Union turned to building the best spaceplane possible—a virtually identical replica of the United States Space Shuttle!

Buran

The final winged spacecraft built by the Soviet Union was, like its predecessors, undertaken behind a veil of utmost secrecy. When it was finally revealed to the world late in 1988, it was, however, like déjà vu. The Buran (Snowstorm) orbiting vehicle was a clone of the American Space Shuttle orbiter, right down to the color and pattern of its heat-absorbing tiles. Identical in shape and configuration to the Space Shuttle, Buran was 118 feet long—only 4 feet shorter—and it had a wingspan of 79 feet compared to 78 feet in the shuttle. The wing area and wing sweep were identical, as was the size and configuration of the payload bay.

Built by Rockwell International and having completed twenty-six heavily publicized flights when Buran was first revealed, the Space Shuttle was about as far from a secret program as any high-tech machine could have been. Virtually every detail of the Space Shuttle's design was public knowledge. It was clear to all that the Soviet Union had absorbed every scrap of this information. Instead of being seen as a technical triumph, Buran was seen as an embarrassing icon of a system that was bankrupt of technical innovation.

Little attention was focused on the differences the two systems. While the winged spaceplanes were virtually identical in appearance, the launch systems were distinctly different. The Space Shuttle utilized two solid rocket boosters to augment its liquid-fueled Shuttle Main Engine (SME). Buran was designed to be launched by the liquid-fueled rocket developed by the Energia design bureau. The rocket, called Energia, was the largest launch vehicle in the world after the United States stopped producing the immense Saturn V that had propelled the Apollo astronauts to the moon. It would be capable of producing nearly 8 million pounds of thrust, more than the Space Shuttle's group of engines.

This huge gun was designed to fire nuclear artillery shells.

The U-2 was the most successful spy plane of the Cold War.

The D-21 drone was designed to be launched from the SR-71. Able to fly at Mach 3, it was the fastest reconnaissance drone ever designed.

The Polaris was the first intercontinental missile which was capable of being launched from a submarine.

The Air Force's Dyna-Soar program was one of the earliest American planes to put a man into space.

The E-3 AWACS is the premier Command and
Control aircraft in the Air Force.

The Sea Shadow is the Navy's first stealth warship. In order to ensure secrecy, all the initial sea trials were conducted at night.

The B-2 bomber has performed well in both the Gulf War
and in Operation Desert Storm.

During Desert Storm, the F-117 destroyed
over 1,600 high value targets.

The Tacit Blue is one of the strangest looking aircraft in the US
inventory. The strange shape is designed to accommodate
a huge, side-looking radar.

The SR-71 Blackbird is the fastest plane ever built. It flew so high and so fast that no Soviet missile could catch it.

Design work on the Buran project dated back to 1971, and the project was formally initiated in 1974. Paralleling the Space Shuttle's development, it was under the direction of Valentin Glushko at the Energia design bureau. As the development of both Buran spaceplane and Energia booster proceeded during the late 1970s, it was imagined that manned space missions with the system would occur by the mid- to late 1980s.

In 1977, NASA had done aerodynamic testing of the Space Shuttle with a full-scale spaceplane bolted to the back of a Boeing 747. In 1983, the Soviet Union secretly began testing a Buran mock-up bolted to the back of a modified Myasishchev M-4. However, the lack of parts dramatically delayed the completion of the operational Buran.

The first ground tests of the engines for the Energia launch vehicle occurred in 1986 shortly after NASA suffered a disastrous setback in the loss of the spaceplane *Challenger* on the twenty-fifth space mission of the Space Shuttle system. This incident would ground the Space Shuttle program for more than two years. It seemed to the upper echelon at the Soviet Ministry of Defense that the Buran project might benefit from the suspension of the Space Shuttle operations, and it was hoped that it might actually make its first flight before the American Shuttles were back in space. However, an epidemic of hardware and software problems were delaying Buran as well.

The long-delayed first launch of the huge Energia rocket occurred in May 1987. As the Buran spaceplane was not ready, the Energia was used to launch the Polyus anti-satellite spacecraft. The Energia worked fine, but the Polyus failed to achieve orbit because of a hardware glitch.

It was a year later before Buran was finally approved for flight operations. The United States Space Shuttles were not yet flying, so there was some degree of excitement at the big Baikinour Kosmodrome launch site that the Reds might beat the Yanks. However, it was not to be. The Space Shuttle returned to flight on September 29, 1988, with the first scheduled Buran mission a month away. The planned October Buran mission was scrubbed because of hardware problems and it did not occur until November 15.

The first flight of the Buran spaceplane was an unmanned orbital mission. The entire mission profile, from launch to orbit to runway landing, was conducted by remote control. The Soviets had demonstrated a working spaceplane, and promised that a crew would be aboard "next time." It was even revealed that a second Buran spaceplane had been completed and that it would soon be ready to join its sister ship in orbital operations.

However, the second flight into space for the Buran vehicle never came. It was carried to the Paris Air Show in 1989 for the world to have a closer look, but a second powered flight was delayed indefinitely. In June 1993, after the end of the Cold War had brought the demise of the Soviet Union itself, Russian President Boris Yeltsin ordered the final cancellation of the Buran program.

The Energia launch vehicle, however, continued to be developed as a means of launching heavy payloads.

CHAPTER 9

Spy Planes

JUST THE TERM *SPY PLANE* IS A PHRASE THAT CONJURES UP the nervous and contentious mood of the Cold War. In May 1960, the shooting down of an American U-2 piloted by Francis Gary Powers was one of the Cold War's milestone moments.

There is something cool and mysterious about the environment of high technology reconnaissance and electronic warfare aircraft. Battles can be won and lost without a shot being fired. Secrets that took years to weave—and nearly as long to disguise—can be compromised in split seconds. The roles of fighters, bombers, transports, trainers and refueling aircraft are all self-evident, but what mysteries lurk beneath the epithet *spy plane*?

Reconnaissance aircraft evolved from observation aircraft, a role to which military airplanes were assigned even before the name *warplane* was coined. The first operational missions flown by military aircraft were observation missions. Italy used them over Libya in 1911 and in World War I, the first military aircraft were observation planes.

In the beginning there were the pilot's eyes, straining through the oil and dust on his goggles to see some surface feature far below. On the next flight he took his binoculars and then a camera to record the same for later interpretation on the ground. By World War II, the large-format cameras carried by reconnaissance aircraft were quite specialized and very accurate. The photos they provided proved to be an essential element in planning and executing the allied strategic-bombing missions that ultimately turned the tide of the war. Reconnaissance photos also provided vital information for surface operations, and were particularly useful in planning amphibious operations.

During a typical wartime strategic operation, reconnaissance aircraft would both precede and follow the bombers, taking before-and-after pictures, first to help in planning and then to help assess the results.

Until after World War II, reconnaissance aircraft were mostly combat aircraft of one sort or another that had their guns replaced by cameras. Reconnaisance birds based on fighters could go low and fast, while those adapted from bombers could provide imagery of strongholds well beyond the front.

During the war, the F-13 reconnaissance plane, a camera-equipped B-29, had mapped the Japanese heartland prior to the big B-29 raids because no accurate cartographic data about Japan existed in Allied files.

The aerial reconnaissance chore in Vietnam was handled in much the same way as in Vietnam and Korea: by converted warplanes. In the early part of the war the McDonald RF-101 was used, an aircraft which had distinguished itself in 1962 during the Cuban missile crisis with low-level runs over Castro's island empire. The McDonald RF-4C, the reconnaissance version of the great Phantom II fighter, replaced the RF-101 after 1967, and remained as the state of the art for use in low-level, day-to-day tactical reconnaissance until the 1980s.

In World War II, reconnaissance missions over enemy territory were an integral part of planning both defensive and offensive operations. During the Cold War, the United States military in general, and the Strategic Air Command in particular, operated under the assumption that in order to prevent or win World War III, such reconnaissance work was essential.

Under his 1955 Open Skies proposal President Dwight
Eisenhower suggested that the world could ensure peace
through a practice of open aerial reconnaissance conducted
by all of the world's major powers. The Soviet Union, then
still contemplating offensive military actions, rejected the
notion. The Eisenhower administration then gave the green
light to Lockheed to proceed with the U-2.

Though the U-2 would be the first aircraft specifically
designed to conduct overflights of the Soviet Union, it
would not be the first to probe the dark secrets of the red
empire. In the Cold War as in World War II, some reconnaissance aircraft were adapted from common aircraft
originally designed for other missions. The Navy modified
Convair PB4Y Privateer and Lockheed P2V Neptune patrol aircraft for the reconnaissance mission early in the
Cold War. Indeed, such aircraft were among the first lost to
Soviet fire during the Cold War. A PB4Y is presumed to
have been shot down over the Baltic Sea in April 1950 by
Soviet interceptors after allegedly violating the airspace of
Soviet-occupied Latvia. In November 1951, a Neptune was
shot down over the Sea of Japan near Vladivostok. No sur-
vivors were reportedly recovered from either incident, although there were persistent rumors that members of the
PB4Y crew were seen in Soviet prison camps later in the
1950s.

Perhaps the most notable of the existing aircraft used
for reconnaisance missions around the periphery of the Soviet Union during the Cold War were the Boeing EB-47
and RB-47, the electronic- and photo-reconnaissance version of the B-47 Stratojet strategic bomber. Ironically, the
American strategic bomber produced in the largest numbers since World War II was never in combat once, but the
reconnaissance variants were in harm's way frequently
during their service at the height of the Cold War.

One of the earliest known shooting incidents involving
a Stratojet came on May 8, 1954. A Boeing RB-47 based at
RAF Fairford penetrated Soviet air space near the naval
base at Murmansk and photographed a number of Soviet

facilities. As it was turning home, the RB-47 encountered Soviet MiG-15s, as well as MiG-17s, which were not known to be operational at the time. The MiG-17s attacked, and the RB-47 returned fire. Moments later, the Stratojet passed into Finnish air space and the Soviets broke off their assault. The RB-47 suffered several hits, but no aircraft on either side was lost.

The first Stratojet loss to enemy action came on April 17, 1955. An RB-47 of the 26th Strategic Reconnaissance Wing operating out of Eielson AFB in Alaska was shot down by MiG-15s near Cape Lopatka, at the southern end of the Kamchatka Peninsula. According to Soviet documents circulated after the end of the Cold War, the aircraft was acquired by radar near Cape Vasiliev and did not actually violate Soviet air space. It was intercepted east of Cape Kronotski and attacked for two minutes. The RB-47 disappeared from radar screens and the crew was reported missing.

Three nonfatal attacks against RB-47s are reported to have occurred during the autumn of 1958 in widely separated locations. These were on October 31 over the Black Sea, on November 7 near Gotland Island in the Baltic Sea, and on November 17 over the Sea of Japan. In each case, the Stratojet involved eluded the Soviet interceptors and returned safely to its base.

On July 1, 1960, two months to the day after the loss of the U-2 piloted by Francis Gary Powers ignited an international incident, an RB-47H was shot down over the Barents Sea. This, too, became an international incident that was widely reported and a topic of intense discussion in the media. The United States government insisted that the RB-47 had never been closer than 30 miles to Soviet territory, and the matter was discussed and debated in the United Nations Security Council during the weeks following the incident.

Assigned to the 38th Strategic Reconnaissance Squadron of the 55th Strategic Reconnaissance Wing, the RB-47H was operating out of RAF Brize Norton. It was piloted by

Major Willard G. "Bill" Palm, with Captain Freeman "Bruce" Olmstead as copilot and Captain John R. McKone as navigator. In the reconnaissance pod were Major Eugene Posa, Captain Oscar Goforth and Captain Dean Phillips. The aircraft was reportedly shot down by a MiG-15 piloted by Vasili Poliakov. Both Olmstead and McKone ejected and survived. Palm's body was recovered and was returned to the United States on July 25. Olmstead and McKone were tried and convicted of espionage in a Soviet court and jailed. However, they were eventually released on January 25, 1961. Reportedly, Posa's body was also recovered, but it was never returned to the United States.

Probably the last shooting incident involving a Stratojet came on April 27, 1965. An ERB-47H was intercepted by a pair of North Korean MiG-17s over the Sea of Japan. Extensive damage resulted in the loss of two engines, although the Stratojet escaped to make an emergency landing at Yokota AB in Japan.

While converted and adapted aircraft can often do an admirable job, it is axiomatic that aircraft which are specially designed for the task can meet their challenge to an even greater degree. Some of the reconnaissance aircraft developed during the Cold War can be counted among the most specialized machines to ply the stratosphere.

Genetrix

Despite the efforts of the RB-47s and others that sniffed at the edges of the Soviet Union, the United States spent the early days of the Cold War craving a means of conducting surveillance operations *over* the Soviet Union. Eventually the Lockheed U-2 and later the Corona spy satellites would solve the problem, but in the early 1950s, the United States turned the clock back to the eighteenth century technology—balloons.

Named for the ancestral mother of the Julian clan by way of Aeneas in classical mythology, Project Genetrix was a U.S. Air Force program undertaken even before the CIA began funding the U-2. As early as 1951, the RAND

Corporation had done a top-secret study of using weather balloons equipped with cameras for extremely high altitude, long-range reconnaisance missions.

The Air Force moved ahead with the development and testing of cameras and film-recovery techniques to turn the concept of the RAND study into a reality. Some of the remotely controlled camera technology developed for Genetrix would prove useful a few years later in the Corona satellite program.

In December 1955, Project Genetrix was ready to go and the Eisenhower administration authorized flights to begin early in 1956. Launching from bases in Western Europe, the Air Force sent literally hundreds of balloons over Eastern Europe and the Soviet Union, many of them operating above 40,000 feet.

Because the prevailing winds blew west to east, the balloons had to cross the entire breadth of Eastern Europe and the Soviet land mass, about 5,000 miles, before they could be successfully recovered. Many drifted off course and came down in remote areas of Siberia or northwestern China. A few were apparently intercepted and shot down. Many were not lost, but rather were recovered by the Soviets. The United States used the cover story that the Genetrix balloons were doing scientific research in conjunction with the International Geophysical Year, but the Soviet Union did not accept this explanation. Their public complaints about Genetrix hastened the decision to quickly terminate the project after less than two months.

Amazingly, nearly fifty Genetrix cameras and film capsules were recovered and more than half of these contained imagery that was deemed by Air Force intelligence to be useful. The Air Force proposed a follow-on program that would use balloons flying at even higher altitudes, but President Eisenhower reportedly intervened personally to stop the Air Force from throwing good money after bad.

Ironically, one of the most useful consequences of this project of reconnaisance balloons masquerading as weather balloons was the weather data that were obtained.

A great deal was learned from high-altitude winds over the Soviet Union that would be vital in planning the future U-2 missions.

The Skunk Works

No discussion of Cold War spy planes is complete without mention of the Lockheed Advanced Development Projects (ADP) office, the legendary Skunk Works. It was here that some of the Cold War's most important secret projects— from spy planes to stealth aircraft—were created. Indeed, it can be said that during the Cold War—not to mention at the turn of the century—the Skunk Works was one of the most secret places in the aeronautical world.

The history of aircraft design and development is filled with many remarkable stories and there are many important design bureaus that have been responsible for truly legendary aircraft. However, there are few stories and few design bureaus that can compare favorably with the Skunk Works. Formed in 1943 by Clarence Leonard "Kelly" Johnson against a backdrop of wartime urgency, the Skunk Works developed and maintained a reputation for creating aircraft that were years—if not decades—ahead of their time, and for doing so quickly and efficiently. In the Byzantine world of corporate and military bureaucracy, the latter is nearly as extraordinary as the aircraft that the Skunk Works produced.

Kelly Johnson will forever be remembered for his straightforward, no-nonsense approach to aircraft design, which resulted in some of aircraft that were the most technologically advanced in the world at the time he and his team created them. He began his career in 1933 as a designer at Lockheed, where he helped to design the Orion single-engine transport, and the Electra twin-engine airliner which first flew in February 1934 and evolved into a long series of transport, patrol and attack aircraft.

Johnson quickly developed a reputation as an ingenious engineer, and in 1937, the Institute of Aeronautical Sciences (now the American Institute of Aeronautics and Astronautics) awarded him the Sperry Award for his design of the Lockheed-Fowler Flap used in the control surfaces of aircraft.

In the late 1930s, Johnson directed the engineering effort that led to the design of the revolutionary Lockheed P-38 Lightning, which was to be the fastest American fighter in the first half of World War II. Used in large numbers by the U.S. Army Air Forces (USAAF), the P-38 also offered exceptional range. All of the top USAAF aces flew the Lightning.

In 1943, the USAAF selected Lockheed to build what was to be America's first operational jet fighter. Kelly Johnson and a hand-picked team were virtually sealed into a canvas-roofed building next to the Lockheed wind tunnel in Burbank, California, and told to design and build a prototype in 180 days. This was the beginning of the ADP office, which continues to be known, because of the conditions in its original home, as the Skunk Works. The name was taken from the place where Al Capp's cartoon character Li'l Abner distilled his "Kickapoo Joy Juice."

Johnson's Skunk Works had the prototype XP-80 jet fighter ready for engine tests in 139 days, and two years later it was the standard fighter in the USAAF.

After World War II, Johnson and the Skunk Works team designed a series of high-performance aircraft including the F-94 Starfire interceptor and the remarkable Mach 2 F-104 Starfighter—known as the "missile with a man in it"—which earned Johnson the Collier Trophy. Also during the 1950s, the Skunk Works was asked to design an extremely long-range and high-altitude spy plane that could be used for flights over the Soviet Union. This top-secret project resulted in the U-2.

After the U-2, the Skunk Works produced the amazing family of aircraft that included the SR-71 family, the fastest and highest-flying jet aircraft ever manufactured. This series, especially the SR-71 itself, was Kelly Johnson's masterpiece. In every part of its design—including its shape, its materials, its components and even its fuel—the aircraft was a revolutionary design unlike anything else. The Collier Trophy that he received was a small measure of recognition for such a design feat. The SR-71 and the Skunk Works's engineering innovations that made it possible were unlike anything of their era and have, for the most part, never been equalled.

Project Aquatone and the Original Spy Plane

The term *spy plane* was coined to describe the Lockheed U-2. High-flying reconnaissance aircraft had existed for half a century before the U-2 came to the attention of the mainstream media, but there was something about the audacity of a secret airplane flying over the Soviet Union in the darkest days of the Cold War that begged for such an epithet.

The impetus for the U-2 was the need by the CIA to gather accurate photographic intelligence concerning weapons development within the Soviet Union. The United States needed a secret weapon that could spy on Soviet secret weapons. President Dwight Eisenhower had advanced his Open Skies proposal, under which reconnaissance aircraft from either country could openly operate in the skies over the other—much as reconnaissance satellites do today. When Soviet Premier Nikita Khrushchev laughed off Ike's Open Skies, the president authorized the CIA to undertake the mission covertly under the code name Operation Overflight.

Richard Bissell, the special assistant to CIA Director Allen Dulles, made contact with Kelly Johnson. Dulles outlined the need for a high-flying aircraft capable of extremely long missions involving flights across the breadth of the Soviet Union. To accomplish this, Kelly Johnson ingeniously based his aircraft on the wings of a glider to give it long-range soaring capability. The aircraft, Lockheed Model CL-282, would be built under the code name Aquatone. When completed, it would receive the U.S. Air Force designation U-2, identifying it only as a "utility" aircraft.

To flight test the Project Aquatone aircraft, Lockheed and the CIA constructed a secret base at Groom Lake in a location in the vast military operating area north of Nellis AFB in Nevada that was once designated by the Atomic Energy Commission with the innocuous appellation of Area 51. Known informally as Paradise Ranch because the desolate high desert was anything but a paradise, the Area 51 site would be home to countless other supersecret projects in later years.

The U-2A had a wing span of 80 feet, and was 49 feet 7 inches long. It had a gross weight of 16,000 pounds and could operate at an altitude of 85,000 feet. Powered by a single Pratt & Whitney J75-P-13 turbojet, it had a range of over 2,200 miles.

The first flight of a U-2 occurred at Groom Lake in August 1955, and the aircraft entered service, overflying the Soviet Union, in July 1956. They would be operated by CIA crews, with operational support provided by the U.S. Air Force. Eventually, the Air Force would take over flight operations as well. Initially the U-2 activity—masquerading as an Air Force weather-reconnaissance squadron—operated from Adana (later Incirlik) AB in Turkey. Later operations were also based at Lahore and Peshawar in Pakistan.

The primary operations involved missions along the southern periphery of the Soviet Union, and overflying missile-test facilities in the central Soviet Union, especially in what is now Kazakhstan. Missions would also involve crossing the Soviet Union, even overflying Moscow itself. In these missions, the U-2s would land at Bodo in Norway. In addition to the overflights of the Soviet Union, U-2s monitored the Middle East, especially during the 1956 Suez Crisis.

For several years, the U-2 operated with impunity. It was impossible to see and when detected by radar, it was soaring too high to be touched. By 1960, however, Soviet surface-to-air missiles had improved to the point where the U-2 finally became vulnerable. On May Day in 1960, veteran U-2 pilot Francis Gary Powers found this out over an ICBM site near Sverdlovsk. He survived being shot down but was captured and put on trial in Moscow.

This very public "show trial" also placed the CIA and the whole Operation Overflight mission in the defendant's chair. A feeding frenzy for the worldwide media, the U-2 scandal quickly became an international incident of enormous proportion. It embarrassed outgoing President Eisenhower, who was about to meet with Premier Khrushchev in a historic summit conference that was to have been the final international event of his eight-year presidency.

Eisenhower's summit was canceled, and so was Operation Overflight. The U-2, however, remained in operation, flying reconnaissance missions over Cuba during the 1962 Cuban Missile Crisis, and over Vietnam during the decade of United States involvement there.

After 1960, operational control of the U-2 aircraft passed to the U.S. Air Force, which assigned them to the 9th Strategic Reconnaissance Wing at Beale AFB in California. For most of the ensuing decades, however, most of the fleet was out on assignment, operating from forward bases throughout the world, especially the Royal Air Force facility at Alconbury in England and Kadena AB on Okinawa.

Among the most closely guarded series of missions undertaken by the U-2 after the Powers incident involved launching the aircraft from U.S. Navy carriers at sea. The idea originated in 1963 with Richard Bissell, who recognized that the land bases from which the U-2 had been operating were known to the Soviets and that carriers would restore some of the secrecy to basing. Under Operation Whale Tale, the sea trials of the spy plane began in August 1963 aboard the USS *Kitty Hawk*. The huge wing span of the U-2 was much greater than that of the typical carrier plane, but the very slow landing speed made touching down theoretically easier than with a typical carrier plane. Lockheed test pilot Bob Schumacher and several CIA pilots trained for and executed a series of takeoffs and landings over a period of several months. For these operations, the spy planes were retrofitted with arrestor hooks and other equipment and designated as U-2G.

The first operational use of a carrier-launched U-2G

was not flown against Soviet targets but rather to monitor the French nuclear tests at Mururora Atoll in French Polynesia. Operation Seeker involved flights that kept tabs on French nuclear tests in May 1964.

The original U-2A was superseded in 1967 by the larger U-2R. The U-2R was powered by an improved version of the Pratt & Whitney J75-P-13 turbojet that powered its older sister. It was 63 feet long with a wing span of 103 feet. The gross weight was increased to 40,000 pounds, the operating altitude was pushed to above 90,000 feet and the range to 3,500 miles. Amazingly, aircraft carrier operations involving the larger U-2R were considered and sea trials were undertaken in November 1969 aboard the USS *America*.

Through the 1960s, the U.S. Navy's role in U-2 carrier operations was merely that of hosting Air Force and CIA aircraft and aircrews. However, the U-2R carrier operations elicited a great deal of interest by the Navy, and in 1973, two specially configured U-2Rs were equipped with ALQ-110 Big Look surveillance radar and delivered to the Navy under the designation U-2EPX. Over the ensuing years, the Navy used their U-2EPX spy planes for a variety of roles, including Operation Outlaw Hawk, in which their radar was linked to other radar sights both aboard surface ships and ashore. There was also consideration given to arming the Navy U-2EPXs with offensive weapons— including nuclear weapons—but this plan is not believed to have been implemented operationally.

In 1980, it was decided the assembly line should be reopened to build twenty-six all-new U-2Rs, which would be delivered under the newer and more appropriate designation TR-1 (Tactical Reconnaissance, first). One of these was delivered to NASA as an Earth resources survey aircraft under the designation ER-2.

In the coming years, U-2s would also be tasked with routine aerial-mapping missions over the United States at the behest of NASA and the Department of Agriculture.

After the end of the Cold War, they were an integral part of U.S. Air Force operations in Gulf War I, the Balkan wars of the 1990s, in Afghanistan during Operation Enduring Freedom and over Iraq in Gulf War II.

Between 1994 and 1998, the entire U-2R/TR-1 fleet was reengined with the General Electric F118-101 turbofan, delivering 19,000 pounds of thrust. Now all redesignated U-2S, these aircraft have a range in excess of 4,500 miles. The U-2Ss also have been upgraded with the Senior Year defensive system and three important sensor packages— Senior Spear for communications intelligence, Senior Ruby for electronic intelligence and Senior Glass for signals intelligence.

Today, the aircrews call her the Dragon Lady, a graceful bird of quiet sophistication that sees it all. Having burst dramatically into public awareness in the darkest days of the Cold War, the U-2 has now long outlived the Soviet Union. Many long decades after its very rude public debut in 1960, the U-2 family remains an extremely well-guarded secret weapon in the twenty-first century.

Mandrake

Often referred to during the 1960s as the "Soviet U-2," this long-range, high-altitude reconnaissance aircraft was a heavily modified variation on a jet fighter that had made its first appearance more than a decade before the Soviet Union captured its first example of the great Lockheed spy plane.

While the famous Mikoyan-Gurevich (MiG) design bureau would dominate Soviet jet fighter aircraft development during the last half of the twentieth century, during World War II, the design bureau of Alexander Yakovlev had produced the definitive Soviet piston-engine fighters. After World War II, Yakovlev and Mikoyan Gurevich moved into jets. While the latter was working on its immortal MiG-15, one of the greatest jet fighters of the early Cold War years, Yakovlev developed the Yak-25. Codenamed Flashlight by NATO analysts, the Yak-25 was a large fighter with a pair of Tumansky turbojet engines slung under its swept wings. Nearly 500 were built during the early 1950s as two-seat, all-weather interceptors.

In 1957, two years after the first flight of the Lockheed U-2, the Soviet air force ordered Yakovlev to create a comparable high-altitude aircraft, and to base it on the durable Yak-25. To create the new aircraft, Yakovlev borrowed Kelly Johnson's idea of very large, glider-like wings. They exchanged the 36-foot swept wingspan of the Flashlight fighter for a straight wing spanning nearly 77 feet, nearly the same as the U-2A.

The new aircraft was officially designated a Yak-25RV, with the suffix (Razvedchik Vysotnyi) standing for reconnaissance, high altitude. Flight testing was conducted in the spring of 1959, reaching altitudes up to about 60,000 feet and demonstrating excellent glider-like aerodynamic characteristics. Over the coming years, 165 Mandrakes were built, including at least a couple that were designed to operate remotely, without a pilot on board.

After Francis Gary Powers and his U-2 were shot down in May 1960, Yakovlev examined the wreckage and incorporated what they learned into the Mandrake, which was in production at the time. The improved Mandrake entered service in 1963. Mandrake operations continued into the 1970s, and the aircraft were observed over the Middle East and China, as well as over the fringes of NATO air space.

Ironically, just as Yakovlev borrowed from Lockheed to create the Mandrake, General Dynamics in the United States would borrow from Yakovlev. In 1962, General Dynamics began work on high-altitude reconnaissance aircraft which involved nearly doubling the wing span of a Martin B-57 tactical bomber from 64 to 122 feet. This project resulted in the RB-57F—retrofitted with an all-new wing—of which 21 were constructed. They flew operational missions from 1963 to 1974. Many of these missions were over the periphery of the Soviet Union and the People's Republic of China. Some flights originated at the U-2 base at Peshawar in Pakistan.

Super Spy Plane

Though it first flew in the 1960s, its top speed is still unknown. All we know is that the Lockheed SR-71 Blackbird is confirmed as the fastest and highest-flying aircraft that ever took off from a runway. The phrase "faster than a speeding bullet" was literally true for the Blackbird.

Of all aircraft ever manufactured, only the experimental North American Aviation X-15—which didn't take off under its own power—was clocked at faster speeds. In 1976, an SR-71 set a world's absolute speed record for airplanes that take off from runways of 2193.167 mph—Mach 3, or three times the speed of sound—but it topped this speed officially on several ocassions, and its unofficial top speed is much faster. The speed record still stood at the beginning of the twenty-first century.

How much faster? At a briefing given by the 9th Strategic Reconnaissance Wing attended by this writer in the 1980s, a spokesman was asked what they would do if someone ever took the speed record away from the SR-71. "We'd just take up one of our birds," he laughed, "and step down a little harder on the accelerator."

Even after its temporary retirement in 1990, the Blackbird's top speed remained secret. Officially, it is rated at "Mach 3+" but the emphasis is always on the "plus." When this writer mentioned 4,000 mph around a group of SR-71 pilots at Beale AFB when the SR-71 was still operational, the question elicited smiles and knowing chuckles.

From its design and engineering to the fuel that it burned in its engines, the Blackbird's family was like no other. The materials used in the construction of these airplanes were experimental at the time, and the overall design and the shape of their fuselage to provide most of the lift was an engineering breakthrough.

The SR-71 evolved from the CIA's mysterious A-12 reconnaissance airplane, which was developed in the early 1960s for clandestine missions behind the Iron Curtain where withering speed and almost-impossible altitude were required for secrecy and safety.

The supersecret project that led to the Blackbird was initiated in 1957 by Richard Bissell of the CIA. The idea was for an aircraft that was capable of flying at extreme altitudes, like the U-2, but which would be faster than any known Soviet aircraft. The performance parameters were Mach 3 and an operational altitude above 90,000 feet.

The two companies who would submit proposals for the new aircraft would be Lockheed and the Convair division of General Dynamics. Convair was then developing its B-58 Hustler, the first supersonic strategic bomber built in the United States.

Convair's proposals centered around a manned parasite aircraft that could be carried beneath a B-58 and air launched at high speed and altitude. The first proposal, designated as Fish, evolved into Convair's Project Kingfish. While wind tunnel models were built and tested, neither Convair aircraft was actually built.

While Convair had its Project Kingfish, Lockheed would have its Project Archangel. At the Skunk Works, Kelly Johnson came up with a series of studies beginning with the A-1 and culminating in the A-12. Most were dart-shaped aircraft, although the A-4 was shaped like an arrowhead. The configuration for several in the series remains unknown nearly half a century later. Indeed, the secrecy at the time was extreme. The President and a handful of CIA and Air Force personnel were the only people outside the two companies who were aware of the projects, and neither company knew exactly what the other was doing.

Late in 1959, the Skunk Works A-12 proposal was chosen by the CIA, and in January 1960 the CIA issued a contract to Lockheed to build a dozen A-12s under the code name Oxcart. Both Perkin Elmer and Eastman Kodak received secret contracts to develop extremely high-resolution camera systems.

Built mostly of titanium to withstand the extreme temperatures encountered at Mach 3, the A-12 also incorporated radar-confusing contours and surfaces that were a prelude to the stealth technology that the Skunk Works would pioneer in the 1970s. The first A-12 prototype was completed at Burbank in February 1962 and delivered to Groom Lake, where it made its first flight on April 26. Within two years, it was being flight tested at Mach 3.2 and higher.

In the meantime, Kelly Johnson suggested that the Air Force consider a variation on the A-12 as a Mach 3 interceptor for its Air Defense Command (ADC). A new generation of supersonic bombers was predicted to be taking shape in the Soviet Union, and an aircraft such as the A-12, which could cruise comfortably at three times the speed of sound, was seen as desirable. The interceptor idea was sound, but the scenario provided the CIA and the Air Force with a secondary benefit. The interceptor version, which was ordered by the Air Force in October 1962 under the designation YF-12, could serve as a cover story for the entire program. By 1962, the rumor that Lockheed was working on a supersecret, high-performance aircraft was circulating in the aerospace industry, and it could now be whispered that the rumor was true and the aircraft was the YF-12.

The YF-12 was, however, a real project. It was equipped with the Hughes AN/ASG-18 air intercept radar system that had originally been developed for the high-speed North American Aviation F-108 interceptor program that was cancelled in 1959. It would be armed with the Hughes GAR-9 (later redesignated as AIM-47) Falcon, an extremely high-performance air-to-air missile capable of speeds up to Mach 6.

The first YF-12 made its debut flight at Groom Lake on August 7, 1963 and began testing the AIM-47 a year later. Only three YF-12s were built and were never placed into service, but they were the fastest interceptors ever flown—before or since—although the Soviet MiG-25, which entered service a decade later, was close.

Even before the debut of the YF-12, the Strategic Air Command saw the A-12/YF-12 Mach 3 capability as desirable for a bomber. As early as 1961, General Curtis LeMay and Kelly Johnson discussed the possibility of an Air Force A-12 that could deliver small, high-yield nuclear weapons. Such an aircraft was ordered in 1962 under the "reconnaissance/strike" designation RS-71 and developed under the project code-named Senior Crown. The designation numeral 71 was the next available in the bomber lineage that had previously used a B prefix, although the North American Aviation XB-70 also flew under the RS-70 designation. By the time the Senior Crown airplane first flew on December 22, 1964, reconnaissance was its sole function, and so its designation was transposed to SR-71 for "strategic reconnaissance."

The CIA's A-12 Oxcart was the first of the family to become operational. Secretly deployed to Kadena AB on Okinawa under Operation Black Shield and supported by the U.S. Air Force, the CIA A-12s began missions over North Vietnam on May 31, 1967. Through the end of the year, eighteen missions were flown over North Vietnam. Some were tracked by radar, but the A-12 easily outflew enemy surface-to-air missiles. After the capture of the USS *Pueblo* spy ship off the coast of North Korea in January 1968, A-12 flights began in that area. The A-12 could cross North Korea in seven minutes and proved impossible to hit.

By May 1968, it was decided that CIA A-12 operations would be terminated in favor of deploying the Project Senior Crown SR-71 as a cooperative effort between SAC and the CIA. A total of fourteen A-12s had been built and thirty-two SR-71s would be built, and the Strategic Air Command SR-21s would be assigned to the 9th Strategic Reconnaissance Wing at Beale AFB in northern California, although at any given moment, much of the fleet would be deployed to overseas detachments, especially at Kadena AB and at RAF Mildenhall in the United Kingdom.

The SR-71 had a wing span of 55 feet 7 inches, the same as the A-12, and a length of 107 feet 5 inches, 62 inches longer than the A-12. The gross weight was 140,000 pounds, up from 117,000 for the A-12. The service ceiling was in excess of 100,000 feet, and it operated routinely above 85,000 feet. At these altitudes, literally at the edge of space, the sky above appears black at midday.

The two JT11D-20B continuous-bleed turbo-ramjet engines, designed specially for these aircraft by Pratt & Whitney, delivered 23,000 pounds of thrust, or 34,000 pounds with afterburner. The SR-71 was the only airplane in the world known to burn JP-7 fuel, which is so nonvolatile that it cannot be lit with a match. It takes a chemical reaction to get the engines started.

The nickname Blackbird was derived from the color of the specially formulated paint applied to the SR-71 surface, which was designed to both absorb radar and to reduce wing temperature.

Internal bays were designed to contain the Blackbird's optical, digital and electronic reconnaissance equipment. There is a two-man crew who wear space suits similar to those worn by astronauts. The pilot and the reconnaissance systems operator manage the hardware secreted behind removable panels that are spread across the belly of the Blackbird.

The first operational SR-71 mission was flown over Vietnam from Kadena AB on March 21, 1968, two months before the A-12s were withdrawn. Their operational career would span the globe and extend for more than a quarter century, with critical high-priority missions being flown from Vietnam to Libya. Many of the missions that the Blackbird flew remain secret, but the skies over Cuba and the Middle East knew her, and there were many stories of her outrunning supersonic air-to-air missiles over North Korea, and of the cat-and-mouse games with MiGs off Vladivostok. Not one SR-71 was ever lost to enemy action.

The Blackbird was, as they said in the 1970s, "high nineties technology that we were lucky to have in the sixties." Ironically, the Air Force announced in 1989 that the Blackbird would be retired, a victim of the end of the Cold War that it helped to win. The last overseas-deployed SR-71 departed from Kadena AB in January 1990, and on

March 6, 1990, a Blackbird was delivered to the Smithsonian Institution's National Air and Space Museum. In this last flight, the aircraft became the only aircraft in history to set a world speed record as it flew to retirement in a museum—it flew from Southern California to Washington, D.C., in 64 minutes and 20 seconds.

No other aircraft has ever had the distinction of having been the fastest operational aircraft in the world from the day it entered service until the day it was retired.

The SR-71's reconnaissance capabilities were greatly missed during Operation Desert Storm in 1991, and an effort was made to reactivate part of the fleet. This was ultimately successful, and several of the world's fastest operational airplanes went back into service with the U.S. Air Force in 1995. Two years later, however, President Bill Clinton killed the reactivated Blackbird with a line-item veto. SR-71s continued to be operated as test aircraft by NASA at Edwards AFB in California until the turn of the century.

D-21 Tagboard

No mention of the SR-71 is complete without a corollary nod to her unmanned sister ship. Just as the Lockheed SR-71 Blackbird was the fastest manned reconnaissance aircraft known to have flown during the twentieth century, the D-21 is the fastest unmanned aerial vehicle of its kind known to have flown during the past century.

The idea for the D-21 program originated with Kelly Johnson, who saw it as a natural extension of the SR-71 program. He could see the value of a Mach 3 reconnaissance drone that could be air launched by the Mach 3 A-12/SR-71 aircraft. No aircraft in the world was fast enough to catch either one, so they could operate with impunity in any hostile airspace.

The CIA, Lockheed's customer for the A-12, showed little initial interest in the Mach 3 drone, but in October 1962, they finally authorized the project under the code name Tagboard. As with the A-12/SR-71 program, the Tagboard drone originated as a CIA project, but in both programs, the U.S. Air Force would ultimately emerge as the dominant player.

Lockheed referred to their new drone as the Q-12, implying that it was to be a drone associated with the A-12. In 1963, as the two aircraft evolved as a joint weapons system, the A-12 carrier aircraft were redesignated with an M for mothership, and the Q-12 was designated with a D for drone, or daughtership. To avoid confusion with other A-12s that would not to be used with Tagboard, the numerals were also inverted. Thus, it would be a D-21 drone aboard an M-21 mothership.

In developing the D-21, Lockheed drew upon past experience with their X-7 experimental aircraft and their working relationship with the Marquardt company, whose RJ43 ramjet engines would be used. The operational D-21 would be 42 feet 10 inches long, with a wing span of 19 feet. Like the A-12/M-21/SR-71, it would have a top speed in excess of Mach 3 and a service ceiling above 100,000 feet. Its range once launched from the mothership would exceed 3,000 miles.

The D-21 was designed to be recovered by parachute after it ejected a module containing its reconnaissance camera and the film exposed on its mission.

Wind tunnel and other tests took place during 1963, and the first D-21 was completed in August 1964. The debut flight of a D-21 mated to the top of its mothership occurred over Groom Lake (Area 51) in Nevada in December 1964, and the first air launch and free flight of a D-21 followed in March 1966.

After three successful launches, a D-21 malfunction on the fourth flight resulted in the loss of both drone and mothership, as well as one of the mothership crewmen. The problem was that the D-21 had to be mounted on top of the M-21. In the wake of this incident, Kelly Johnson proposed that they switch to using a B-52 as a mothership, because in this scenario, the D-21 could be mounted under the mothership. This would be safer than launching from the top of an M-21, because the drone could be dropped before it fired its engines.

There were still bugs to be worked out, but finally, after a series of failed launches, the first successful launch of a D-21 from a B-52 occurred in June 1968.

After more testing, the CIA and the Air Force requested and received presidential authorization to use the D-21 on an operational photo-reconnaissance mission over North Vietnam. In November 1969, the first such deployment failed when the data link failed and the D-21 "vanished." Three further operational missions between December 1970 and March 1971 were all deemed as failures when the camera modules were lost or damaged in recovery. Other missions are said to have been flown, but they've never been confirmed.

The Tagboard program is said to have been officially canceled in July 1971, although its existence would remain classified as top secret until 1977. Many of the D-21s still remained in storage at the turn of the century, ready to accept the call to reactivation.

Foxbat

Just as Yakovlev's Mandrake was the Soviet Union's answer to the Lockheed U-2, the Mikoyan-Gurevich MiG-25 Foxbat was seen during the Cold War as the Soviet aircraft to match the high-performance aircraft that emerged from United States drawing boards in the late 1950s and early 1960s. In terms of speed and altitude, this era saw the advent of a generation of high-performance aircraft that has no precedent before or since. In addition to the Lockheed Blackbird family, there was also the North American Aviation XB-70 Valkyrie strategic bomber that *cruised* at three times the speed of sound (Mach 3). Also from North American Aviation in this era was the planned F-108 Rapier Mach 3 interceptor, and the rocket-powered X-15 research aircraft, an air-launched aircraft that routinely exceeded Mach 5 and had a top speed of Mach 6.7 (4,520 mph).

As the 1950s came to a close, it was clear to Soviet planners that American aviation technology was going higher and faster at an accelerating rate. To be able to confront the challenge of this new generation of aircraft, the Soviet air force ordered Mikoyan-Gurevich to create an interceptor aircraft that could equal their speed and altitude capabilities. The mandate was to "catch the Valkyrie."

In 1964, Mikoyan-Gurevich rolled out the first of several prototypes for what would eventually enter service as the MiG-25. Like the MiG-25, these prototypes were large, heavy aircraft constructed primarily of steel and given a pair of very powerful Tumansky turbojet engines. The basic design, modeled after the U.S. Navy's A3J Vigilante attack bomber, sacrificed maneuverability and range for maximum speed and altitude. One prototype achieved an unofficial speed record for jet aircraft of 1,665 mph (Mach 2.8) in 1965.

As news of this new high-speed fighter reached the West, there was a great deal of concern because by then both the F-108 and XB-70 programs had been terminated, as had the YF-12 interceptor version of the SR-71. With this in mind, NATO assigned an especially sinister code name to the new Soviet superjet—Foxbat.

Though there was a two-seat trainer version, the standard MiG-25 interceptor carried a crew of one and was typically armed with up to four AA-6 air-to-air missiles. The operational aircraft varied between 71 and 73 feet in length, depending on the specific subvariant and had a wing span of 46 feet. The big steel frame and capacious fuel tanks gave then a gross weight of more than 40 tons, but they could cruise at Mach 3 for 900 miles. At slower, more fuel-efficient speeds, this range could be doubled.

The Foxbat had entered service with the interceptor squadrons of the Soviet Troops of Air Defense (Protivo Vozdoshnaya Oborona Strany [PVO Strany]) by 1970, and was soon adapted for the reconnaissance role. During the 1970s, lone Foxbats on reconnaissance flights were often seen in the skies over the Middle East, often in Algerian, Libyan or Syrian markings.

Carrying the externally mounted air-to-air missiles created a certain amount of air-to-air drag and compromised both speed and range. However, when it was stripped down for use in the reconnaissance role, the Foxbat was virtually immune to interception and thus a truly remarkable weapon. They were often used as reconnaissance aircraft during the various Arab-Israeli confrontations that paralleled the Cold War. Israeli F-4 Phantom II fighter aircraft would try to catch them, but it was futile.

Of course, when the Foxbat interceptor was matched against the SR-71, the much faster Blackbird could always easily slip away from a Foxbat.

The Foxbat was the much-feared mystery villain of the Soviet air force until 1976, when Lieutenant Viktor Belenko defected to the West, landing his MiG-25 in Japan. The U.S. Air Force went over this Foxbat with a fine-tooth comb, discovering that, for all its raw power, the Foxbat was really a very technologically unsophisticated airplane.

Roughly 1,200 Foxbats were produced though 1983—most of them as interceptors—when the type was superseded by the MiG-31. Code-named Foxhound by NATO, the MiG-31 was a great improvement over its predecessor, although outwardly it was virtually indistinguishable in size and shape from the Foxbat. By the 1980s, the paradigm had shifted from the brute strength ideals of the "higher and faster" 1960s to the more subtle all-seeing eye of modern radar systems. Equipped with SBI-16 Zaslon fixed phased array radar, the Foxhound was the first Soviet fighter to match the look-down, shoot-down radar capability of American jets such as the F-15 Eagle and F-16 Falcon. The new Soloviev D-30F6 engines gave the Foxhound no better top speed than the Foxbat, but it extended the range.

By 1987, more than 100 Foxhounds had been deployed by the Soviet Union, and they would remain both in service and in production after the end of the Cold War. In 1992, Mikoyan-Gurevich and the Russian government entered into an agreement with the People's Republic of China whereby a variation of the MiG-31 would be produced in limited numbers by the Chinese at Shenyang.

CHAPTER 10

Stealth Aircraft

THE TERM *STEALTH AIRCRAFT* ENTERED THE POPULAR LEXI-
con during the 1980 presidential campaign. Jimmy Carter, a
president with a reputation for being weak on defense, was
running for reelection and he needed a card to play to the
media to counter this perception. In his hand, he had the
card of a top-secret military program with unbelievably advanced technology, and he played it. The Carter administration let it be known that the U.S. Air Force was working on a
supersecret technology called "stealth" that would absorb or
deflect radar so as to render an aircraft virtually invisible.

It was not the first time that a sitting president had revealed an extremely top-secret, high-technology aircraft
program during an election year. Lyndon Johnson had
done so by revealing the SR-71 in 1964. Had 1980 not
been such a contentious election year, the existence of
stealth technology would have remained buried behind a
wall of secrecy for most of the coming decade. Indeed, it
would not be until 1988 that the general public would actually get to see one of these invisible airplanes.

The once-mysterious stealth technology can render an airplane invisible to radar. To create such an aircraft, aircraft designers had first studied the nature of radar. For instance,
radar doesn't perceive size, only contour, shape and surfaces.
A glossy, light-colored surface reflects light and also re-

flects radar back to its receiver, so to defeat radar, designers would paint the airplane with a dark, flat radar-absorbing paint. Metallic surfaces also reflect radar, so the use of a non-metallic plastic material like Kevlar would go a long way toward reducing radar detectability. Until the 1970s, when advances in nonmetallic structural materials made new techniques possible, it wasn't possible to build such an aircraft. Conversely, if not for advances in radar and radar-guided antiaircraft missile technology during the same period, it would not have been necessary. Jet engines, especially when they are hanging under a wing on pylons, are very easy for radar to spot, so designers of stealth aircraft would conceal them entirely within the wing or fuselage.

The efforts that led to stealth aircraft began in the mid-1970s within the Defense Advanced Research Projects Agency (DARPA) and the U.S. Air Force with the super-secret Air to Surface Technology Evaluation & Integration (ASTEI) program and the Covert Survivable In-Weather Reconnaissance/Strike (CSIRS) program. The technology was ultimately developed into real aircraft both by the Northrop Corporation and at Lockheed's Advanced Developments Projects office, known informally as the Skunk Works.

F-117 Nighthawk

Before it was officially revealed in November 1988, the Lockheed F-117 had been the subject of intense speculation for nearly a decade. Though the existence of stealth was revealed in 1980, almost nobody knew what the airplane looked like. There was a sizable number of guesses, but all were wrong. Some were very wrong.

Stealth was a strange technology that few people understood. Among those who did were those at the Lockheed Skunk Works. Presided over by Clarence "Kelly" Johnson, the Skunk Works had been responsible for some of the greatest and most secret aircraft of the Cold War, from the U-2 to the SR-71. Ben Rich, who succeeded Johnson as the head of the Skunk Works in 1975, would lead the team that built the mysterious F-117.

Early in 1977, DARPA gave Lockheed a contract to go ahead with a pair of stealthy test aircraft that would be built under the code name Have Blue. Managed by the U.S. Air Force Systems Command, Have Blue was one of the most secret programs in existence at that time.

Have Blue would also be one of the strangest in appearance as well. The Skunk Works had discovered that a faceted fuselage would provide the lowest possible radar cross section, and by building an aircraft whose surface contained no right angles and was composed entirely of triangular and trapezoidal surfaces, its radar "signature" could be virtually eliminated. Beyond this, radar could be absorbed by coating the aircraft's surface with a fibrous boron-polymer resin material called Fibaloy.

Constructed at the Air Force–controlled Plant 42 near Palmdale, California, the two Have Blue prototypes were completed late in 1977 and taken to the Groom Lake test facility north of Nellis AFB in Nevada that was once known as Area 51. Flight testing began in early 1978, and proceeded through the year. The test program went reasonably well, although one of the Have Blues was damaged beyond repair in a landing accident unrelated to the stealth configuration of the aircraft.

The aircraft were flown against a number of different types of airborne and ground-based radar systems, and the stealth technology was shown to work amazingly well. Though the second Have Blue was lost in July 1979, the stealth concept had been shown to have fulfilled its promise. The aircraft were, in fact, virtually invisible to radar.

Under the top-secret project name Senior Trend, Lockheed was then given a contract to build a small production series of fifty-nine stealth aircraft based on the Have Blue. Just as few knew what this new aircraft would look like, nobody guessed what it was called. Most outside observers assumed that it would be designated as F-19, because that was the next number available in the new nomenclature system that had been adopted in 1962. Instead, it was numbered in the old pre-1962 numbering sequence. To this day, though higher numbers have been assigned, the F-19, if it exists, has not been identified. Nor, for that matter, have the F-112 though F-116.

The Skunk Works went back to the drawing board and came up with an aircraft that was similar to the Have Blue, but a bit more than half again larger. Both aircraft had two vertical tail surfaces that were not vertical. In Have Blue, they were tilted inward, toward each other. In the F-117, they would be tilted outward in a V configuration.

Powered by a pair of General Electric F404 nonafterburning turbofan engines, the F-117 would be 63 feet, 9 inches long and have a wing span of 43 feet, 4 inches. It would weigh 52,500 pounds and have the capability of carrying a wide variety of air-to-surface weapons—especially guided "smart" bombs—in its internal bomb bay. No weapons would be carried externally, because weapons on external pylons have a large radar signature.

While they would be operated under the "F for Fighter" designation F-117, the aircraft would be used as bombers. Their mission would be to attack highly important targets that were well protected by radar. During the Cold War, such targets would have included Soviet command and control facilities that would have been targeted in the first hours of a World War III scenario.

The F-117 would be equipped with infrared targeting systems and an inertial navigation system for operations in complete darkness and all weather conditions. For this reason, it would be given the official name Nighthawk, although it would receive a number of unofficial nicknames, such as the simple and ubiquitous Black Jet. Because it is inherently unstable aerodynamically to increase its maneuverability, the F-117 was also widely known as the Wobblin' Goblin.

The first flight of an F-117 occurred on June 18, 1981, at Groom Lake and by 1982, five test aircraft had been flown over Area 51. In 1983, the production series F-117 aircraft were coming out of the Lockheed factory, so the Air Force created the 4450th Tactical Fighter Group, and established it at a base for the near Tonopah, which is north of Groom Lake at the upper end of the restricted-access Nevada Test Range.

For the next five years, the F-117 was one of the most successfully kept secrets in the Air Force. The 4450th Tactical Fighter Group flew them only at night. Finally, in November 1988, the Air Force chose to officially bring its stealth fighter in from the darkness, and the existence of the airplane known as F-117 was finally revealed. Two years later, in July 1990, the last of the F-117s was delivered to the Air Force.

In 1989, the 4450th Tactical Fighter Group was redesignated as the 37th Tactical Fighter Wing (later to become the 49th Fighter Wing), and the Nighthawks were relocated to Holloman AFB in New Mexico in 1992.

The baptism of fire for the F-117 Nighthawk came in December 1989, during Operation Just Cause, the multiservice mission in Panama which successfully captured dictator General Manuel Noreiga, and returned an elected government to power. Unfortunately, the attack by a half dozen F-117s missed their targets during a nocturnal strike due to the pilots having been given the incorrect targeting coordinates.

The F-117 labored under the burden of a failed first mission for only 14 months. In January 1991, during Operation Desert Storm, the Nighthawk became the star of the show. Beginning with some of the first missions of the air campaign, the F-117s hit and destroyed about 1,600 high-value targets, such as command-and-control centers, fortified bunkers and bridges. In general, they targeted highly sensitive targets where absolute precision was a must. They were the only American or coalition aircraft to strike targets in downtown Baghdad.

The Nighthawks were never once detected by the Soviet-designed and Iraqi radar installations. Although the Iraqis put up a withering barrage of antiaircraft fire, they never found or hit an F-117.

In 1999, Nighthawks were deployed to Aviano AB in Italy and Spangdahlem AB in Germany to support NATO's

Operation Allied Force. An F-117 led the first United States strike against Yugoslavia in March 1999. One of the two dozen Nighthawks involved in the operation was lost to enemy fire near Belgrade, but it is not believed that it was acquired by radar.

Four years later, in the wee hours of March 19, 2003, a pair of Nighthawks of the 379th Air Expeditionary Wing dropped the first bombs of Operation Iraqi Freedom. As in Gulf War I, F-117s operated with complete impunity over the most heavily defended targets in Iraq throughout Gulf War II.

B-2 Spirit

Known simply as "the stealth bomber" for years before it was officially unveiled in 1988, the B-2 is one of the most remarkable, secret and expensive aircraft conceived during the Cold War. During the B-2's gestation period in the 1980s, the Soviet Union had successfully created the most elaborate radar defensive network in history, so the Strategic Air Command countered by creating the largest radar-invisible bomber in history. The B-2 was conceived, developed and originally deployed as a means of delivering a nuclear strike against the most heavily defended targets within the Soviet Union.

In the 1980s, the project was known formally as the Advanced Technology Bomber (ATB), but it was well known that the "advanced technology" was stealth. For eight years after the existence of the ATB was first leaked in the press, no details—not even its shape—was officially announced. However, despite the secrecy, its price tag was correctly rumored to be such that it was the most expensive airplane program in history. When calculating the program cost to include the development of a whole level of technology, each of the B-2s cost more than it would have if it'd been made of solid gold.

The Northrop approach to stealth technology had many similarities to the Lockheed approach, but one major difference. A large portion of an airplane's radar signature is in its fuselage. As had been demonstrated at Northrop several decades before anyone had heard of stealth technology, an airplane doesn't need a fuselage to fly, it only needs a wing. Therefore, a wing may be thickened (radar doesn't discern size, only contour) and the crew, engines and weapons can be put inside the wing. The result is a "flying wing."

Experiments conducted by Jack Northrop in the 1940s proved the validity of the flying-wing design. It was out of these that Northrop developed the U.S. Air Force's great flying-wing strategic bombers—the YB-35 and YB-49—in the late 1940s and early 1950s. These airplanes, whose wing span was roughly the same as the B-2, were never ordered into production because of control problems, but by the early 1980s, control was much easier to achieve with fly-by-wire controls than it had been with hydraulics in the 1940s. When it was announced in 1983 that Northrop was building the stealthy ATB, many people began to suspect that it, too, would be a flying wing.

Hard edges and sharp angles are always very radar visible, so every effort would be made to smooth out corners and edges. Even the Rockwell B-1A bomber had 10 percent of the cross section of the Boeing B-52 because it had the engines partially blended into the fuselage and there was a smoother contour between the fuselage and wings.

The confluence of wing and fuselage and the multitude of sharp and even right angles in an airplane's tail would present a final and unique challenge to a stealth designer, yet one which easily could be solved just by getting rid of it. Because of fly-by-wire control, the B-2 needs no tail. Moving surfaces in the trailing edge of the wing act as aileron, elevator and rudder functions.

In 1987, it was announced that the Air Force would be buying 132 ATBs, which would be built at the highly secure Plant 42 factory complex at Palmdale in the California high desert. The number was slashed to seventy-five before the first flight and, finally, to a mere twenty-one, enough for two squadrons and a few test aircraft. A slow rate of production, and the fact that the enormous research and development costs had to be amortized over just 16 percent the number of aircraft originally planned made the B-2 the most expensive aircraft in history.

The first flight of a B-2 took place on July 17, 1989 and the second aircraft made its debut in 1990. Six B-2s were delivered for avionics and operational testing by 1993, and the first operational B-2 was delivered to the 509th Bomb Wing at Whiteman AFB in Missouri in December 1993 after the Cold War had ended, and a year after the Strategic Air Command was merged into the new Air Combat Command. The 509th's first B-2 squadron, the 393rd Bomb Squadron became fully operational in 1997, and a second squadron, the 715th Bomb Squadron was formed.

Officially named Spirit, the B-2 has a wing span of 172 feet, a length of 69 feet and a gross weight of 376,000 pounds. It has a service ceiling of 50,000 feet and an unrefueled range exceeding 11,000 miles. It is powered by four General Electric F118-GE-100 turbofan engines, each delivering over 19,000 pounds of thrust. The engines are concealed by scalloped over-wing intake ducts and have shielded over-wing, trailing-edge nozzles.

The B-2 can carry a variety of air-to-ground munitions including 20 B61 nuclear bombs, 16 B63 nuclear bombs or conventional gravity bombs and precision-guided smart bombs. The B-2's bomb bays can be equipped with either racks or rotary launchers, and, in addition to bombs, it was designed to carry AGM-69 SRAM or AGM-131 SRAM II Short Range Attack Missiles.

Under the Cold War–era Single Integrated Operational Plan (SIOP), the B-2 would have carried 25,000 pounds of nuclear weapons, although it has a total payload capacity of 40,000 pounds.

The B-2 was equipped from the outset with an Inertial Navigation System (INS) as well as a Hughes APQ-181 multimode, phased array radar system and a targeting system aided by Global Positioning System (GPS)—for precision bombing.

Though the B-2 was arguably the most sophisticated

strategic bomber developed during the Cold War, it was not operational until after the Cold War era ended. It existed at the time of Gulf War I, but missed that conflict as well. The Spirit's operational baptism of fire came in 1999, during the U.S. Air Force support of NATO's Operation Allied Force in what is now the former Yugoslavia.

During the first eight weeks of Allied Force, the B-2 fleet was responsible for destroying 33 percent of all the Serbian targets attacked during the whole operation. In flying these missions, the 509th Bomb Wing crews flew nonstop round-trip missions to Kosovo from Missouri. These flights, the longest operational bombing missions in history, were topped two years later.

In the autumn of 2001, when the United States retaliated against the al-Qaeda gangsters and their Taliban hosts in the mountains of Afghanistan, the B-2s were back in action. Again, the mission plan involved nonstop, round-trip flights from Whiteman AFB.

Black Manta

The existence and configuration of the F-117 and B-2 were kept secret through the 1980s, but indications are that they were only two of perhaps a dozen stealth aircraft programs that were ongoing in the United States during that time. One of the most widely reported was the Northrop TR-3 Black Manta. The TR-3 has never been officially acknowledged by the Department of Defense, so information about it is generally speculative. It almost certainly exists, but as this book was being written, it was still a "black" program, shrouded under the highest secrecy and still deniable.

The "TR for Tactical Reconnaissance" designation was created in the 1980s for redesignating the Lockheed U-2R as TR-1 for tactical battlefield surveillance, so the TR-3 designation would suggest that the Black Manta is a tactical reconnaisance aircraft.

It is widely believed that the TR-3, like the F-117, had its origins in the mid-1970s with the supersecret Air Force Air to Surface Technology Evaluation and Integration

(ASTEI) program and the Covert Survivable In-Weather Reconnaissance/Strike (CSIRS) program. It has been suggested that the F-117 was the Strike aircraft while the TR-3 was the CSIRS Reconnaissance aircraft.

Reportedly, Northrop received a contract in late 1978 to build a Tactical High Altitude Penetrator (THAP) prototype. This aircraft, the XTR-3 or YTR-3, first flew in 1981 at Groom Lake in Nevada, and the success of the flight testing led to the production of up to thirty TR-3As. These were, in turn, often observed from the ground in the general area between Nellis AFB, Nevada; Edwards AFB, California; and White Sands, New Mexico. Occasionally, TR-3s were seen in the company of F-117s or KC-135 refueling aircraft.

During both Gulf Wars, in 1991 and again in 2003, TR-3s were reported to have flown reconnaissance missions over Iraq in support of F-117 combat operations. Probably powered by two General Electric F404 turbofans buried in its wings, the TR-3 is said to be quieter than the F-117 and about the same size.

Aurora

A virtual poster child for speculation about supersecret, or "black" aircraft programs, Aurora is probably the most whispered about airplane "never seen." This phantom craft was first observed in the fiscal year 1986 as a line item for $80 million in the Department of Defense budget. A year later, the budget for the unexplained project called Aurora was up to $2.2 billion. Virtually nothing official has been heard since, so it may have been canceled or submerged in another top-secret program. The latter may have included the U.S. Navy's mysterious Chalk Coral and Retract Amber programs.

Persistent rumors—which could, of course, originate with deliberate misinformation—and mysterious sightings have kept Aurora fresh in the minds of black-aircraft speculators.

It is possible that Aurora is, or was originally intended

to be, a stealthy replacement for the SR-71 reconnaissance aircraft. The SR-71 was withdrawn from service in 1990 at about the time that an Aurora aircraft—if it existed—would have been flying. An analysis of data that has been made public indicates that Lockheed's Skunk Works had been conducting studies of hypersonic aircraft to replace the SR-71. Some studies even suggest liquid hydrogen as a fuel for such an aircraft.

Since the end of the Cold War, a hazy and somewhat incomplete picture of this invisible mystery ship has emerged. Aurora is thought to have been flown at speeds up to Mach 7, and has been observed as a fast, bright light in the sky at 50,000 feet. Sightings have occurred near the Groom Lake site at Area 51 in Nevada where the SR-71 and F-117 were tested, as well as over Scotland and in the Pacific. Speculation has included mention of a secret base in the Pacific, perhaps on an atoll near Kwajalein, which is used by the U.S. Air Force for missile testing. In the late 1990s, a mystery aircraft thought to be associated with the Aurora project and using the call-sign Gaspipe is known to have been operating at Edwards AFB.

The fact that Tacit Blue remained secret through its entire test program and that the appearance of both the F-117 and B-2 remained classified until the U.S. Air Force chose to make the aircraft public, is a clear indication that if Aurora does exist, it could be successfully kept secret.

Mothership

If the Aurora project had been the poster child for black-aircraft speculation since the last decade of the Cold War, then the so-called Mothership is the child of those with one foot in the black-aircraft world and the other placed among those who speculate seriously about the extraterrestrial origin of Unidentified Flying Objects (UFOs).

Leaving the speculation aside, reports of the Mothership are based on serious observations. Most of these sightings have occurred in the high-desert area of California's Inyo, Kern and San Bernardino counties. These areas are within

less than an hour's flying time of three bases from which secret aircraft routinely operate—Edwards AFB, the China
Lake Naval Weapons Center and the vast Nellis AFB range
that contains the Groom Lake facility at Area 51.

The name derives from the fact that the aircraft is especially large and usually seen in the company of other,
smaller aircraft, usually F-16s and F-117s. The latter may
be present as chase planes, or possibly the Mothership is
refueling them. The Air Force typically uses F-16s as
chase planes for evaluating test aircraft. Others suggest
that the mystery aircraft air-launches smaller aircraft.
Other observers report a very narrow aircraft with a length
of perhaps 200 feet that looks somewhat like the XB-70
aircraft of the late 1960s. Such an aircraft would still look
futuristic in the twenty-first century.

Based on seeing it with other well-known aircraft, some
observers estimate the wing span as roughly 150 feet,
which places it in the same size range as the Northrop B-2.
The observers are sure that the mystery aircraft is not a
B-2, although it is typically seen at dusk or at night and
hence is hard to evaluate.

Tacit Blue

While speculation swirled around Aurora, the Mothership
and other mystery aircraft, the U.S. Air Force successfully
operated the unique Tacit Blue aircraft in absolute secrecy
more than a decade earlier. When the Air Force officially
unveiled the Tacit Blue Technology Demonstration Program in a news conference at the Pentagon in April 1996,
jaws dropped. Here was an aircraft that could not have
been mistaken for any other and it had never been suggested or described in the popular press.

The clumsy-looking Northrop Tacit Blue aircraft resembled a rounded boxcar with a straight, tapered wing
and a V tail. So boxy was the Tacit Blue's appearance that
pilots are said to have joked that it looked like someone
had forgotten to take the airplane out of its packing crate.
The reason for the boxcar shape was the need to incorpo-

rate a huge, side-looking, single-aperture radar. It used a secret, smooth, curvilinear surface to redistribute electric energy to create a low radar reflection.

The 15 ton craft was 55 feet 10 inches long and had a wing span of 48 feet two inches. A single flush inlet on the top of the fuselage provided air to two high-bypass turbofan engines. Tacit Blue employed a digital fly-by-wire flight control system to help stabilize the aircraft. Two Tacit Blue airplanes were built, but only one was flown. The second was kept in reserve in case something happened to the first.

When the program began in 1978, Tacit Blue was originally conceived as a platform for demonstrating that a stealth surveillance aircraft with intercept radar and other sensors could operate close to the forward line of battle with a high degree of survivability. The idea was that such an aircraft could continuously monitor a ground situation behind enemy lines and provide real-time targeting information to ground commanders.

Among the operational systems that were tested aboard the Tacit Blue were the Air Force's Pave Mover and the U.S. Army Stand-Off Target Acquisition and Surveillance (SOTAS) program. The idea behind these projects was to develop radar that could track vehicles on the ground as easily as radar tracked aircraft in the sky. In 1982, Richard DeLaver, the Undersecretary of Defense for Research and Engineering (USDRE), merged Pave Mover and SOTAS into a multiservice joint program that would ultimately be known as the Joint Surveillance Target Attack System (J-STARS), or Joint STARS.

Based in the former Area 51 on the Nellis AFB range in southern Nevada, Tacit Blue made the first of a reported 135 flights in February 1982. The Air Force reported that when flight testing ended in 1985, Tacit Blue was placed in storage and kept under wraps until after the end of the Cold War because many of its design characteristics were considered too advanced and innovative to be revealed publicly. The second airframe was reported to have been disassembled without having been flown.

When this "black" aircraft—which was actually painted bright white—came out of the darkness, it was not only made public, but it was sent to the U.S. Air Force Museum at Wright-Patterson AFB in Ohio for public display.

In the meantime, the U.S. Air Force and the Department of Defense made the decision to contract with the Grumman Corporation (now part of Northrop Grumman) to put the Joint STARS technology into a Boeing 707 airframe. The first such aircraft made its service debut under the designation E-8 during Gulf War I in 1991.

CHAPTER 11

Airborne Command and Control

IN ANY WAR, IT IS ESSENTIAL FOR FIELD COMMANDERS AND their bosses to have a real-time grasp of the battlefield and an up-to-the-minute view of the location of their own assets—and those of their opponent. To pursue the chess analogy, commanders want to see the chessboard. Even if you can't read the mind of the opposing commander, seeing what he's doing and the "how and when" of what he's doing can help you intuit what he's thinking.

From the days of the Roman legions until World War I, command and control was as simple as riding your horse to the nearest high ground and scanning the battlefield. For the half a millennium before World War II, commanders could rely on telescopes to aid their real-time intelligence, but that was about the best they could do. In both world wars, aerial reconnaissance provided commanders with fast and recent information, but few commanders risked flying over battlefields to see for themselves from an aerial vantage point.

The theory, which evolved into today's Airborne Warning And Control System (AWACS) operations, is that a mobile radar station that is 30,000 feet in the air is a useful and extremely flexible addition to any defensive radar network involving fixed sites on the ground.

During the Cold War, advances in technology—including

imaging, sensing and communications technology—helped to finally make real-time command and control a reality. Commanders had unprecedented views of the battlefields. Of course the technology continued to evolved to the amazing levels seen in the Gulf Wars of 1991 and 2003.

As the airborne command-and-control technology revolution unfolded during the years of the Cold War, aerial platforms (as well as the real-time space-based platforms discussed in chapter 2) have become an essential part of the command-and-control arsenal available to commanders at all levels of a conflict.

Warning Star

The precursor to the modern airborne command-and-control centers was the Lockheed Warning Star. The airframe was that of the highly popular Lockheed Constellation, one of the most widely used four-engine airliners of the postwar years, and the last piston-engine propeller airliner built by Lockheed. Inside, instead of passengers lounging in the Pullman-style comfort of the golden age of air travel, the aircraft was a hive of radar and sensors operators.

The project originated with the U.S. Navy and began soon after World War II. As the name implies, the Warning Star evolved from a need to develop an effective airborne early warning system to protect the United States coastline and the U.S. Navy fleet at sea. In the beginning, the Navy tried packing its cumbersome electronic gear into the cramped interior of a B-17 bomber (Navy designation PB-1W). More space was needed, so the Navy gravitated to the notion of using an off-the-shelf commercial airliner with lots of internal volume.

In 1951, the Navy ordered two Lockheed Model 749 Constellations under the designation PO-1W (later WV-1) as test airplanes, and 124 larger Model 1049 Super Constellations under the designation WV-2 as operational Warning Stars. An additional eight 1049s were later ordered as WV-3s and equipped for weather reconnaissance. The WV-2s were distinguished from Constellation airliners by the addition of a massive APS-20 search radar dome under the belly and a huge APS-45 radome atop the fuselage that looked like a stubby shark's fin.

The first Warning Stars joined the Navy in 1953. They carried a crew of between two and three dozen, mostly assigned the task of monitoring the supersecret surveillance gear in the Combat Information Centre (CIC). From 1953 until the Distant Early Warning (DEW) Line of land-based radar sites was completed across the Arctic in 1961, the Warning Stars flew continuous 12-hour missions over the North Atlantic approaches to the United States. After that date, they continued into the 1970s to fly missions out of such bases as Keflavik in Iceland, monitoring the airspace between Greenland and the United Kingdom.

In the Pacific, Warning Stars were constantly on patrol in the area from the west coast of North America westward to a line generally between Midway Island and Adak Island in the Aleutian chain west of Alaska. During the Vietnam War, secret electronic reconnaisance versions, designated as WV-2Q, are known to have operated throughout southeast Asia.

The Warning Stars would continue to serve as geographic extensions of the DEW Line well into the 1970s. Even today, many of the details of their Cold War activities remain shrouded in mystery.

Big Eye

In 1951, the U.S. Air Force ordered ten airborne early warning aircraft essentially like the Navy's WV-2 Warning Star, under the designation RC-121C. They were equipped with the enormous radomes described in the previous discussion of the Warning Star. An additional seventy-two RC-121Ds were ordered through 1955. Operationally, these aircraft were tied into the Air Defense Command mission and into that of the joint United States-Canada North American Air Defense Command (NORAD).

The Air Force Military Air Transport Service (Military

Airlift Command after 1966) would also own and operate a number of C-121 aircraft in strictly a transport configuration. Among these was President Dwight Eisenhower's Air Force One, nicknamed *Columbine*, after the state flower of Colorado, his wife's home state. While some of the Air Force's C-121 Constellations were transferred to the Air Force from U.S. Navy orders, the RC-121s were ordered directly from the manufacturer.

By the 1960s, the RC-121s had been redesignated as EC-121s to reflect the dominant electronic component of the mission. With significant hardware and software upgrades, including improved NORAD interface, some forty-two of the EC-121Ds were redesignated as EC-121H. These are known to have operated with the 551st Airborne Early Warning and Control Wing. A further block of EC-121Ds were upgraded with APS-95 search radar for special operations in Vietnam under the designation EC-121Q. It was these aircraft, assigned to the 552nd Airborne Early Warning and Control Wing, that formed the nucleus of Operation Big Eye.

Operation Big Eye was undertaken in 1965 in response to North Vietnamese interceptor activity in southeast Asia. The Air Force wanted a means to monitor the MiGs that threatened United States aircraft that were flying the Operation Rolling Thunder bombing missions over North Vietnam. An aerial command post had an advantage over any of the land-based early warning sites in South Vietnam because it could be moved close to North Vietnam and operate well above ground interference.

The first deployment involved five EC-121s from the 552d Airborne Early Warning and Control Wing based at McClellan AFB near Sacramento, California. Established in 1955, the 552d Airborne Early Warning and Control Wing had earlier been involved in radar tracking during the recovery of film capsules from the Corona spy satellites over the Pacific.

At first, the Big Eye task force was based on Taiwan, but

operations were generally flown from forward bases, including Tan Son Nhut in South Vietnam or from Royal Thai bases in Thailand, including Ubon RTAFB, Udorn RTAFB and Korat RTAFB. In October 1967, the official base of operations would move to Korat RTAFB. Shortly after being deployed to Southeast Asia, the Operation Big Eye task force was redesignated as College Eye.

College Eye

The College Eye Airborne Command and Control Center (ABCCC) EC-121Q aircraft became not only an essential part of air operations in Vietnam, but a prototype for U.S. Air Force ABCCC operations everywhere. It was in October 1967 that a College Eye aircraft became the first aerial command post to vector a United States fighter to successfully intercept and shoot down an enemy fighter in wartime.

Though College Eye was a southeast Asia operation, it transformed the way that the Air Force structures air operations for the remainder of the Cold War and beyond. As such, it is useful to examine College Eye in some detail. Indeed, much of the ABCCC activity elsewhere during the Cold War remains shrouded in secrecy or has simply been forgotten.

Beginning in 1966, College Eye was integrated into the complex command-and-control network that radiated from the command headquarters of the U.S. Air Force Seventh Air Force. Located near Saigon and code-named Motel, this headquarters had the responsibility for controlling the missions entering North Vietnam. The command-and-control network included the U.S. Navy Positive Identification Radar Advisory Zone (PIRAZ) early warning ships in the Gulf of Tonkin that were code-named Crown, as well as two land-based radar sites. These were the site at Dong Ha that was code-named Waterboy, and the site code-named Invert at Nakhon Phanom RTAFB in Thailand. Waterboy was the northernmost Air Force radar site in South Vietnam.

Management and operational integration of the data streams from these locations flowed through the U.S. Air Force control-and-reporting center, or Tactical Air Control Center (TACC), which was located at the supersecret compound on Monkey Mountain near Danang AB in South Vietnam. Both Air Force and U.S. Navy bombers were managed through this network.

Another ground-based radar system, located at Udorn RTAFB in Thailand and code-named Brigham, provided navigational assistance to aircraft going north. It was the primary radar facility for aiding in the rendezvous of aerial refueling tankers with other aircraft.

While Waterboy provided good coverage to the south and to the east, it had blind spots looking to the north, and this made College Eye an essential part of the program. Waterboy's radar was limited to about 180 miles, so it could neither adequately handle air operations north of Thanh Hoa, nor over the Hanoi area. Thus, Waterboy would "hand off" the bombers to the College Eye ABCCC as they passed north of Thanh Hoa.

In support of operations over Hanoi, the College Eye EC-121s flew elliptical flight paths over the Gulf of Tonkin about 30 to 50 miles from the port of Haiphong that were code-named Ethan Alpha and Ethan Bravo. In addition, there was an ellipse above northern Laos code-named Ethan Charlie. In April 1968, College Eye also began working with forward air controllers that were supporting air to ground operations in Laos.

Beginning in July 1967, the College Eye ABCCCs were equipped with the QRC-248 IFF (Identification, Friend or Foe) system, which greatly improved their ability to manage aircraft in the congested aerial-combat zones over Hanoi and Haiphong.

In March 1968, the College Eye EC-121Qs were augmented by the addition of the EC-121K aircraft. Code-named Rivet Top (later Rivet Gym), these aircraft carried secret, special-purpose electronic equipment that provided not only improved antiaircraft radar capability, but a capability to defend United States aircraft from the surface-to-air missile threat that was prevalent in North Vietnam.

In addition to their work in monitoring strikes against North Vietnam, College Eye EC-121s were the unsung heroes in preventing North Vietnamese air attacks against United States bases in South Vietnam. On at least two known occasions, in October 1965 and February 1968, the North Vietnamese air force launched such missions. In both cases, these were detected by the EC-121s and United States aircraft were scrambled to prevent the attacks from getting though. This was clearly a capability that would have been essential on the Central European Front had the Cold War turned hot.

During the "bombing halt" period from 1968 to 1972, when air operations over North Vietnam were limited, College Eye continued to be active elsewhere in southeast Asia. In May 1972, when the offensive against North Vietnam resumed during the Operation Linebacker, a new control facility at Nakhon Phanom was used. Code-named Teaball, it was analogous to the Motel facility that had been the command-and-control center during Operation Rolling Thunder between 1965 and 1968. During Linebacker, College Eye was augmented by a force of specially modified EC-121T aircraft that were operated under the code name Disco.

After the Paris Peace Accords signed in January 1973 effectively ended active United States combat operations, College Eye remained in support of South Vietnamese operations. The last College Eye mission would be flown in August 1973 and the 552nd Airborne Early Warning & Control Wing detachment in Thailand returned to the United States having logged nearly 14,000 missions in support of more than 135,000 tactical missions.

Batcat

No discussion of the C-121 Constellation in the secret-operations role is complete without a mention of the EC-121R Batcat. While the EC-121D and EC-121Q had the familiar Warning Star radomes above and below the fuselage, the EC-121R Batcat did not. Except for its three-tone jungle camouflage paint, a paucity of cabin windows and dozens of small antennas, the Batcat could have been mistaken for a Super Constellation airliner. There were 30 EC-121Rs, all of them formerly U.S. Navy EC-121K (formerly WV-2) or EC-121P (formerly WV-3) aircraft that had been stripped of their distinguishing radomes.

Though the Batcat was less immediately identifiable as a special-operations aircraft than those assigned to the College Eye task force in southeast Asia, their mission was even more secret. Assigned to the 553rd Reconnaissance Wing at Korat RTAFB, the Batcats operated as the relay aircraft for the Igloo White operation between 1967 and 1971. As discussed in chapter 14, Igloo White involved sensors that were dropped along enemy infiltration routes to monitor troop movements. The Batcat crews were responsible for encrypting and relaying the data from the Igloo White sensors to the command post at Nakhon Phanom.

In 1971, Batcats were replaced by the smaller Beechcraft QU-22 aircraft operating under Operation Pave Eagle, and were returned to the United States. The 27 EC-121R aircraft that survived the war in southeast Asia—three were lost in accidents—were all cut up and scrapped between 1972 and 1976. None of these quite-specialized secret aircraft survived the Cold War and the full details of their activities during five years of service remain undisclosed.

Rivet Brass and Rivet Amber

When the Boeing Model 707 jetliner entered service in 1958, it forever revolutionized commercial air travel, carrying nearly twice as many passengers twice as far and twice as fast as the leading propliners of that era. When the prototype for the 707—the Boeing Model 367–80 "Dash Eighty"—first flew in 1954, it also served as the prototype for a military transport that was to be similar to the 707. This aircraft, the Boeing Model 717, entered service with the U.S. Air Force in 1957 under the designation C-135.

Of the 806 military 717s that were built, 754 would be delivered as air-refueling tankers—a dozen delivered to the French air force as C-135F, and the rest to the U.S. Air Force under the KC-135 designation. Most of the rest went to the U.S. Air Force as C-135 transports, but a majority of these aircraft were subsequently converted for use as surveillance or electronic-warfare aircraft.

The exact number of these after-market conversions was top secret during the Cold War, and is still not known. However, it is known that nineteen of the aircraft were delivered by the Boeing factory already in special mission configuration. These included five Model 717 airframes that were designated as EC-135C, and fourteen similar Model 739 electronic reconnaissance airframes that were designated as RC-135A or RC-135B.

As noted, the full dimensions of the conversion programs were top secret during the Cold War, and are still classified. By late in the Cold War, most of these secret projects were officially acknowledged, although few details have yet been released.

Rivet Brass is known to have been the code name assigned to a group of three C-135As and one KC-135A (NKC-135A) that were converted as telemetry intelligence–surveillance aircraft in 1962 and 1963. They emerged with large, thimble-shaped radomes in their noses and fence-like antenna arrays along the tops of their fuselages. Redesignated as RC-135D, these aircraft flew secret combat missions code-named Combat Apple that involved surveillance missions of the airspace over North Vietnam and other areas of interest in the Far East. At least one RC-135D was upgraded to become an RC-135S Cobra Ball surveillance aircraft.

Rivet Amber was an electronic intelligence–gathering aircraft that was similar in appearance to the RC-135D Rivet Brass. Under a U.S. Air Force contract beginning in 1963, Ling Temco Vought installed a huge seven-megawatt phased-array radar antenna under a 240-square-foot fiberglass panel in the fuselage of at least one C-135B. Having been thus converted to Rivet Amber configuration, the air-

craft was redesignated as RC-135E and tasked with monitoring Soviet ICBM tests and tracking the splashdown of
their reentry vehicles in the Pacific Ocean. Nicknamed
Lisa Ann, the Rivet Amber aircraft could reportedly track
objects as small as a basketball.

The Rivet Amber aircraft were assigned to the 6th
Strategic Reconnaissance Wing of the Strategic Air Command, and based at Eielson AFB near Fairbanks, Alaska.
The actual missions were flown out of Shemya AFB, at the
tip of the Aleutian Island chain. Known as the "Black Pearl
of the North Pacific," Shemya is the westernmost point in
the United States. It is so far west that the International
Dateline is curved westward for a few degrees to accommodate it within the same day as the rest of the United States.
These top-secret flights took the RC-135E over the Pacific
and close to the Soviet Union's Kamchatka Peninsula.

In June 1969, shortly after a routine take off from Shemya, the pilot of the Rivet Amber aircraft reported that the
RC-135E was encountering intense shaking just before the
aircraft disappeared from radar. A massive search turned
up no shred of debris. Lisa Ann was lost without a trace,
becoming one of the little known, but still unexplained,
mysteries of the Cold War.

Cobra Ball

The secret U.S. Air Force program known as Cobra Ball involved retrofitting a small number of aircraft with infrared
telescopes and electro-optical sensors for tracking ballistic
missile tests at long range. Because of the need to reduce
light reflection when using the sensor gear, the upper side
of the right wing of each Cobra Ball was painted flat black,
while the left wing was grey and the fuselage and tail were
white.

When the program started is not known for sure, but the
second of the Cobra Balls is known to have been deployed
in 1972. All were retrofitted under the very top-secret Big
Safari hardware modification program, all were designated
as RC-135S, and all were assigned to the 55th Strategic

Reconnaissance Wing based at the Strategic Air Command headquarters at Offutt AFB in Nebraska. Operationally, the RC-135S aircraft would be forward deployed to locations such as—but not limited to—Shemya AFB in the Aleutian Islands.

The Cobra Ball operations often involved flying in the proximity to Soviet air space near the Kamchatka Peninsula. In September 1983, when a Korean Air Lines Boeing 747 jet-liner was shot down by Soviet interceptors off Kamchatka, it was reportedly because they mistook it for a Cobra Ball.

Sensors aboard Cobra Ball aircraft are known to have included signals intelligence (SIGINT) and measurements and signatures intelligence (MASINT) systems, with the latter including a Real Time Optics System (RTOS) and a Large Aperture Tracker System (LATS).

After the end of the Cold War, the wing was redesignated simply as the 55th Wing, and the Cobra Ball aircraft were tasked with flying tactical, as well as strategic, missions. This involved using their unique capability to monitor tactical missile launches in the event of a repeat of the Scud barrages launched from Iraq during Gulf War I. Newer and more sophisticated sensors were installed, including a medium-wave infrared array, a real-time optical system and an interface with the tactical-information broadcast service.

Beginning in 1997, Big Safari upgraded the RC-135S fleet to the new and improved Cobra Ball II configuration. Much of the work would be done behind a high fence and high security at a closely guarded Raytheon E-Systems facility located east of Dallas, Texas.

Though newer sensor technology has eliminated the concern for glare, the right wings of the twenty-first-century Cobra Balls are still black for the sake of a connection to their Cold War legacy.

Cobra Eye

Late in the Cold War, a single RC-135S was retrofitted with a cryogenically cooled, infrared telescopic sensor subsystem under the Optical Aircraft Measurement Program (OAMP). The resulting aircraft was redesignated as RC-135X and code-named Cobra Eye. The top secret OAMP system was designed by Ball Aerospace to analyze objects in four dimensions—spatial, temperature, spectral and radiometric, meaning its brightness in the infrared portion of the spectrum.

Rivet Joint

Rivet Joint was a U.S. Air Force electronic intelligence and battlefield management program that emerged in the 1970s and incorporated hardware and software that evolved directly from the Big Eye and College Eye programs. Rivet Joint would be a contemporary of the E-3 Sentry AWACS program discussed below. The first Rivet Joint converted aircraft was delivered under the designation RC-135V in August 1973. Five RC-135Vs were added during 1975, and eight more Rivet Joints joined the fleet between 1977 and 1984. The last seven Rivet Joint aircraft were delivered with a slightly different electronics package and were designated as RC-135W.

Like all RC-135s, the Rivet Joints had the large radomes in their noses that distinguish them from KC-135s, but the Rivet Joints are further identifiable by the large, flat panel phased array antennas that protrude from either side of their forward fuselages.

The Rivet Joint fleet was assigned to the 55th Strategic Reconnaissance Wing, based at the Strategic Air Command headquarters at Offutt AFB in Nebraska, although the fleet was typically forward deployed during most of the Cold War years. The Rivet Joint mission was to be prepared to provide reconnaissance information and electronic warfare support directly to theater commanders and combat forces if the Cold War turned hot. They operated both data and voice links for combat advisory broadcasts and imminent threat warnings. In addition to these activities, Rivet Joints are capable of conducting electronic intelligence—and communications intelligence—intercept operations.

After the Cold War, as the wing became simply the 55th Wing, the Rivet Joint aircraft were used in the Balkans during the 1990s in Operation Joint Endeavor and Operation Allied Force. They also would take part in U.S. Air Force operations in southwest Asia after the turn of the century, often working in cooperation with other airborne platforms such as AWACS and Joint STARS. In the meantime, the U.S. Air Force had decided to expand the Rivet Joint fleet, adding four new RC-135W conversions in 1998 and 1999.

Looking Glass

Throughout the Cold War, the nerve center of the United States nuclear strike capability was the command-and-control center deep beneath the Strategic Air Command (SAC) headquarters at Offutt AFB in Nebraska. So important and so sophisticated was this center that it became the centerpiece of the United States Strategic Command (STRATCOM) when SAC was merged into the Air Combat Command in 1992. So important and so sophisticated was this center that it here that President George W. Bush traveled on September 11, 2001, after the United States was attacked.

Because of the importance of Offutt's underground command-and-control center, it was obvious to SAC planners that it was high on the Soviet first-strike target list. With this in mind, SAC decided that an alternative backup site was needed. Because any such location would become an instant target, SAC created an airborne command post, locating the backup equipment in an EC-135C aircraft. If Offutt AFB was destroyed, control would be assumed seamlessly by a command post whose location was constantly changing. Because the EC-135C's capability would mirror that which was on the ground at Offutt AFB, it was code-named Looking Glass.

Eventually, Looking Glass served not only as a mirror of the capabilities at Offutt AFB, but of those at the National Military Command Center in the Pentagon as well. The Pentagon maintained an alternate National Military Command Center at Fort Ritchie in Maryland, but the desirability of also having an airborne mirror was obvious.

The SAC outfitted several EC-135Cs to perform the Looking Glass mission, deciding that at least one should always be airborne. The EC-135C was a Boeing Model 717, very similar to the RC-135s discussed above, and the Boeing KC-135 (also Model 717) aerial refueling tanker. Unlike the majority of RC-135s, the EC-135 aircraft had a refueling boom like the KC-135 and could perform aerial refueling operations.

During the Cold War, the Looking Glass aircraft were assigned to the 55th Strategic Reconnaissance Wing and were operated by two airborne command-and-control squadrons, one at Offutt and one at Ellsworth AFB in South Dakota.

The Looking Glass Airborne Command Posts flew a random pattern over the United States, usually on an 8-hour shift, always staying aloft until the next shift's aircraft had taken off and established all necessary communications with SAC headquarters, the National Military Command Center and the strategic nuclear forces on alert around the world.

To perform its mission, Looking Glass carried the same type of battle staff that were underground at Offutt AFB. The commander, or Airborne Emergency Actions Officer, was always a flag officer, if not an Air Force general, then a U.S. Navy admiral drawn from Submarine Group Nine, Pacific (COMSUBGRU NINE) and Commander, Submarine Group Ten, Atlantic (COMSUBGRU TEN). This officer had the authority to order forces in the field to execute nuclear strikes if directed by the president of the United States.

The staff included command control, operations, plans, intelligence, logistics, and communications personnel. The Airborne Launch Control System (ALCS) would also permit Looking Glass to control the entire Minuteman fleet if any or all of the ground launch control centers were put out of action.

The first Looking Glass took off from Offutt AFB on February 3, 1961, and at least one was airborne 24 hours a day, 365 days a year for more than 29 years. On July 24, 1990, the continuous Looking Glass airborne alert was terminated, although they continued to remain available 24 hours a day. The Looking Glass crews had accumulated more than 281,000 accident-free flying hours. Two years later, the Looking Glass mission was transferred from SAC to STRATCOM. In October 1998, the U.S. Navy's E-6B Mercurys, also based on the Boeing 707 airframe, replaced the EC-135C fleet for the Looking Glass mission.

Constant Phoenix

An Offutt AFB hangar mate of Looking Glass during the long, dark days of the Cold War was another Boeing 717 airframe designated as WC-135W and code-named Constant Phoenix. The WC-135W was essentially a weather monitoring aircraft that was tasked with the special mission of collecting particulate and gaseous debris from the atmosphere in accordance with the 1963 Limited Nuclear Test Ban Treaty. Assigned to the 55th Strategic Reconnaissance Wing, Constant Phoenix supplied data to the Air Force Technical Applications Center (AFTAC), which was accountable for the detection and verification of nuclear discharges and the effects thereof.

Through the years, Constant Phoenix flew missions along the periphery of the Soviet Union to monitor nuclear tests, as well as atmospheric radiation debris from other incidents, such as the 1986 meltdown of the Soviet nuclear reactor at Chernobyl. Still operational, Constant Phoenix has also kept tabs on Chinese, Indian and Pakistani nuclear weapons testing.

AWACS

Floating lazily through the sky like a 707 airliner being followed by an especially friendly flying saucer, the E-3A

Airborne Warning and Control System (AWACS) is one of the most sophisticated airborne command posts devised during the twentieth century. Had the Cold War turned hot, a handful of them could have controlled air operations throughout the European Theater.

As was demonstrated in the regional conflicts that followed the end of the Cold War, few Cold War–era weapons revolutionized wartime command and control more than the AWACS. In the field of electronic warfare and battle management, AWACS revolutionized the potential Cold War battlefield in the 1980s, and has proven its value to field commanders since 1991.

The experience gained during the Vietnam War with secret programs such as College Eye convinced the U.S. Air Force to develop such a capability permanently and to apply it to the potential Cold War aerial battlefield. After the war, a revolution in the world of electronics also made possible a far higher level of technical sophistication.

To accommodate this new equipment, the Air Force chose a larger and more sophisticated aircraft than the Vietnam-era C-121s. The airframe chosen was the Boeing Model 707, which was similar to the 717 and 739 airframes already in service with the Air Force as KC-135s, RC-135s and EC-135s. This airframe was, in turn, designed to be configured with the leading edge of state-of-the-art electronics, and then topped off with a 30-foot rotating radome, or "rotodome."

Work on what would evolve into the AWACS began even before the United States concluded its military role in the Vietnam War in 1973, and the first airframe was delivered under the designation E-3A in 1975. Engineering, test and evaluation began in October of that year, and in March 1977 the 552nd Airborne Warning and Control Wing (later the 552nd Air Control Wing) at Tinker AFB in Oklahoma became operational with the first E-3As, now given the name Sentry.

The most distinguishing feature of the E-3A is the 30-foot skunk-striped rotodome, but inside, it has more tactical battlefield information processing capability than any aircraft ever flown. Its radar and computer subsystems were able to provide air commanders with broad and detailed real-time battlefield information, including position and tracking information on enemy aircraft and ships, as well as the location and status of friendly aircraft and naval assets. The information could be transmitted to major command-and-control centers in rear areas or aboard ships. Then, as now, this data could—and has been—forwarded in real time to the president and secretary of Defense back in the United States.

In its air-defense role, the AWACS can detect, identify and track airborne enemy forces at great distances and direct interceptors to engage those targets. It can also provide information for commanders of air operations to gain and maintain control of the air battle, and, when operating in support of air-to-ground operations, the AWACS can provide direct information needed for interdiction, reconnaissance, airlift and close-air support for allied ground forces.

The AWACS is capable of monitoring hundreds of airborne targets from the Earth's surface up into the stratosphere, over land or water in any weather or visibility situation. It can be refueled while airborne and remain aloft for eight hours between refuelings.

Between 1977 and 1984, 34 E-3A aircraft were delivered to the U.S. Air Force. A round of updating began to turn the E-3As into E-3Bs and E-3Cs in 1984. The improvements included increasing the number of situation display consoles (SDC), improving the Have Quick radar jammers and upgrading the Joint Tactical Information Distribution System (JTIDS) and Tactical Digital Information Link (TADIL). When TADIL tattles, the crew members at the SDC listen, and the more clearly they hear, the safer everyone is.

The first and continuing assignment of the U.S. Air Force E-3 fleet would be with NORAD, guarding the periphery of North America. During the Cold War, much of the AWACS fleet was forward deployed to Europe, the Far East and other trouble spots. During the two Gulf Wars, AWACS were forward deployed to that theater. E-3s have also been active in Operations Desert Fox, Southern Watch and Allied Force. Beginning in September 2001, they were also used to monitor United States air space as part of Operation Noble Eagle. Suddenly, AWACS found itself eyeing commercial airliners—instead of bombers—as potentially lethal weapons. It was something that was almost never imagined during the Cold War.

In addition to those delivered to the U.S. Air Force, NATO acquired eighteen AWACS, with the first delivered in January 1982. The NATO aircraft operate with multinational crews but carry the national insignia of Luxembourg, NATO's smallest member. The United Kingdom has also received seven AWACS of its own, France has four, and Saudi Arabia ordered eight. The Saudi AWACS are unique in that they are KE-3s with the capability to refuel other aircraft in flight. During the 1990s, the British, French and NATO AWACS monitored the air space over the Balkans.

Kneecap

As became painfully clear on September 11, 2001, a decade after the end of the Cold War, the centers of government in Washington, D.C., are vulnerable to attack from the air. If the Pentagon and Offutt AFB needed Looking Glass as an airborne analog, they were not alone.

While Looking Glass performed the airborne command-and-control function for the Pentagon, the overall command and control of United States military forces resides not with the Pentagon but with the entity known as "the National Command Authority." This euphemism refers ultimately to the President of the United States, the Commander in Chief, although it encompasses his national defense staff, including the secretary of defense.

Realizing the vulnerability of Washington two decades before 2001, the Pentagon moved to create the National

Emergency Airborne Command Post (NEACP), whose acronym was traditionally pronounced Kneecap. The airframe chosen for Kneecap was the Boeing 747 jumbo jetliner, which had just been introduced into airline service, and which had about three times the floor space of the EC-135 or RC-135. Three specially configured 747s were ordered under the U.S. Air Force designation E-4A, and the first was delivered in 1974.

The NEACP aircraft were originally managed by the Strategic Air Command. One was placed on 24-hour-alert status at the south end of the Andrews AFB taxiway, 11 miles from the White House. The big white aircraft waited a short distance from the 89th Military Airlift Wing hangar where Air Force One was pampered. Kneecap's ominous presence here over the years earned it the nickname "Doomsday Plane."

In the event that a Soviet nuclear missile launch occurred while the president was in Washington, he would have been taken to Andrews AFB and the E-4A would take off immediately. Inside, the president and a hastily assembled battle staff would settle into their respective work areas in the 4,350 square feet of floor space and go to work. With the communications equipment available to them, they would be able to communicate with American air, sea and ground forces worldwide. Before the big plane had crossed Chesapeake Bay en route to its station, the president could be following up the counterstrike that he might have ordered earlier from his office. Before the first Soviet ICBM could impact an American target, Minuteman reentry vehicles would have been plunging back through the atmosphere toward Pinsk and Minsk and Omsk.

Beginning in 1978, the E-4As were upgraded to E-4B standard and a fourth aircraft was added. An E-4B crew may include up to 114 people, including a joint-service operations team, a maintenance and security component, a communications team and others.

In 1995, NEACP was redesignated as the National Airborne Operations Center (NAOC), and since 1998, the

E-4Bs have also supported the Federal Emergency Management Agency (FEMA) as needed in times of natural disaster. In this role, it would serve as the FEMA command-and-control center until a ground center could be established.

Today, Offutt AFB serves as the E-4B main operating base, but the small fleet has numerous forward operating bases throughout the United States at locations such as Andrews AFB.

Joint Stars

Since World War II and throughout the Cold War, it had been a fantasy of military commanders on the ground to have a radar system that could track military vehicles on the ground the way that radar could track aircraft. The technological impediments to such a dream were many. Essentially, the sky is a vast, three-dimensional space filled with few solid objects, and the largest of those are the objects that are desirable to track on radar—airplanes. The ground environment is essentially two dimensional, and filled with what radar operators call "ground clutter." This includes trees, houses, hillocks and cows, among myriad other large objects.

The United States armed forces, especially the Army, desired a system that could be used to track tanks and troop movement in the event of the massive Soviet invasion of Western Europe that was projected as the opening ground action of World War III.

The problem of a practical ground-scanning radar had been addressed by numerous failed projects throughout the Cold War, but by the 1980s, two projects were getting close. These were the Air Force's Pave Mover and the U.S. Army's helicopter-based Stand-Off Target Acquisition & Surveillance (SOTAS) program. In 1982, the undersecretary of defense for research and engineering (USDRE) combined these into a single multiservice joint program that would ultimately be known as the Joint Surveillance Target Attack System (J-STARS), or Joint STARS. Neither program had achieved the desired breakthrough and the merger seemed to be what the doctor ordered.

Under the management of the Air Force Electronic Systems Division (ESD), Joint STARS gradually took shape and the Grumman Corporation was selected as the lead contractor to integrate the system into an airborne platform. It was decided to use an airplane rather than a helicopter, and for awhile, the supersecret Tacit Blue aircraft was considered. Finally, it was decided to use a Boeing 707 airframe, which was essentially the same aircraft that was then being used as the Air Force's E-3 AWACS aircraft.

The first 707, a used commercial airframe, was fitted with Joint STARS equipment and turned over to the Air Force under the designation E-8A in April 1988, and it was fully flight tested with all systems up and running eight months later. After two E-8As were thus retrofitted, the Department of Defense decided to buy twenty-two all-new 707 airframes from Boeing under the designation E-8B. When this turned out to be too expensive, they went back to using "previously owned" 707 airframes, to be acquired under the designation E-3C.

In the world of defense hardware acquisition, one is accustomed to stories of programs that lag for years behind their initially projected deadlines. With Joint STARS, however, the opposite would be true. The initial operating capability for Joint STARS had been planned for 1997, but they actually would have their baptism of fire in 1991.

The Department of Defense correctly predicted that Operation Desert Storm would see the largest military action involving massed movements of vehicles in a generation. It was a situation that was tailor-made for Joint STARS. The two E-8A reproduction prototypes were still being tested, but they were nevertheless rushed to the Gulf War Theater and put into action. They performed in spectacular fashion. Joint STARS was praised for tracking Iraqi mobile forces, including tanks, troop transports and Scud missiles during forty-nine combat missions comprising more than 500 combat hours.

In one case, Joint STARS detected eighty Iraqi vehicles bound for the town of Khafji after the battle there involving the United States Marines. This information went to tactical air commanders, who promptly took out the Iraqis. The radar images that Joint STARS provided of the streams of Iraqi vehicles retreating from Kuwait are among the icons of Desert Storm.

The Joint STARS aircraft were also active during American and NATO involvement in the Balkans between 1996 and 1999, as well as during Operation Enduring Freedom in 2001 and Operation Iraqi Freedom in 2003.

The operational E-8C would incorporate the systems proven in Gulf War I, as well as the lessons learned. These modified Boeing 707-300 series commercial airframes have been extensively remanufactured and modified with the radar, communications, operations and control subsystems required to perform its operational mission. They still look like airliners except for their flat grey paint and the prominent 40-foot, canoe-shaped radome under the forward fuselage that houses the side-looking, phased array antenna.

The radar and computer subsystems can gather and display detailed battlefield information on both enemy and friendly ground forces and relay it to Army ground commanders. The radar antenna can be tilted to either side of the E-8C to provide a field of view covering nearly 19,000 square miles. It can detect and identify targets that are more than 150 miles away, distinguishing low-flying helicopters and rotating antennas.

Though it arrived in the last breath of the Cold War, Joint STARS has clearly demonstrated how it might have transformed Allied ability to operate on the central European battlefield of World War III. An airborne battle-management, command-and-control, intelligence, surveillance and ground-reconnaissance platform without parallel,

Joint STARS will provide United States ground and air commanders with real-time ground surveillance to support targeting and attack operations well into the twenty-first century.

CHAPTER 12

Communications

THE CAPABILITY TO COMMUNICATE IS AN ESSENTIAL ASPECT of all integrated military operations as well as in all aspects of civilian life. Long ago, battlefield communications involved such rudimentary methods as smoke signals and bugles. The use of signal flags evolved during the middle ages, and is still part of naval operations in the twenty-first century. During the nineteenth century, the telegraph made it possible to communicate well beyond line of sight. In World War I, telephone communications were a natural extension of the promise of the telegraphic revolution, and by World War II, radio communications were standard.

During the Cold War, communications equipment and methods continued to evolve. This chapter emphasizes just a few of the interesting highlights related to strategic, espionage and military communications. We have omitted mention of the likes of satellites for communications and data relay. While this might have been a secret novelty in the 1960s, today, it is something that nearly everyone in the industrialized world uses every day—and which we take for granted.

Red Phone and Hot Line

The term Red Phone was one of the important buzzwords of the Cold War. Both the United States and the Soviet

Union created immense nuclear arsenals in preparation for annihilating one another if one side should deliberately launch an attack. As unthinkable as such a scenario seems, it was a scenario less feared by the two sides than the accidental launch of an annihilating nuclear attack.

During the 1962 Cuban Missile Crisis, the United States and the Soviet Union came very close to nuclear war. During those dark days in October, any slip or miscalculation might have resulted in an unprecedented disaster. While both sides reserved the right to destroy the other, nether wanted such an event to happen by accident. With this in mind, they later agreed to install an instantaneous direct line of communication between the White House and the Kremlin.

An understanding signed on in June 1963 in Geneva called for the creation of this direct communications link that would come to be known by another important Cold War buzzword—the Hot Line. Initially, the receivers at either end were teletype machines, but the system was later upgraded to actual red telephones, hence that other famous buzzword.

In the 1960s, telephone technology was quite different from what it is in the twenty-first century. Telephones themselves were mostly rotary dial machines, and most telephone communication was carried by copper wire landlines. The first Hot Line was a duplex wire landline circuit, routed from Washington to Moscow via London, Copenhagen, Stockholm and Helsinki. The backup was a duplex radiotelegraph circuit routed through Tangier, Morocco. Perhaps the first use of the Hot Line was in 1967 during the six-day war between Israel and its Arab neighbors.

In 1971, the two sides agreed to upgrade to satellite technology. One circuit was via the United States Intelsat system, the other via the Soviet Molniya II system. After the satellites became fully operational in 1978, the radiotelegraph circuit was discontinued, but the landline remained in service as a backup system.

In 1983, President Ronald Reagan proposed that the

Hot Line be upgraded through the addition of a fax line. The Soviets agreed and this went into service in 1986.

Red Phone, Giant Talk and Giant Star

In addition to its use to describe the Hot Line telephone, the term *Red Phone* was also used during the Cold War to describe the Strategic Air Command Primary Alerting System (PAS). The PAS, or Red Phone, was used to rout information simultaneously to more than 200 SAC operating locations around the world.

The heart of SAC's Command Control Communications system, and managed by the Strategic Communications Division, the PAS was routed through two widely separated lines. The primary line went directly to the bomber wing command posts and to the 152 underground ICBM launch control centers and hardened alternate command posts. The second Red Phone line went to the same locations by way of the Eighth and Fifteenth Air Force command posts. In the event of a nuclear war, the Red Phone lines would transmit the "go-code" to the crews in the cockpits and at the missile control consoles.

In addition to the Red Phone, SAC used what was then state-of-the-art digital transmission media to transmit written communications to the operating locations. Through the 1980s, these transmissions were by means of the Strategic Air Command Automated Command Control System (SACCS) and were transmitted simultaneously to all of SAC's North American command posts.

In turn, the frontline crews in the bombers and silos were tied into the network through a high-frequency (HF), single-sideband radio system that was code-named Giant Talk. Because HF radio was not always reliable in the Arctic, where many of SAC's airborne alert missions were flown, Giant Talk was augmented by Green Pine, a system of ultra-high-frequency (UHF) radio stations located in an arc stretching across the top of North America from Keflavik, Iceland, to Adak near the tip of the Aleutian island chain.

The UHF and HF radio systems were, in turn, backed up by a Survivable Low Frequency Communications System (SLFCS), which operated in the low-frequency and very-low-frequency ranges. Through the 1970s, the Emergency Rocket Communications System (ERCS) could have utilized a Minuteman II booster launched from a Minuteman site to place a communications package into a suborbital trajectory. This package would have, after separation from the booster, transmitted prerecorded information on two UHF frequencies.

Beginning in 1983, much of the Strategic Air Command communications load was carried by AFSATCOM, the Air Force Satellite Communications System, of which the Strategic Air Command portion was code-named Giant Star. AFSATCOM was integrated with the Navy's older Fleet Satellite Communications System (FLTSATCOM) to provide communications integration to SAC ground and airborne command posts as well as bombers and other aircraft.

Radio Station One

The Cold War saw amazing advances in communications technology and extraordinarily complex communications systems. On the opposite end of the spectrum were the small, portable devices that were used by individuals, whether they be soldiers in the field or clandestine operatives operating behind enemy lines. Indeed, the communication equipment used by the Central Intelligence Agency's clandestine operatives constitute some of the most secret of the Cold War's secret weapons.

The idea of placing agents in enemy territory with portable transmitting devices was a cornerstone of espionage activities during World War II. The United States Office of Strategic Services ran many agents throughout German-occupied Europe and throughout southeast Asia between 1942 and 1945. Their radio of choice for these operations was the SSTR series, especially the SSTR-1.

The SSTR family of clandestine operative radios were built by a little-known company called the Radio Development & Research Corporation (RDR Corp). Founded in 1938 and originally based in New York City, RDR relocated to Jersey City, New Jersey, in the late 1940s. While the company was building radios for clandestine operatives, it was also building a small number of strange consumer products. Of these, none is stranger than the 1947 Model 504 Magic-Tone "whiskey bottle radio." It was a real radio encased in a real brown-glass bottle with a label that appeared like a liquor bottle label that carried the slogan "the radio that soothes your spirits." The glow of the vacuum tubes within the bottle was actually quite soothing.

After World War II, RDR also resumed its relationship with the American espionage services. The United States had disbanded the Office of Strategic Services immediately after the war, but the need for such an organization was apparent, so the National Security Act of 1947 contained a provision for the creation of the Central Intelligence Agency (CIA). The agency turned to RDR for a radio transmitter system that was based on the company's World War II radios.

RDR's answer to the CIA requirement for a clandestine operative radio was designated as RS-1, an acronym for the ambitiously conceived Radio Station One. The high-frequency transceiver that became a ubiquitous part of CIA activities through the 1950s and beyond was conceived as not just a radio, but a radio station.

Entering service in about 1950, the RS-1 consisted of an RR2B receiver and RT3 transmitter that together weighed 24 pounds in their original configuration. The entire unit measured 10 inches wide, 8.6 inches deep and 5.5 inches high. They were portable, reliable and durable enough to withstand the jolt of an air drop. They were waterproof to the extent that they could be buried for prolonged periods, and they could be operated from a variety of power sources.

After initial prototyping by RDR, many of the units were manufactured by Admiral until the early 1960s. They were used in covert operations in Eastern Europe and

Cuba, and were widely used during the Vietnam War. In Vietnam, they were installed at field locations throughout the country for clandestine operatives to stay in contact with their headquarters.

Later American Clandestine Communications Devices

Meanwhile, a miniaturized variation on the RS-1 was produced under the designation RS-6. In the 1950s, transistors had been invented, but were not yet in widespread use, so miniaturization relied on creating vacuum tubes that were as small as possible and this would be the cornerstone of the RS-6 system's RR6 receiver and RT6 transmitter. The whole system weighed around 10 pounds and was less than 10 inches on its longest dimension. The RS-6 is known to have been widely used by both the CIA and the U.S. Air Force Strategic Air Command.

During the early 1950s, RDR is known to have received a license from Bell Laboratories (later Lucent Technologies) to develop transistor technology. Germanium Products, an RDR subsidiary, was one of the first to mass produce transistors, possibly marketing them to the defense industry before transistor pioneer Raytheon.

In about 1961, the U.S. Army began to acquire the RS-1 high-frequency transceiver under the designation GRC-109. Initially, it was for use by Special Forces operating behind enemy lines in the Central Highlands and along the Laotian border, but it eventually became common with many forward-deployed units. The GRC-109s remained in production by Admiral through the 1960s.

A very heavy-duty version, designated as GRC-109A, was introduced in 1969. It would be manufactured exclusively for the United States miliary by Oklahoma Aerotronics through 1973. These radios remained in clandestine service for some time, although the full details of their later deployment remain unknown.

A portable version of the RS-6 that was designed to fit in a metal suitcase was reportedly designated as RS-511. It was one of many suitcase radios used during the Cold War, which, like the suitcase radios of World War II, have always been popular with moviemakers creating films about spies and their activities.

The RS-511 was an improvement over the RS-6 in that the components, especially the transmitter and receiver modules, were combined into a single unit. The dials and other user interfaces were also simplified and made easier to use. The compactness of the RS-511 made the unit lighter and less cumbersome than earlier systems and the single-unit format eliminated the need for the operator to have to manually connect cables and wires. Under field conditions, when visibility and time were limited, this process was not always easy. Imagine a clandestine operative having to plug in his cables while crouched in a basement with a jackbooted enemy searching for him above the creaking floorboards.

BR-3U "Svir"

After World War II, both the United States and the Soviet Union created new agencies of espionage with which they would do battle with one another during the Cold War. During World War II, as the principal international espionage directorate for the United States was the Office of Strategic Services (OSS), the rough equivalent in the Soviet Union was the Narodny Kommisariat Vnutrennikh Del (NKVD), the People's Commissariat for Internal Affairs. After the war, the functions of the OSS eventually migrated to the CIA. In the Soviet Union, the NKVD was superseded by the Komitet Gosudarstvennoy Bezopasnosti (KGB), the Committee for State Security. The agents of both organizations needed communications equipment.

As the CIA developed the RS-1 system for use by its clandestine operatives, the KGB developed a variety of transceiver systems, notably the BR3 transmitter/receiver, nicknamed Svir for the river near Leningrad. Weighing more than 30 pounds, these radios were compact units measuring 4 inches high by nearly 10 inches deep and 13 inches wide. Like the American RS-1, they were designed to take rough treatment and adverse weather conditions. They were also equipped with magnetic-tape keys for automatic transmission at up to 750 words per minute.

These radios were used by Soviet agents operating in Western Europe, including neutral nations such as Switzerland. Because they were too heavy to be easily transported by one person, they were often hidden in secret locations rather than being carried. Since the Cold War, many have been found buried in locations from Belgium to Italy. More sinister than merely a novelty of a bygone era, the Soviet radios were often booby trapped and therefore presented a hazard to those who may have stumbled across them.

Burst Coding Systems

When a special-operations military force is operating behind enemy lines, when a military aircraft is operating in enemy airspace or when a clandestine operative is operating under cover, there is a necessity to maintain radio silence in order not to be detected by adversaries scanning radio channels.

However, occasionally it is necessary to make a transmission. This is especially true of the clandestine operative whose mission requires him or her to report the results of an espionage mission. In such cases during the Cold War, the data would be recorded onto magnetic tape without the transmitter turned on, and then transmitted with through "burst coding," in which coded information would have been sent out via Morse code as a quick burst at a much higher rate of speed than a person could have tapped out a message with a telegraph key. Often the burst lasted no more than a few seconds. Then the radio was quickly shut down to prevent the enemy from taking a "fix" on the location. On the receiving end, the burst would be recorded on magnetic tape and played back slowly.

Though such transmissions are taken for granted today in the digital age, in the early years of the Cold War, burst coding was an important innovation, and one that was still highly secret.

For the United States, one of the most important burst coding systems was the venerable AN/GRA-71, which was used by the CIA, by the U.S. Army Special Forces, and by U.S. Air Force as well as by other agencies. Manufactured by Arvin Industries, the GRA-71 accommodated two CA-3B tape cartridges with a spring-operated automatic rewind. The burst coding system featured two coding wheels, one with ten numerals and one with two sets of twenty-six letters, each rendered clockwise.

The receiver station for the GRA-71 was designated as GSH-71. It included a three-channel audio-frequency recorder using three-track, continuous-loop magnetic tape. Two channels were used to record incoming data, while the third recorded the "cue" tone, or control signal.

The successor to the GRA-71 is reported to have been the somewhat mysterious AN/PYC-1 and AN/PSC-2 systems.

Solid-State Equipment for Clandestine Operatives

By the middle 1960s, advances in transistor technology made it possible for espionage and military intelligence agencies to begin fielding solid-state radio transceivers. On the United States side, one of the most important was the RS-49 high-frequency radio, which is reported to have made its debut in about 1964. At least some of the systems are known to have been manufactured by Delco, the radio division of General Motors.

With an RT-49 transmitter and an RR-49 receiver, this "radio station" was similar to the RS-6, but the solid-state components allowed for it to be much smaller and lighter. This, of course, was a welcome innovation for clandestine operatives in the field.

The RS-49 system weighed just over 2 pounds, with the receiver measuring 4 inches on its longest dimension and the transmitter just 5.35 inches long. Each component was less than 2 inches thick. For the 1960s, this amounted to extreme miniaturization. The RS-49 continued to be manufactured and used in the 1970s.

A contemporary of the RS-49 was Delco's Model 5300

family of solid-state, high-frequency transceivers that were used by U.S. Army Special Forces and by the Australian Special Air Service under the designation AN/PRC-64. A four-channel system, the Model 5300 weighed 7.5 pounds with its battery and measured 5 inches by 10 inches, and was 4.5 inches wide.

Autonomous Transmission Systems

The notion of using a small radio transmitter to eavesdrop on a conversation in a closed room has always been a mainstay of espionage operations. The technical problem of making such devices small enough to avoid detection consumed a great deal of time at the CIA and the KGB throughout the early days of the Cold War. Eventually, they were miniaturized to the point that they could justifiably wear their most popular nickname and be referred to as "bugs."

The CIA's Technical Services Division created myriad bugs during the Cold War, many of which are still secret and known only to a few. Among the earliest such devices that was widely used was designated as ST-2A, for Surveillance Transmitter, Second. Cumbersome by modern standards, or even by the standards of the solid-state sixties, the ST-2A was 5.6 inches long, 3 inches wide and 1.25 inches thick. It was typically used as we have seen in those classic black-and-white espionage films from the 1950s—hidden in a hotel room and monitored from an adjacent room.

In the latter years of the Cold War, as solid-state technology allowed greater miniaturization, bugging transmitters grew smaller, more ubiquitous and more secret.

CHAPTER 13

Secret Naval Vessels

THOUGH ARMIES HAVE BEEN THE MOST COMMONLY USED weapon of international conflict, naval power has been an important part of national defense since 480 B.C., when the Greeks under Themistocles changed to course of history by defeating the Persians under Xerxes at the Battle of Salamis. During the nineteenth century, the British Empire became the world's first truly global superpower, not because of its army, but because of its navy. In the years between World War I and World War II, naval power was seen as the key element in force projection for all the world's major military powers not located in continental Europe, namely Japan, the United Kingdom and the United States. The battleship was the ultimate weapon.

In December 1941, the battleship quickly proved *not* to be the ultimate weapon. The Japanese used airpower to destroy the cream of the U.S. Navy battleship fleet at Pearl Harbor, and three days later, they sank the backbone of British Royal Navy power in the Far East, the HMS *Repulse* and the HMS *Prince of Wales*.

During World War II, naval power began to be measured, not by battleships, but by aircraft carriers. Beyond the 1940s, only the U.S. Navy would continue to keep battleships in its arsenal, and then only a single four-ship class, the World War II-era Iowas, and it was only during the 1980s that all four would be in commission at the same time during the Cold War.

By nature, few naval surface ships can be considered as secret weapons. They're too big. On the other hand, submarines are secret by definition. In both world wars, Germany's submarines were clearly its ultimate naval weapon. In World War II, American submarines certainly were an effective weapon not only in taking out Japanese shipping, but in rescuing downed flyers—including future President George Herbert Walker Bush—and in landing commandos behind enemy lines for special operations.

At one point during the Cold War, an American submarine officer explained to this writer over a cup of coffee aboard his vessel that there are two types of ships in any navy—"submarines and targets."

Certainly if this book were about secret operations of the Cold War rather than secret weapons, the exploits of submarines and submariners would consume a great many pages. Possibly the closest thing to open, armed conflict between the Soviet Union and the United States during the Cold War occurred between submarines beneath the waves of the Atlantic and the Pacific. Of course, the subs of both navies routinely shadowed the surface ships of the opposing sides as well—often undetected.

Nuclear power for submarine propulsion began with the commissioning of the USS *Nautilus* in 1954 and was soon followed by that of the Soviet submarine K-3. As sizable numbers of these joined the two fleets, the nature of submarine operations—and potential submarine warfare—changed forever. No longer were submarines hindered by the need to refuel. With nuclear propulsion, they could conduct patrols involving tens of thousands of miles and remain at sea for months.

After the advent of ballistic missile submarines, a key activity of both navies was using nuclear attack subs to follow the ballistic missile subs of the opposite side. Following without detection became a game for both sides, and often they succeeded in doing so for days.

So secret were most exploits of the submariners during those years that they remained unknown, even long after the Cold War ended. Indeed, many of the secret missions and secret weapons of the submarine services may never be known. In the U.S. Navy, submariners were typically required to ascribe to secrecy oaths that would not expire for decades.

In this section, we present a selection of ships from the Cold War that were specially designed and beyond the ordinary.

Cobra Judy and *Observation Island*

Displacing 13,000 tons and 564 feet in length, the United States Naval Ship (USNS) *Observation Island* was owned by the U.S. Navy and used for a wide variety of missions, both routine and sensitive. For the last dozen years of the Cold War, she was operated by the U.S. Air Force as a highly sophisticated, floating, missile-observation post. Using the once supersecret Cobra Judy radar, she monitored both American and Soviet missile launches and spied on other activities. Her work would continue after the Cold War and beyond the turn of the century.

Her keel was laid down in the autumn of 1952 at a shipyard in Camden, New Jersey. When she was launched the following year she was commissioned as the commercial merchant ship SS *Empire State Mariner*. In 1954, she went out of service as a transport and was mothballed as part of the U.S. Navy's Maritime Reserve Fleet, to be brought into naval service in a time of national emergency. In 1956, she was transferred to the Navy and sent to Maryland Shipbuilding and Drydock in Baltimore to be converted for use as a test facility for the Fleet Ballistic Missile Weapons System. It was not until 1958, however, that the Navy actually took delivery of the ship.

Officially recommissioned as the USS *Observation Is-*

land (EAG-154) in December 1958, the ship was extensively refitted as literally an "observation island." Her primary mission under new ownership was to monitor the launch at sea of the Polaris Submarine Launched Ballistic Missile (SLBM). However, initially, she served as the first floating launch platform for Polaris. The missile had previously been launched from land and would eventually be launched from submarines, but in the meantime, the first launch at sea would be from the surface so that program managers could observe closely. This first Polaris sea launch from the deck of the USS *Observation Island* came in September 1959, with the ship anchored off shore from Cape Canaveral, Florida.

Through 1962, the USS *Observation Island* operated in the Atlantic Test Range, alternating between observing submarine launches of Polaris SLBMs and launching them herself when a new version needed a first test-firing at sea. From 1962 through 1972, the ship continued these activities, alternating between the Atlantic and the Pacific Test Ranges. Six days before he was assassinated in November 1963, President John F. Kennedy came aboard the USS *Observation Island* to watch a Polaris A2 launched from the submerged nuclear ballistic missile submarine, USS *Andrew Jackson*. In December 1969, she test-fired the first Poseidon SLBM launched from a ship.

The USS *Observation Island* was held in reserve by the United States Maritime Administration from 1972 to 1977, when she was reactivated by the U.S. Navy and retrofitted as a Range Instrumentation ship. On August 18, 1977, she was recommissioned as the USNS *Observation Island* (AGM-23) and assigned to the Special Mission Ships Program in the Pacific. The AGM prefix stands for Missile Range Instrumentation Ship, a role not unlike that which she had performed as EAG-154.

Between 1979 and 1981, she went back into Maryland Shipbuilding & Drydock for further work and emerged with AN/SPQ-11 Cobra Judy phased array radar and a new official assignment to the U.S. Air Force Technical Applications Center and Electronic Systems Center at the Eastern Space Missile Center, which, in turn is headquartered at Patrick AFB in Florida.

Based at Pearl Harbor, *Observation Island* would spend the remainder of the Cold War detecting, tracking and collecting intelligence data on Soviet and other nations' strategic ballistic missile tests over the Pacific Ocean. Bolted onto a mechanically rotated steel turret on the aft end of the ship, Cobra Judy stands more than four stories high and weighs 250 tons. The large, octagonal S-band radar array, composed of a dozen separate antenna elements, is 23 feet across.

In 1985, Raytheon installed an X-band radar system antenna to complement the S-band phased array. The five-story parabolic dish of the X-band dish antenna was installed aft forward of the phased array. Because X-band offers a better degree of resolution and target separation, this addition was intended to improve Cobra Judy's capability to collect data on the terminal phase of distant ballistic missile tests.

Since the end of the Cold War and especially since the turn of the century, Cobra Judy's electronic eyes have been turned toward the activities of the unstable warlords of North Korea.

Halibut and Ivy Bells

In the annals of clandestine naval activities during the Cold War, few ships are more deserving of a mention than the submarine USS *Halibut* (SSN-587), and few operations are more intriguing that Operation Ivy Bells.

The USS *Halibut* was a Gato Class ship laid down at the Mare Island Naval Shipyard in Vallejo, California, in April 1957 and commissioned on January 4, 1960, as SSGN-587. Not the first submarine to carry the name, SSGN-587 succeeded the World War II–era USS *Halibut* (SS-232), which was launched in April 1942 for an extensive service career in the Pacific Theater.

The N in the *Halibut*'s designation identified the 350-

foot vessel as having nuclear propulsion, the G identified her as being a guided missile launch platform. In the days before the ballistic missile submarines designed to launch Polaris, Poseidon and Trident SLBMs from vertical tubes, the *Halibut* was the first of a family of submarines specifically designed to launch the Regulus cruise missile. The missiles were carried in a large "hangar" that was located on the deck of the submarines in order to keep them above the wave tops when the vessel was operating on the surface. Discussed in chapter 5, the Regulus was launched horizontally from the deck of the submarine while she was on the surface.

Though innovative and forward looking when it was conceived in the 1950s, the U.S. Navy's Regulus program was short-lived. After several deployments and a number of successful missile launches, the *Halibut* departed in May 1964 on what was to be the last patrol by a Regulus-equipped submarine in the Pacific. Though this was the end of her missile career, this was really just the beginning for the *Halibut*. As for the USS *Growler*, her ultimate mission would be to serve as a permanent public display of a Regulus submarine. Today, both the ship and a Regulus may be seen and visited at the Intrepid Sea-Air-Space Museum in New York City.

Between February and September 1965, the USS *Halibut* was completely overhauled at Pearl Harbor. The reconfigured *Halibut* was the brainchild of a U.S. Navy scientist named John Craven, who could see the enormous potential of taking clandestine sleuthing beneath the waves of the world's oceans.

The missile-firing gear was removed from the 50-foot hangar on her deck and she was redesignated as SSN-587. The capacious hanger was essentially remodeled as a special-operations center and fitted with state of the art Sperry Univac mainframe computers. Known as the Bat Cave to the clandestine operatives who worked in it, this section of the ship would prove ideal for the secret missions that lay before it. Another feature of the *Halibut* that was attractive for its new career was the enormous hatch on the Bat Cave, which was more than ten times larger than that on any other nuclear submarine. Of course, the fact that she was a nuclear submarine gave the *Halibut* the ability to travel submerged for a virtually unlimited duration. This was also important for secret operations.

The specific secret operations for the *Halibut* initially involved underwater surveillance, for which she was equipped with gear that was so state of the art that few people—even within the Navy's submarine service—knew that it existed.

One of *Halibut*'s first missions was Operation Winterwind, locating and photographing artifacts from Soviet missile tests. For both sides, ICBM test-firings usually ended with the missiles splashing down in the Pacific Ocean. It was assumed that they would then be hidden from view forever. The Winterwind project was designed to find them.

Soon, the *Halibut* received an ocean floor surveillance mission of extreme importance. In March 1968, the K-129, a Soviet Golf II–class nuclear ballistic-missile submarine, was lost with all hands about 1,700 miles northwest of the Hawaiian Island of Oahu. At the time, this disaster was unknown to all but a select few in the Soviet and United States navies, and the Soviet navy would never figure out exactly where the submarine had gone down.

Even past the turn of the century, the exact nature of the loss remains unknown. The U.S. Navy maintains that the K-129 suffered an internal explosion—not an unusual circumstance aboard Soviet submarines. The Soviets, meanwhile, would always maintain that the K-129 collided with the U.S. Navy submarine USS *Swordfish*, which was later observed by a Soviet spy with damage consistent with a collision. The U.S. Navy dismissed the *Swordfish* damage as having been caused by an ice fragment in the Sea of Japan. In any case, the *Halibut* was tasked with locating the K-129.

In July 1968, the *Halibut* succeeded in locating the sunken Soviet submarine and over the ensuing month, the crew in the Bat Cave succeeded in obtaining more than 20,000 detailed images of the K-129, including pictures of the uniformed skeleton of a sailor. No inch of the K-129 went undocumented.

Though the mission would remain top-secret until after the Cold War, it was an immediate sensation in the dark corners of the United States espionage services and at the highest levels of government. Incoming President Richard Nixon was elated when he heard about this intelligence coup in early 1969, and the CIA was so excited that they wanted a piece of the *Halibut*. They also wanted a piece of the K-129. This led the CIA to come up with Project Jennifer, which is discussed in the following entry.

In the meantime, the CIA also went so far as to convince the Office of Naval Intelligence to form a supersecret joint venture to be known as the National Underwater Reconnaissance Office. This was an analog to the National Reconnaissance Office for space-related surveillance, which was a joint venture of the CIA and the Air Force.

In 1970, the U.S. Navy and the National Security Agency concocted what would be the USS *Halibut*'s ultimate mission—Operation Ivy Bells. The idea—not revealed until after the Cold War—was so audacious that it is still compared to espionage fiction. North of Japan is the Kamchatka Peninsula, which is separated from the land mass of Russia by the vast and inhospitable Sea of Okhotsk. On the sparsely populated peninsula were the big Soviet naval base at Petropavlovsk and myriad secret and high-priority military sites associated with ICBM testing, early warning radar and the like. During the Cold War, the main line of communication between Kamchatka and the mainland of the Soviet Union was an underwater cable on the bottom of the Sea of Okhotsk. *Halibut*'s mission was as simple as it was difficult—to put a wire tap on the cable!

Tapping the Sea of Okhotsk cable would be an intelligence coup of unimaginable proportions. It would also be an extremely dangerous task. Operating at the bottom of the sea in the frigid latitudes was bad enough, but it was a certainty that any United States naval vessel caught in the Sea of Okhotsk would be sunk.

The *Halibut* was extensively modified and fitted with an airlock system to allow divers to leave the submerged vessel and install the tap. The tap itself weighed six tons and was nuclear powered to permit long-term operations. It was sophisticated enough to be capable of individually monitoring the dozens of lines that ran through the Soviet cable. These data were, in turn, recorded on wide bands of tape to be picked up later. The first wire tap was installed in the summer of 1972, and the *Halibut* and other reconfigured submarines, such as USS *Parche* (SSN-683), made repeated trips to the Sea of Okhotsk to change out the tape reels.

During the 1970s, Operation Ivy Bells provided an intelligence windfall that is yet to be fully comprehended. Most of what was recorded was straight, unencoded conversation. The Soviets had no idea what was happening until 1980, when a National Security Agency staffer named Ronald Pelton sold out the program to a Soviet spy. By 1981, the Soviets had located and removed the wire tap.

Meanwhile, the *Halibut* and the *Parche*, as well as their sister ship, the USS *Seawolf* (SSN-575) had continued with other clandestine operations—including more cable tapping—the details of which are still classified long after the end of the Cold War.

The *Halibut* and the *Seawolf* were both decommissioned later in the Cold War, and were scrapped in 1994 and 1997, respectively. The *Parche*, which was commissioned in 1974, two decades after the others, remained in service past the turn of the century. Pelton was sentenced to three consecutive life terms in federal prison. Kamchatka is still home to secret Russian facilities.

Project Jennifer and the *Glomar Explorer*

It is interesting to look at the history of sensational revelations of secret information against the backdrop of desperate efforts to control these revelations. These events burst suddenly into the headlines and are all the buzz from the folks around the office water cooler to the television talk shows. Within official circles a panic ensues in an impossible effort to do damage control.

It is hard to imagine that these events will not form a permanent part of the collective unconscious, yet a decade or so later, it is hard to find anyone who remembers them. Those who tried so hard to control the leak have gotten their way. That which had ceased to be secret is now forgotten.

In 1975, it was hard to find anyone who was not aware of a bizarre CIA operation called Project Jennifer, and of the strange ship called the *Glomar Explorer*. Today, as the Cold War itself is becoming a less distinct memory, more often than not, these names elicit blank stares. The CIA, which tried so hard to control this leak, got its way. The secret has faded from public consciousness—but it no longer matters.

As noted previously, the Soviet Golf II class nuclear ballistic missile submarine designated as K-129 sank in the Pacific northwest of Oahu in March 1968. The U.S. Navy sent the submarine USS *Halibut* on a secret mission to locate and photograph the K-129. It was not only a mission accomplished, but one that was accomplished so well that the CIA came up with the idea to go back and raise the K-129.

However, it was not until the early 1970s that Project Jennifer was officially initiated. It was one of the deepest secrets in the CIA at the time, and only a handful of people knew about it. This was problematic because the enormous technical problems associated with the recovery of a huge naval vessel from 17,000 feet of water would involve a great deal of complex engineering and a great many engineers.

Never short on imagination, the CIA wove an equally enigmatic cover story that would be a credit to the most accomplished spy novelist. The story even included an idiosyncratic billionaire who hadn't actually set foot in his own office in decades and whose very name was synonymous with the idea of a man of mystery.

Just as we have cited sensational news stories that fade completely from the public view, so, too, we might mention public figures that make the transition from household name to virtual obscurity in a generation's time. In the early 1970s, one such household name was that of Howard Robard Hughes. Known as "the world's richest man," which he probably was, Hughes captured the imagination of the tabloid-reading public because he was also an eccentric's eccentric. He had not been seen in public for more than a dozen years and was rumored to spend all of his time lying in a bed in a darkened hotel room. In fact—as this writer has learned from individuals who had access to those dark rooms during this era—the rumors were true.

Hughes had inherited from his father an extraordinarily lucrative patent on oil drilling equipment and had multiplied this fortune through a variety of projects ranging from two aircraft companies to a controlling interest in TransWorld Airlines to the then-largest concentration of hotels in Las Vegas. Among the interests into which the corporate tentacles of the Hughes Summa Corporation reached was an interest in deep ocean mining.

It is well known that the floor of the Pacific Ocean is littered with "nodules" composed of manganese and other metals such as nickel and cobalt. Because of the great depth, it has always been considered prohibitively expensive to harvest these nodules. However, such a venture was a perfect cover story for Project Jennifer. Summa, in cooperation with the CIA, created an entity called the Deep Ocean Mining Project, which got under way in 1973. By this time, Hughes himself was incapacitated from a broken hip suffered in a fall in the bedroom (of course) of his London hotel suite and was so heavily medicated that he was probably unaware of any of the actual details of the project.

The recovery of the nodules was to be carried out by a specially configured vessel called the *Glomar Explorer*, which was built by Sun Shipbuilding and Drydock Company for a mining company known as Global Marine Development. The recovery tool itself would be a huge multi-fingered claw that would be extended beneath the ship by 60-foot sections of pipe. The sections would be attached to one another one at a time until the pipeline, with the claw at the bottom, extended more than three miles beneath the waves. The submarine would be grasped, and then the pipeline would be raised by disassembling it one section at a time. It would be a long laborious process during which anything could go wrong at any step.

The *Glomar Explorer* was put to sea in June 1974. Soviet espionage agents had been eyeing this massive 619-foot ship, with the complex forest of cranes and scaffolding on deck. They did not entirely believe the manganese-nodule cover story, but they were still uncertain what the ship was really up to. In fact, the Soviets actually watched the recovery efforts without knowing what was going on. The Soviet Union never ascertained the mission of the *Glomar Explorer* until their agents read about it in American newspapers months later.

For the *Glomar Explorer*, finding the K-129—whose location was still unknown to the Soviet Union—was the easy part. However, an analysis of the earlier photos indicated that the submarine was extremely fragile, having been damaged when it crashed into the ocean floor in 1968 and having been subjected to intense pressure under the weight of the ocean.

After one failed attempt, the *Glomar Explorer*'s claw succeeded in grasping its quarry. The crews raised the entire submarine about half the way to the surface when it began to crumble and break apart. Eventually, when the claw finally came out of the water, it grasped less than a quarter of the submarine. The items most coveted by the CIA, including code books and missiles, had been lost. The secret mission of the *Glomar Explorer* had failed.

However, the *Glomar Explorer* was about to face an even more tenacious enemy—the American media. This was the era of Watergate. Richard Nixon had resigned the presidency while the *Glomar Explorer* was at sea. Bob Woodward and Carl Bernstein of the *Washington Post* had become folk heros for exposing the Watergate scandal and for bringing down a presidency. Every reporter in America wanted to become an investigative journalist and to achieve folk hero status by exposing the next big government scandal. The government was on the defensive. The CIA was now fair game for muckrakers and Project Jennifer represented the kind of enticing muck that sold papers. It had everything from an outlandish scheme to the outlandish Hughes.

Hard to keep under wraps, rumors about the true mission of the *Glomar Explorer* had begun to leak, and the *Los Angeles Times* broke the story in February 1975. They got the ocean wrong—they placed the recovery project in the Atlantic—but the essential details were more or less correct. The *New York Times* joined in, and CIA Director William Colby leapt into damage-control mode. If the United States was concerned about the cover of Project Jennifer being blown, so, too, was the Soviet government. They were humiliated at having it revealed that they had both lost a sub and failed to find it. Not only had the Americans found it, they had raised at least part of it. Both governments made discrete overtures to the American news media to stop running stories.

The CIA managed the leaks by deliberately leaking a cover story that the *Glomar Explorer* had recovered most of the Soviet submarine, and giving the location as 750 miles from Hawaii, instead of 1,700.

As for the *Glomar Explorer* and her now-blown cover, there was discussion of a second attempt at raising the sub. However, the USS *Seawolf* surveyed the scene and returned some bad news. Because the part of the vessel that had broken off had crumbled on its way back down, fragments had returned to the ocean floor like so much confetti. There was no sense in trying again.

In 1976, ownership of the *Glomar Explorer* passed from Global Marine to the U.S. Navy, and the following year she was transferred to the United States Maritime Administration, which manages the U.S. Navy's mothballed fleet. For most of the next two decades, she remained in mothballs, parked with the a large group of mothballed naval vessels in Suisun Bay, northeast of San Francisco. In 1996, she was leased back to Global Marine use in commercial ocean-mining operations. As she slipped under the Golden Gate Bridge, bound for deep water, few noticed or remembered her brief moment of fame and controversy during the Cold War.

Wing In Ground Effect

"If only ships could be made to fly," sounds like a phrase uttered by desperate mariner or a hopeless dreamer. In fact, flying ships that are neither hydrofoils nor airplanes do exist. During the Cold War, the Soviet Union secretly built numerous such craft to take advantage of the little-known phenomenon of Wing In Ground Effect, which is better known by its acronym, WIG.

What is WIG and why is it desirable?

Technically, ground effect is a cushion of air that is compressed beneath an aircraft when it is very close to the ground. This is why an airplane gains a bit of additional lift just before it lands. Such a phenomenon would be desirable for a surface vehicle, because contact with the surface of the Earth creates drag and works to slow down any vehicle on the surface. This is why the fastest speed boats operate with the smallest possible area of their hulls in contact with the water. They seem to be flying over the surface of the water, but they aren't. A WIG vehicle, on the other hand, actually *is* flying over the surface of the water. With no drag, such vehicles can travel faster than the fastest speed boat.

A hovercraft also operates on a cushion of air, but the cushion is generated by huge fans. In a WIG craft, the cushion is created through aerodynamics. As in an airplane, lift is created by wings.

Naturally, WIG is more desirable over water than over land, because land surfaces are typically uneven. This would disrupt the ground effect, something that would be disastrous at high speeds. Nevertheless, many of the early WIG theorists considered using it over land. In Finland in 1935, an inventor named T. J. Kaario built a WIG sleigh for use in traveling over snow.

Alexander Lippisch is best known for designing delta-wing aircraft in Germany during World War II, notably the Messerschmitt Me.163 rocket fighter. Less well known is his postwar work with WIG vehicles, especially his experimental X-112 craft. He was even able to secure the Collins Radio Company (later a component of Rockwell International) in the United States as an investor. A small vehicle with two open cockpits and T tail, the X-112 was certainly successful as a concept demonstrator, but Collins saw no future in it and withdrew from the project.

Parenthetically, it has been said that the massive H-4 wooden flying boat built during World War II by Howard Hughes would never have worked as an airplane, but might have been an ideal WIG vehicle. Hughes flew the huge "Spruce Goose" one time in 1947, and then only a few feet off the water in the harbor of Long Beach, California. Analysts have suggested that it did not actually fly but it merely operated in ground effect. Hughes is said to have known this, and it is why he neither went higher on the H-4's only flight, nor made any additional flights in the big craft.

Though small privately funded experiments continued elsewhere in the world, only the Soviet Union saw the promise in very large military WIG vehicles. In the Soviet Union, such craft are referred to by the Russian word *Ekranoplan*, meaning screenplane. By the early 1960s, the design bureau headed by Rostislav Alexeiev was developing hydrofoil ships when it turned to Ekranoplans as well.

Meanwhile, Soviet premier Nikita Khrushchev was well known for dreaming grandiose dreams when it came to technology in the service of national prestige. He had insisted that the Soviet Union have the world's first orbital spacecraft and his scientists gave him Sputnik. He had insisted that the Soviet Union have the world's first man in space and his scientists gave him Vostok 1 and Yuri Gagarin's famous flight. He had insisted that the Soviet Union have the world's first man on the moon, and his scientists were working on that. Closer to the Earth's surface, Khrushchev saw the technological promise of Ekranoplan technology and committed the resources of the Soviet Union to this project as well.

Beginning work in 1963, Alexeiev designed a series of Ekranoplan vehicles of gradually increasing size, notably one that was designated as SM-2, and an unrelated craft designated as SM-2P7. These small prototypes were used to test various configurations for an eventual craft that would be of truly monumental size. This feature would certainly have pleased Premier Khrushchev, but he would not remain in office long enough to see this dream come true.

Kaspian Sea Monster

Rumors of the so-called Kaspian Sea Monster first began to circulate in 1966, but it was not until September 1991 that the existence of this huge Ekranoplan was first confirmed by Soviet authorities.

Though Khrushchev was deposed in 1964, work on the Ekranoplan program continued, culminating in the KM, a 550-ton WIG craft that was built at a secret factory in the closed city Gorky. The obsession with secrecy within the Soviet Union was so pathological that even the city itself was secret. Now called Nizhny Novgorod, Gorky was notable as being a major city into which no outsiders were permitted during the Cold War.

Of course, by the mid-1960s, the United States Corona spy satellites were imaging Gorky routinely, drawn with a curiosity nurtured by the Soviet paranoia. When the KM was rolled out and trucked to the Kaspian Sea for its initial testing, American photo interpreters thought that it was a seaplane. Given the appearance of Soviet Ekranoplans, it was an easy mistake to make. Ekranoplans look like stubby-winged seaplanes, and no American analyst had ever seen anything else that remotely resembled a Soviet Ekranoplan.

The KM was the largest WIG craft ever constructed. It was 350 feet long, longer than any airplane of any kind, and it was built with a wing span of 100 feet. It would later be retrofitted with wings spanning 130 feet. It had a high T tail that was actually a V at the top of a tall rudder. The craft was powered by eight Dobryin VD-7 turbojet engines located at the front of the fuselage to produce additional lift.

The KM made its first "flight" in October 1966 and remained in operation for more than a decade. Though only one was built, it underwent frequent modifications and changes of configuration. Markings also changed often, so the different numbers seen in photographs that have leaked out of Russia since the end of the Cold War convey the erroneous suggestion that there were multiple KMs.

The Monster came to its death in December 1980 when it crashed on takeoff in high seas. The biggest Ekranoplan in history was written off as a total loss, but it was not the end for big Soviet WIG craft.

Orlan

The technological successor to the huge KM was the substantially smaller A90.150 Orlan (Orlyonok) Ekranoplan. Weighing 125 tons, the Orlan was also developed and produced in Gorky by the Alexeiev Central Hydrofoil Design Bureau. The first flight occurred on the Volga River in 1973, and a total of five craft were eventually built. Plans to build more than 100 Orlans were apparently shelved after a 1974 crash with some high-ranking passengers aboard. The first operational Orlan finally joined the Soviet navy in 1979. During the 1980s, Orlan Class vehicles were observed in the overall gray livery of the Soviet Navy and the blue and white colors of Aeroflot, the Soviet (now Russian) airline.

The Orlan Class vehicles had a cruising speed of 250

mph—much greater than any hovercraft—and a range of 1,250 miles. The Orlans were powered by two Kuibyshev NK-8 jet engines, which provided lift by directing their blast downward and aft, under the winglets. Forward motion is delivered by two Kuibyshev NK-12 turboprops mounted in the vertical tail surfaces that drive two huge contra-rotating propellers. They were 188 feet long, with a payload capacity of over 20 tons and a passenger capacity of up to 150 in a single-deck configuration. One double-decked Orlan existed and was capable of carrying 300 passengers. Though originally envisioned as troop transports, at least one of the craft was configured as an offensive warship designed to carry SS-22 antiship missiles.

It is believed that the Russian navy continued using the Orlans until the autumn of 1993, after which they were parked outside, open to the weather, at a naval base and allowed to deteriorate.

Lun

At the same time that they were developing the Orlan Ekranoplan transport craft, the Alexeiev Design Bureau was also working on an offensive WIG craft for the Soviet navy. The long-planned but often-delayed construction of the first Lun Class Ekranoplan warship began in 1983. The initial "flight" tests began on the Volga River in July 1986 but moved to the Caspian Sea in 1987. Larger than the Orlan, the Lun was like the earlier KM, and like it, was powered by a brace of eight jet engines. In the case of the Lun, these were Kuibyshev NK-87 turbofans. Lun was distinguishable from other Ekranoplans by its having three pairs of missile launching tubes arrayed atop its fuselage.

Only one Lun was built, although a second one was partially complete when a tentative decision was made in 1991 to convert it to a search-and-rescue Ekranoplan under the name Spasatel. According to reports, the original Lun was damaged in an accident on the Caspian Sea and the Spasatel was mothballed before completion and has remained virtually untouched in the Alexeiev facility for more than a decade.

Since the Cold War, Alexeiev has moved on to its eight-passenger Volga 2 commercial Ekranoplans. Meanwhile, companies in Germany and elsewhere are adapting the once-secret world of WIG craft for possible commercial applications.

Sea Shadow

In 1988, when the U.S. Air Force officially revealed the appearance of the Lockheed F-117 stealth fighter aircraft, the existence of such an aircraft had been known for 8 years. As discussed in chapter 10, the details of the F-117 had been a closely held secret, but it had been generally known since 1980 that the United States had been working on the technology to produce aircraft that were virtually invisible to radar.

While observers knew that stealth aircraft were in the pipeline during the last decade of the Cold War, few imagined that Lockheed and the U.S. Navy were also developing a stealth warship.

Work on the stealth warship project was undertaken during the mid-1980s in a joint project involving the Defense Advanced Research Projects Agency (DARPA), the Navy and Lockheed Missiles & Space Company. The result was the ship known as *Sea Shadow* (IX-529), which had an appearance unlike any military ship ever seen. It incorporated the Small Water Plane Area Twin Hull (SWATH) design, in which the hull, which looked somewhat like the forward fuselage of the F-117, was suspended above the water on angled pontoons. The faceted, flat black surfaces of the *Sea Shadow* were completely smooth. Any protruding antenna or weapon would have dramatically increased the vessel's radar signature.

The *Sea Shadow* was constructed in absolute secrecy inside the enormous Hughes Mining Barge (HMB-1), moored at Redwood City, California, near the Lockheed

Missiles & Space Company headquarters at Sunnyvale.

During the Cold War, sea trials were conducted on San Francisco Bay and in the Pacific only at night. The ship slipped under the Golden Gate Bridge in the moonlit darkness and returned to its lair inside the Hughes Mining Barge—like a character in a Hollywood vampire movie—before daylight.

Powered by a diesel electric engine with a twin-screw diesel electronic drive, the ship was 164 feet long, with a beam of 68 feet, a draft of 14.5 feet and a displacement of 560 tons. It was designed to be operated by a crew of eight to ten.

The existence of the strange ship was finally officially revealed in April 1993, as the Navy began daylight testing of *Sea Shadow* off the coast of southern California. A year later, the *Sea Shadow* was integrated into naval battle group exercises. Both the *Sea Shadow* and the Hughes Mining Barge were relocated to a new home port at Naval Station San Diego by the end of 1994.

The operation of the ship has generally been at the hands of a specialized crew from Lockheed (Lockheed Martin since 1994), though newly developed onboard combat systems such as the Automated Combat Identification System (ACIDS) and the Tactical Action Advisor (TAA) are almost certainly manned by U.S. Navy personnel.

For five years, the *Sea Shadow* was officially laid up in San Diego, but in 1999 the ship was reactivated in order to provide a test platform for technology that the U.S. Navy hoped to incorporate into its DD-21 21st Century Land Attack Destroyer development program. Once again based on San Francisco Bay, the *Sea Shadow* took part in the Third Fleet's Battle Experiment Echo in 1999 and Battle Experiment Hotel in 2000. The *Sea Shadow* was also used for DARPA's High Performance Distributed Experiment (HiPer-D) program.

The vessel's SWATH technology has been adapted for the somewhat more conventional Victorious and Impeccable Classes of T-AGOS ocean surveillance ships. Some of the low-observable technology pioneered by the *Sea Shadow* design has also been incorporated into the recent Arleigh Burke Class destroyers. Having been aboard such ships, the author has noted that many of the bulkhead surfaces that are traditionally vertical are now slanted, a method for helping to deflect radar.

CHAPTER 14

Unorthodox Weapons

WHEN DISCUSSING UNORTHODOX WEAPONS, ONE MOVES through the gray area of plausible deniability to the dark world of the *The X-Files* that may or may not exist. Even those in the military refer to these programs on the dark side as "black" programs. Arguably, this is the world where the real secret weapons are kept. These are the things that the public does not know about—and where those who do know would be summarily executed for revealing their secrets.

Among the weapons and tactics developed during the Cold War, there are some which defy categorization and some which defy belief. Some, such as Project Stargate, are cases of truth being stranger than fiction. Others, such as MK-Ultra are cases of truth and fiction being so intertwined with one another that history is left with a virtually indecipherable hybrid. Other very strange, rumored Cold War weapons and programs are probably fiction, but nobody is completely sure.

Hollywood loves these mysterious projects, and its creative minds have probably created a much larger "black" world than really existed. It was into this imaginary world that the aliens from that July 1947 crash at Roswell, New Mexico, were taken. It was here that the "alien autopsy" was conducted, and this is the place that the dozen people said to comprise the "Majestic 12" wanted to be kept secret. If there really *was* something to be kept secret here, it still is.

Majestic-12 (MJ-12) is alleged to have been a high-level secret committee that was established by President Harry Truman in 1952 to oversee the investigation of Unidentified Flying Objects. The existence of Majestic 12 has been consistently denied by official sources, but widely discussed by those interested in the theory that UFOs are of extraterrestrial origin. According to the conspiracy theories, members of Majestic 12 included scientists such as J. Robert Oppenheimer and Edward Teller, as well as Defense Secretary James Forrestal and Air Force officers General Nathan F. Twining and Hoyt Vandenberg. The chairman is said to have been Dr. Vannevar Bush, a former president of the Carnegie Institute and a former chairman of the National Advisory Committee for Aeronautics and of the National Defense Research Committee, who served as director of Office of Scientific Research and Development, which controlled the Manhattan Project during World War II. No hard evidence confirming the existence of Majestic 12 has ever been made public.

A belief in the reality of the Roswell story presupposes the existence of technology beyond the comprehension of human inventors because it came to us—albeit by accident—from a world where intelligent life would have mastered the ability to travel throughout the galaxy with ease. On the other hand, other strange weapons used technology that was much more basic, even if it was taken to ridiculous lengths. Take, for example, an actual—but little known—secret program from the 1960s that would have involved placing an enormous mirror in geosynchronous orbit over Vietnam. The purpose would have been to focus the reflection of the sun on the battlefield at night.

Some secret projects, such as Igloo White, are notable as cases where enormous resources were devoted to various unorthodox secret programs that were truly unorthodox. The prevailing mystery of Igloo White is why so much time, talent and treasure was devoted to something that was so unlikely to succeed. However, before we write this sort of project off as folly, we should remember that a great many important discoveries have come from creative minds operating "outside the box."

This chapter discusses a mere handful of the many strange secret projects—and rumored secret projects—that were perused during the Cold War.

Igloo White

Now largely forgotten, although it was publicly documented in the late 1970s, the Igloo White project was a poster child for one of these "most secret and most unusual" programs. Indeed, some aspects were not declassified until the late 1990s and many details of Igloo White are still classified.

The idea behind Igloo White was to use miniaturized sensors to monitor foot and vehicle traffic on the Ho Chi Minh Trail, a network of infiltration routes that reached into southern and central South Vietnam from North Vietnam by way of Laos and Cambodia. These sensors were air-dropped onto the trail disguised as twigs and pieces of detritus that would blend into a mountainous jungle environment.

So sophisticated were these sensors that they could detect not only the noise and the vibration of passing vehicles, but things as subtle as body heat. The Doppler effect of multiple sensors could also determine the direction that a vehicle or person was moving. These data could theoretically be relayed to attack aircraft, which could then attack the site without seeing the target visually.

The proposal for this far-fetched scheme reached the desk of Secretary of Defense Robert McNamara in the autumn of 1966. Being enamored with the potential of any emerging advanced technology, McNamara ordered that the project be implemented and given a high priority. As it was being developed, the project was known variously as

Air Launched Acoustical Reconnaissance (ALARS) or
Trails & Roads Interdiction, Multisensor (TRIM).

The sensors themselves were based on the air-dropped
sounding buoys (sonobuoys) that were then used by the
U.S. Navy to track Soviet submarines. The idea was to apply the same process to land operations. The first sensors
were acoustic buoys (acoubuoys). Sonobuoys recorded the
acoustic "signatures" of the sounds of the engines and propellers of various Soviet submarine types. The recordings
were kept in libraries and used to identify and track Soviet
vessels and monitor Soviet technology.

During Igloo White, the Americans built their "library"
ahead of time by recording the sounds of captured North
Vietnamese vehicles on various types of roadways to use
as a reference for evaluating data from the sensors.

Acoubuoys were only one of the types of sensors that
were included in the project. While the acoubuoys detected
sound, other sensors detected vibration and others monitored temperature anomalies. Some sensors were tiny,
while others were several inches square and weighed several pounds. They were very sophisticated for the time,
given the fact that they had to be designed to distinguish
between the sound and/or vibration of a user of the trail,
versus distant thunder or artillery fire. Tens of thousands of
the sensing devices would be manufactured and sent overseas through 1972.

The sensors were designed to be air-dropped at very low
altitudes over the jungle trails, a process that was not always easy, but often dangerous. Initially, the sensors were
sown by a dozen Lockheed P2V Neptune patrol aircraft assigned to a secret U.S. Navy "observation" squadron designated as VO-67 (OBSRON 67) that operated under code
name Sophomore between November 1967 and June 1968.
Seven Neptunes were also operated by the U.S. Air Force
under the designation B-69.

In 1967 and early 1968, the Navy operated under such
operational code names as Dye Marker and Muscle Shoals.

It was not until the U.S. Air Force took over the management of the project in June 1968 that the Igloo White code name was assigned. The Air Force 21st Special Operations Squadron used H-3 helicopters to sow the sensors, although fixed-wing aircraft continued to be utilized. South Vietnamese troops also placed many of the sensors by hand.

One of the amazing features of Igloo While was its scale. Eventually, Igloo White would be funded to the tune of a billion dollars annually (more than five times that in today's dollars). It ran from 1967 to 1972, headquartered in the largest building in southeast Asia, a place known as the Infiltration Surveillance Center (ISC). This massive facility at the Royal Thai air base at Nakhon Phanom (aka Naked Phantom) was also the largest computer and data processing center in southeast Asia during these years.

The transmitters on the sensors had a relatively short, 20-mile range, so the data from the sensors were relayed to Nakhon Phanom by aircraft flying over the Ho Chi Minh Trail. For this purpose and for detecting targets on their own, the Navy Neptunes were equipped with APQ-92 search radar, an airborne moving-target indicator and Black Crow vehicle-ignition detectors. They were also equipped with SUU-11 Gatling gun pods, 40mm M149 automatic grenade launchers and bombs for attacking targets along the trail.

After the Air Force took over management of the sensor program, Navy Neptunes of Attack Squadron 21 (VAH-21/HATRON-21) continued to fly coordinated attack missions from Cam Ranh Bay until June 1969.

From 1968 through 1971, the Air Force data relay missions were flown by the EC-121R Batcats of the 553rd Reconnaissance Wing, based at Korat RTAFB in Thailand. Each was equipped with eight ARR-52 data receivers for "listening" to the sensors hidden below. Typical Batcat missions involved 12 hours of flight time, most of it spent overflying the Ho Chi Minh Trail, recording and transmitting data from the sensors. In order to ensure seamless coverage, each EC-121R would remain on station over the trail until the next one arrived from Korat to take over.

In 1970, the EC-121R Batcats were replaced by the smaller Beechcraft QU-22 Quackers in the Igloo White operations. Deployed under Operation Pave Eagle, the QU-22s were assigned to the 554th Reconnaissance Wing at Udorn RTAFB. They would eventually replace the Batcats and continue the relay operation through 1972. The Q prefix is an indication of an Air Force plan to fly the Quackers by remote control on the Igloo White mission, although it is believed that all of the operational missions were flown by on-board human pilots.

The data from the Batcats and Quackers went back to the climate-controlled ISC, where a staff numbering in the hundreds worked with a huge mass of IBM 360 and IBM 2400 mainframe computers to evaluate the data. The total computing power at the ISC was virtually unmatched at that time anywhere in the world. The IBM 2250 monitors displayed detailed views of the Ho Chi Minh trail on which individual sensors tracked individual infiltrators who could not imagine the technology that kept track of them. So capable were the big IBMs that they could tell how fast vehicles were traveling and the weight of their loads.

Ideally, the information could then be relayed to attack aircraft—including AC-47, AC-119 or AC-130 gunships or F-4 Phantom fighter bombers—which could strike quickly before the enemy "got away." This worked well in theory, but often times, even though the staff at the ISC could "see" an enemy, the process of getting bombs on the target was delayed by the necessity of sending a request for targeting authority through the chain of command.

Even today, it is hard to determine the effectiveness of Igloo White. Because of the nature of the jungle terrain, and of the targets, aerial reconnaissance photos documented little serious damage. Igloo White–related damage assessments at the time were little more than guesses.

It is known that the enemy was very adaptive. They found many of the sensors and learned how to distort the data being streamed back to the ISC. Furthermore, a great deal of enemy material continued to reach South Vietnam throughout the Igloo White period. The enemy continued to push a substantial volume through the Ho Chi Minh Trail using feet and bicycle traffic instead of motor vehicles. The bikes were detectable, but virtually impossible to hit from the air.

The final assessment is that Igloo White may have made it harder for the enemy to use the Ho Chi Minh Trail, but it never stopped them. One of the most technologically advanced battlefield programs of its era, it became a case study in why and how a system that depends on high technology can be overcome by people on the ground. As would be demonstrated to the United States forces in Afghanistan a generation later, an enemy on foot can be injured by high technology, but they cannot be reliably neutralized—except by foot soldiers.

Igloo White was not an overall success, certainly not sufficiently so to justify the price tag. What it did provide was a test case in the dos and don'ts of high-technology warfare.

Unsuspecting Subjects

The history of clandestine operations during the Cold War is filled with incidents of secret weapons being tested on unsuspecting civilians. Both the United States and the Soviet Union did it within their own territory, although incidents within the United States are better documented within the public record.

During the Cold War, there was a constant fear on both sides that the other would unleash a chemical or biological attack. It was mutually understood that the other side had, if not necessarily the will, certainly the capability to covertly launch such attacks. Such weapons are particularly insidious in that they are silent killers, impossible to see or hear, and difficult to detect or to track—until it is too late. As with other weapons, defense against chemical and biological agents required understanding them, and this required testing them.

In 1977, it was reveled during Senate hearings on health

and scientific research that various United States government agencies had tested biological agents in domestic populated areas between 1949 and 1969. These tests primarily involved low-threat chemical and biological agents and were designed to determine the patterns by which the germs spread in order to plan ways to defend against a covert attack by the Soviet Union.

For example, between 1950 and 1953, the CIA and the Department of Defense released nonlethal bacteria over San Francisco, New York and other cities and had monitored infection rates. In the late 1950s, similar tests were done in Florida, and in 1966, the New York City subway system was the subject of a bacterialogical experiment.

It is widely assumed that there were other projects that still remain secret. Rumors still circulate and from time to time something purported to be "documentary evidence" surfaces. Generally, it is impossible to sort out fact from rumor, or deliberate disinformation from idle conjecture.

This dark forest of little-known and officially unconfirmed projects also includes the MK family of chemical weapons defense programs. MK programs mostly seem to embody some aspects of mind control, which became a topic of interest after United States service personnel were brainwashed during the Korean War. Having had its own people subjected to mind control, the United States armed forces and intelligence community sought to explore and understand it both to be able to turn the tables and to defend against it in the future.

Based on what information is in circulation, MK-Delta seems to have been an effort to use long-range, high-frequency, VHF and UHF radio waves to transmit subliminal messages to human beings for behavior-programming purposes. MK-Naomi has been variously described as a biological- and/or chemical-warfare program and an effort to stockpile such agents. One particularly strange conspiracy theory in circulation at the turn of the century associated MK-Naomi with a deliberate effort in the early 1970s to create what is now known as the human immunodeficiency virus (HIV). MK-Search and MK-Ultra, discussed below, are rumored to have been the cover designations for experiments conducted in the 1950s and 1960s with mind-altering drugs.

MK-Ultra

MK-Ultra is described in a large number of conspiracy theories as having been a CIA mind-control program that was initiated during the Korean War, certainly active by 1953 and in business until at least 1964. MK-Ultra is said to have been headquartered at the U.S. Army's Camp Detrick in Maryland, and to have been headed by Dr. Sydney Gottlieb. The centerpiece of MK-Ultra is rumored to have been a series of human experiments using various drugs, including heroin and sodium pentothal—better known as "truth serum"—as well as the hallucinogenic drug Lysergic Acid Diethylamide (LSD).

First synthesized in Switzerland in 1938 by Albert Hofmann at the laboratories of the Sandoz pharmaceutical company (now a division of Novartis AG) as a circulatory and respiratory stimulant, LSD was not known to be hallucinogenic until 1943. Considered as a possible treatment for schizophrenia, LSD was studied clinically through the 1950s. Dr. Timothy Leary of Harvard University discovered LSD in the 1960s, and was soon advocating its use on "trips" of self-discovery. Beginning in about 1966, illicit LSD would rapidly become the drug of choice for the growing counterculture movement.

On the other hand, the LSD experience has been likened to a form of artificial madness. Throughout the Middle Ages, there were widespread incidents of mass madness called St. Anthony's Fire. This phenomenon was later attributed to LSD, which is found in the ergot mold that forms on rye bread. A well-documented case of St. Anthony's Fire struck the population of the French village of Pont-Saint-Esprit in 1951.

CIA and U.S. Army studies of LSD are generally

thought to have occurred throughout the 1950s, possibly under the umbrella of MK-Ultra. The subjects of these experiments are said to have included CIA employees and military personnel, as well as prostitutes, mental patients, and members of the general public. While some were told that they were taking LSD, it is believed that most were unaware that they had consumed this tasteless and colorless substance.

The results of the tests varied because the hallucinations were unpredictable and could not be accurately documented. It is believed that some of the LSD experiments ended with the subject committing suicide. The first of these incidents is said to have involved Dr. Frank Olson, who jumped to his death from a tenth floor hotel window in New York City in November 1953. Other theories about Olson's death suggest that he was murdered.

Apparently, not all of these LSD experiences were bad. Gottlieb himself is thought to have taken the drug several dozen times. Of course, he was probably never an unsuspecting subject.

It has been said that most of the official MK-Ultra documentation was destroyed in about 1972 on the orders of CIA Director Richard Helms, but there is no firm evidence of this. Five years later, individuals alleged to have been involved with MK-Ultra testified before Congress, but the proverbial smoking gun was never made available. Dr. Sydney Gottlieb died in 1999 at the age of eighty having never confirmed the existence of the project.

Since the end of the Cold War, speculation has continued to swirl around MK-Ultra and its fellow MK programs and they have become staples of conspiracy theoreticians. Just as LSD moved from the laboratory to counterculture and pop culture in the 1960s, MK-Ultra has moved from the darkened recesses of the clandestine services to the world of turn-of-the-century pop culture. Between 1994 and 1999, MK-Ultra was adopted as the name of a West Coast rock band.

Back in the USSR

In terms of the cultural history of the years that coincided with the Cold War, few single factors were more far reaching and more important than a rock band from Liverpool, England known as the Beatles. They were arguably the most important and popular musical phenomenon in the twentieth century. They came together by chance to form an almost alchemical reaction that could be seen, heard and felt, yet could not be fully understood. They were the catalyst that launched a youth culture among baby boomers that helped change numerous aspects of Western society. Even in the twenty-first century, the influence of the body of work that they created between 1962 and 1970 is an indelible presence in both popular music and popular culture.

Having said all this—and it was said ad infinitum during the last four decades of the twentieth century—few people would stretch the hyperbole far enough to refer to the Beatles as secret weapons of the Cold War—at least not seriously. However, the few who did refer to the Beatles as such were in the Kremlin.

Recently, Dr. Yuri Pelyoshonok, a Soviet-born Canadian academic, revealed that he found evidence in Soviet Cold War–era archives that indicates that the Soviet Union interpreted the Beatles as a secret weapon because Soviet youth "lost their interest in all Soviet unshakable dogmas and ideals, and stopped thinking of English-speaking persons as the enemy."

Stargate

For those who lived through the 1970s, it is hard to forget either the Cold War or the popular culture fascination with a variety of occult practices. It was a decade before the term *New Age* entered the popular lexicon, but buzz words like Extra-Sensory Perception (ESP) were commonly seen in supermarket checkout lines.

Among the myriad books that graced the best-seller lists during this wave of psychic fascination was *Psychic Discoveries Behind the Iron Curtain* by Sheila Ostrander and Lynn

Schroeder, which was published in 1973. Among the phenomena that the book added to pop mythology was "Kirlian photography," in which visual images of a person's "aura" can be captured on film. While one must take most of these "discoveries" with a grain of salt, the book was important insofar as it stated that the Soviet government was officially taking psychic phenomena seriously. Whatever one wishes to believe about Kirlian photography, this much was true: The Soviets really were investigating the weapons and espionage applications of psychic phenomena.

This fact was not news, however, for United States intelligence services. As early as the mid-1960s, word had leaked out that the Soviet Union was looking at ESP. As the CIA monitored various Soviet programs, they discovered that the budgetary outlays for psychic research would more than quadruple between 1970 and 1975.

Not to be outdone, and perhaps fearing a "psychic gap" if ESP was real, the CIA quickly got into the business of investigating ESP. So, too, did the Department of Defense's Defense Intelligence Agency. However, the American agencies chose to refer to these as "remote viewing" programs, rather than as ESP programs. Perhaps the latter term was a bit too much a part of the pop occultist culture for the government agents.

There were a number of separate remote-viewing projects ongoing behind the secret walls of the American services during the 1970s. Inside the Department of Defense, there were Project Sun Streak and Project Center Lane. The U.S. Army also had remote viewing operations called Gondola Wish and Project Grill Frame. The principal CIA remote-viewing programs seem to have been those which were code-named Scanate and Stargate.

The United States government remote-viewing research enlisted the services of the Stanford Research Institute of Menlo Park, California. In ESP, there are said to be practitioners who are particularly gifted in mind reading, so the initial objective of the program was to identify persons that were thus gifted.

Apparently, remote viewing was used literally hundreds of times by both the CIA and the United States armed services from the mid-1970s though the end of the Cold War and beyond. It has been admitted that most of the things "seen" by the "seers" were erroneous, but the government psychics are credited with having been accurate on several occasions. Among these were the 1974 identification of a Soviet nuclear test site near Semipalatinsk and the location of the crash site of a Soviet bomber in Africa. In the latter case, the psychic is said to have been off by only a few miles in naming the coordinates. In 1979, a psychic is said to have correctly described a new type of Soviet submarine that had not yet been launched, and which would not be observed by photo reconnaisance for four months. During Gulf War I, however, the government psychics are said to have failed to locate Iraqi Scud missile sites and other high-value targets.

An official 1995 analysis would determine that the remote-viewing practitioners had been right about 15 percent of the time, which is considered to have been greater than would have met the laws of probability for random guesses.

The United States remote-viewing projects remained completely secret until 1984, when news of them began to leak out. Despite the ridicule heaped upon America's clandestine agencies, supporters in Congress, such as Claiborne Pell of Rhode Island and Charles Rose of North Carolina, continued to support Stargate and the other projects with encouragement and appropriations.

Perhaps it is significant that it took Hollywood until 1994 to adapt the code name Stargate as a movie title. One would suppose that you'd have to be a mind reader to figure out why that was.

CHAPTER 15

Nuclear-Powered Vehicles

THE POWER OF THE NUCLEAR ENERGY THAT ENDED WORLD War II in 1945 was frightening and promising. Having achieved nuclear fission, the scientific community imagined that it was on the threshold of unlocking the secrets of the universe. On a more practical level, nuclear fission promised a bright future. The Atomic Age had arrived. It was now theoretically possible to generate all electric power using nuclear energy and that such power would be virtually limitless.

In a speech to the General Assembly of the United Nations on December 8, 1953, President Dwight Eisenhower outlined the doctrine of Atoms for Peace, an initiative for bending the destructive power of the nuclear sword into a powerful plowshare for the peaceful service of humanity.

Meanwhile, nuclear energy was being imagined as not only powerful, but economical. Consumers were told that in the future—which meant by the middle 1960s—nuclear power would be so cheap that the electric meters at everyone's home would be obsolete.

The same was true, at least theoretically, with vehicles. A nuclear-powered vehicle could cruise for years without refueling. While nuclear-powered automobiles might be a bit impractical for the average family, the military saw a great many applications for larger vehicles.

When the euphoria of the potential of nuclear vehicles gave way to the need for practical engineering, it became clear that the major impediment was the shielding necessary for protecting the occupants of the vehicle from the deadly radiation of the nuclear reactor. Ultimately, the only practical nuclear vehicles would be ships and submarines because they could be made large enough to support both the reactor and the necessary shielding.

Early in the Atomic Age—which was coincidently early in the Cold War—there were those who imagined an all-nuclear fleet for the U.S. Navy, but eventually, the only widespread use of nuclear propulsion by either the U.S. Navy or its Soviet counterpart was in submarines. Nuclear propulsion gave the undersea vessels not only great range, but allowed them to approach the dream of all submariners—silent running.

The first nuclear submarine was the USS *Nautilus* (SSN-571), commissioned in 1954, and the first Soviet nuclear submarine was the K-3 (later *Leninski Komsomol*), which was put to sea three years later. The U.S. Navy experimented with nuclear surface ships as well, commissioning its first nuclear cruiser, the USS *Long Beach* (CGN-9) in 1961, but nuclear propulsion for most surface ships was soon deemed unnecessarily complex and expensive. The exception among surface ships would be aircraft carriers. The U.S. Navy commissioned its first, the USS *Enterprise* (CVN-65) in 1961, and at the end of the Cold War, seven were in service. This was in contrast with dozens of nuclear submarines.

With these exceptions, nuclear propulsion for vehicles never fulfilled the promise that it had held at the dawn of the Atomic Age. In large part, it was a matter of expense. The engineering required to make it work in vehicles smaller than enormous oceangoing vessels was too costly.

However, early in the Cold War, money was no object when national defense was at stake, and numerous secret projects were undertaken. Some of these resulted in truly amazing secret weapons.

Nuclear-Powered Aircraft

Shortly after World War II, as the U.S. Navy was working on plans for nuclear ships and submarines, the U.S. Air Force (USAAF until 1947) got into the act with plans for nuclear aircraft. It was more than interservice rivalry—a strategic bomber with unlimited range was the ultimate fulfillment of the doctrine of strategic air power. Accordingly, the Nuclear Energy for Propulsion of Aircraft (NEPA) program was initiated in 1946.

In 1947, the Atomic Energy Commission (AEC), a United States government agency responsible for the development of nuclear reactors, was created. This organization would work up the initial parameters for the design of shipboard nuclear reactors for the Navy, and it would absorb the activities of NEPA as well.

In turn, the commission established the National Reactor Testing Station. It opened in 1949 in a remote location in the lightly populated high-desert country of southern Idaho near the town of Arco.

In 1951, the commission decided that it was theoretically possible to produce a reactor for an airplane. The problem, of course, would be the size and weight of the reactor, as well as its radiation shield and cooling system. Therefore, it would have to be a very large airplane.

Because no one had ever designed a nuclear-powered aircraft before, the development process would be methodical, moving step by step. Before a nuclear-powered strategic bomber could become an operational reality, a nuclear-powered experimental aircraft would have to be tested as a proof-of-concept demonstrator. This aircraft would be built under the designation X-6.

Before the X-6 could fly, however, it was necessary to build and fly a functioning nuclear reactor aboard a conventional aircraft in order to evaluate shielding techniques.

As a reactor test bed for the eventual X-6, the U.S. Air Force chose the largest aircraft in its fleet, the enormous Convair B-36 bomber. First flown in 1946, the B-36 was

162 feet long, with a wing span of 230 feet—a larger wing span than any other military aircraft ever in service in the United States. It was powered by six Pratt & Whitney R4360 Wasp Major piston engines with 21,000 aggregate horsepower, and later models would also have four General Electric J47 turbojet engines. Even without the jets, the B-36 could take off with a quarter-million pounds of gross weight and fly more than 8,000 miles.

Early in 1951, as the AEC undertook the construction of the first airborne nuclear reactor, designated as R-1, the Air Force ordered Convair to specially modify a B-36 test-bed aircraft under the designation NB-36H. Convair was also given the contract to modify a pair of B-36s that would become the first two nuclear-powered X-6 aircraft. The NB-36H would simply fly with a functioning reactor aboard. The X-6s would fly under nuclear power, with the R-1 reactor powering General Electric turbojet engines. The total propulsion system, incorporating the reactor and engines, was designated as P-1.

The design of the propulsion system would allow the engines to transition between nuclear power and jet fuel, permitting a conventionally fueled takeoff followed by an extremely long cruise under reactor power. Nuclear cruise would easily permit a flight around the world.

Meanwhile, work was under way to construct a test base for the X-6 program. While the NB-36H flights were conducted from Carswell AFB—across the runway from the Convair factory near Fort Worth, Texas—the Air Force wanted a location for the X-6 project that was farther from the prying eyes of just anyone. The site chosen for what was to be designated as Test Area North was near the small town of Monteview, in the Idaho desert, about 40 miles northeast of the AEC National Reactor Testing Station.

The huge hangar that was constructed at Test Area North had thick, lead-lined walls and was designed to contain radiation if necessary. General Electric moved its nuclear power plant operations here and installed robotic equipment so that work could be done on the engines and reactors without exposing humans.

The plan was that the first X-6 flight would come in 1957. The first operational nuclear bomber would, in turn, follow the X-6 in the early 1960s. The first operational wing of such aircraft was to be in service in 1964. Not only Convair, but Boeing, Douglas and Lockheed were invited to submit proposals for the development of these bombers.

Late in 1951, the Air Force made a change in the X-6 test bed, deciding to replace the B-36 with the Convair B-60. The latter was essentially a swept-wing version of the B-36 that was powered by eight Pratt & Whitney J57 turbojets. The first of these aircraft had already been built and was scheduled to fly in the spring of 1952. The nuclear-powered version of the J57 would be the P-3. These changes did not affect the construction of the NB-36H, which was then under way.

In 1953, however, the incoming Eisenhower administration revisited the concept of nuclear-powered aircraft and terminated the X-6 program. The conventional B-60 program would also get the ax, as the U.S. Air Force chose to acquire the Boeing B-52 instead. Once again, though, the NB-36H remained a live program, as did numerous feasibility studies for nuclear-powered operational aircraft for the future. While the X-6 was not to be the first of this new breed, the concept of a nuclear-powered aircraft remained alive and well.

At Test Area North, work on the 15,000-foot runway that was planned for the X-6 program was not begun, but the other work continued. In 1955, the AEC initiated a series of Heat Transfer Reactor Experiments at Test Area North's big nuclear-shielded hangar. These experiments were part of the ongoing development of airborne nuclear power plants, but the engines tested were much larger than the P-1 that had been earmarked for the X-6. The idea was to refine the concept, then scale down the reactor. The goal was a thermal output of at least 50 megawatts delivered by a reactor the size of the one-megawatt reactor that would be test-flown in the NB-36H.

Also in 1955, the NB-36H was finally ready for its debut. Except for a completely redesigned nose section, it was similar in outward appearance to a conventional B-36. Inside was a different story. The gross weight had been pushed up to 360,000 pounds. The one-megawatt reactor itself weighed nearly 18 tons, and the crew shield—consisting of lead plates and water tanks—added another 24,000 pounds.

The first flight of the NB-36H occurred on September 17, 1955, and the first top-secret flight tests of an airborne nuclear reactor were soon under way. These missions were considered so sensitive that on every flight, the NB-36H was accompanied by a transport aircraft carrying paratroopers. Should the NB-36H have crashed, or been forced to land at a civilian airport because of mechanical difficulties, it would be the job of the paratroopers to surround the aircraft and prevent any unauthorized individuals from reaching it.

During eighteen months of flight testing, all phases of airborne nuclear-reactor operations—from shielding to power output—were evaluated. When the NB-36H made its 47th and last flight on March 28, 1957, sufficient data now existed to move ahead to the next phase of nuclear-aircraft development.

Back in the remote Idaho desert, the Heat Transfer Reactor Experiments continued both during and after the NB-36H flight test program. A test reactor assembly designated as HTRE-1 had been built and first tested in 1955. A water-cooled uranium reactor, HTRE weighed more than 100 tons and was mounted on a rail car. It also demonstrated a power output in excess of 20 megawatts. Over the coming years, it was rebuilt several times. In its HTRE-3 configuration, it generated as much as 35 megawatts.

The HTRE-3 was also optimized for weight savings, using light aluminum structural components and hydrided zirconium as a moderator. The HTRE-3 experiments were conducted between April 1958 and December 1960, with the goal being a flight-ready hybrid turbojet-nuclear engine. Built by General Electric, this power plant reportedly would have been designated as XNJ140, with the three letters standing for Experimental Nuclear Turbojet.

At this point in history, the next step would have been to select an airframe design from the several that had been submitted by various aircraft makers, and to proceed with the new engine as had been originally planned with the P-1/X-6. However, three months after the HTRE-3 tests ended, the incoming Kennedy administration ordered the airborne nuclear-propulsion program to be terminated. Secretary of Defense Robert McNamara had little enthusiasm for manned bombers of any kind. He was fascinated with the potential of ICBMs and wanted the Air Force to pursue this line of strategic thinking.

During the remainder of the twentieth century, nuclear propulsion for aircraft would not again be examined officially in the same depth as it had under the X-6 umbrella. However, late in the Cold War, as Single-Stage-to-Orbit (SSTO) spaceplanes were being studied, the notion of nuclear power often seemed to worm its way into a footnote here or there. The well-publicized X-30 National Aerospace Plane (NASP) concept, as well as secret programs such as Science Dawn and Science Realm, generally relied on conventional rocket propulsion.

Test Area North remained an active site even as the Cold War finally came to an end, and the National Reactor Testing Station (now known as the Idaho National Engineering and Environmental Laboratory) is still in operation.

Soviet Nuclear-Powered Aircraft

While the Soviet Union never explored nuclear propulsion for aircraft to the extent that the United States did, this fact would have surprised intelligence analysts during the 1950s. It was widely believed in the secret circles of Western espionage that the Soviet Union was not only working to build a nuclear-powered strategic bomber, but that such a project had moved more quickly than the X-6 program in the United States.

By the autumn of 1958, the United States had test flown the NB-36H with its nuclear reactor and work was still under way in the Idaho desert on a functioning nuclear powerplant. Meanwhile, a year had now passed since the Soviet Union had beaten the United States into orbital space flight with the Sputnik family of satellites. This demonstration of technological prowess led Western intelligence to fear that if the Soviets were ahead in space, they could easily be ahead in nuclear propulsion. Then came the bombshell.

A secret photograph had been taken and it was handed to President Dwight Eisenhower. It showed a large, sleek aircraft with a pencil-shaped fuselage and four engines arrayed on its delta wing. This, the president was told, was the Soviet nuclear aircraft, and it was already being flight tested.

The December 1, 1958, issue of *Aviation Week* magazine carried the report that "A nuclear-powered bomber is being flight tested in the Soviet Union. Completed about six months ago, this aircraft has been flying in the Moscow area for at least two months. It has been observed both in flight and on the ground by a wide variety of foreign observers." The media quickly spread the story of this new technological breakthrough from the Soviet Union.

Though it would not be confirmed for more than a year, the airplane in the photograph and in the articles was not a nuclear-powered aircraft, but the conventional turbojet Myasishchev M-50. The M-50 prototype, code-named Bounder by NATO, would be flight tested through the early 1960s, but never put into production. After the end of the Cold War, the prototype that had caused such a fuss in 1958 was put on public display at the Monino Air Museum near Moscow.

Project Pluto

While the development of a nuclear/turbojet aircraft engine had been one of the first ongoing Department of Defense programs eliminated by the incoming Kennedy administration in 1961, a similar program involving a hybrid of nuclear and ramjet power continued through Kennedy's entire presidency and beyond.

A ramjet engine operates on the principle of "ramming" large volumes of air through its intake at high speed. It can theoretically accelerate to higher speeds than a turbojet, but it functions well only after it has been taken to high speed by other means, such as by a rocket engine. Hence, a ramjet is less versatile and adaptable than a turbojet, and it is impractical for most applications except where very high speed is required. Such applications include high-speed cruise missiles.

Project Pluto was a supersecret project undertaken in 1957 with the goal of producing a nuclear ramjet engine for use in a cruise missile. The work began at the Atomic Energy Commission's Lawrence Radiation Laboratory (now known as the Lawrence Livermore National Laboratory) under the auspices of the U.S. Air Force. Pluto soon outgrew the confines of the Lawrence lab in the foothills east of San Francisco and was moved a new site that was constructed for it at Jackass Flats in the sprawling Nevada Test Site complex owned and operated by the Atomic Energy Commission.

The Project Pluto engineers in Nevada faced challenges similar to those dogging the Heat Transfer Reactor Experiment team working on an aircraft powerplant in the Idaho desert—size and weight. Aside from this, the applications had very different aspects. Whereas the nuclear aircraft engine had to be reliably used over and over, the nuclear ramjet cruise missile would be used for just one 7,000-mile, one-way trip to the Soviet Union. Furthermore, a nuclear-powered bomber would have a crew that had to be shielded from radiation. A cruise missile would not have a crew aboard.

Of course, without a shield, such a missile would be very radioactively "dirty." Presumably, a bit of radioactive filth spread along the route would be insignificant if the object of the mission was to attack a target with a nuclear weapon.

The cruise missile itself, known as the Supersonic Low Altitude Missile (SLAM), was to be developed by Vought, the company that was already producing the RGM-6 (formerly SSM-A-8) surface-to-surface cruise missile for the U.S. Navy. Marquardt, a well-known, California-based rocket-motor company, would build the rocket that would accelerate the SLAM to supersonic speed, where the nuclear ramjet would take over. For low-altitude operations, the SLAM would be equipped with the terrain-comparison (TERCOM) guidance system that had earlier been developed for the Air Force's Martin MGM-1 (formerly B-61) Matador cruise missile.

Having described the "what, where and when" of Project Pluto, one might ask the reason "why?" Why would it make sense to develop an extremely radioactive weapon at great expense when ICBMs were then in development that could attack targets in the Soviet Union without flying at low altitude? The answers were several. In 1957, ICBMs were still in their infancy and the concept was not yet proven. For example, the Convair SM-65 Atlas, the early mainstay of the Strategic Air Command ICBM fleet, was not first successfully flown until September 1957. Second, there was still a great deal of concern about improvements in Soviet radar and antiaircraft weapons. Flying low and fast was still a key tactic for going undetected by radar.

In terms of flying low and fast, the United States had a number of first-generation cruise missiles in 1957 that could do this. However, Project Pluto's SLAM could offer what these could not—range, and plenty of it. If the other cruise missiles could fly low and fast, they did so with a robotic eye on the gas gauge. Flying low and fast are two things that drink fuel at a high rate. A conventional cruise missile started out with limited range and had to get to its target by the shortest means possible. The Project Pluto SLAM had no concern about fuel. It could fly for days if necessary, taking any circuitous route that its controllers chose.

Project Pluto finally bore fruit two months after the nuclear-powered aircraft engine program was terminated. On May 14, 1961, the world's first nuclear ramjet engine, code-named Tory IIA, was test fired at Jackass Flats for several seconds. The program continued with renewed enthusiasm, culminating in the spring of 1964 with the Tory IIC test, in which a Project Pluto reactor producing over 500 megawatts of energy for five minutes powered a ramjet at 35,000 pounds of thrust. The next step would have been flight testing the nuclear powered SLAM. Because nobody wanted to be present for the recovery of the vehicle after its first flight, the decision was made to crash the SLAM into a deep ocean trench.

However, by 1964, ICBMs had come into their own and there was no longer a compelling need for SLAM. Those who were squeamish about dirty reactors screaming across the Far West on test flights—or around the globe at treetop level and at three times the speed of sound—finally got their way. Project Pluto was canceled and its radioactive detritus was sealed into long-term storage in the Nevada desert.

The acronym SLAM was too good to let lie dormant. In the late 1980s, when the McDonnell Douglas AGM-84 Harpoon antiship missile was adapted for use against land targets by attack aircraft, it was designated as AGM-84E and given the name Standoff Land Attack Missile, or SLAM.

Project Rover and NERVA

As we've seen, the United States Atomic Energy Commission undertook studies of nuclear propulsion for a wide range of vehicles during the 1950s. Arguably the most ambitious was the one which envisioned nuclear power for virtually unlimited human activities in outer space—beyond Earth orbit.

The notion of nuclear propulsion for space applications

originated as a weapons program in 1955 at the AEC's Los Alamos Scientific Laboratory in New Mexico. Three years later, the program evolved into what would become the effort to develop a space-launch vehicle capable of taking people to Mars.

Project Rover began in 1955 as a U.S. Air Force–sponsored effort to develop a flight-rated, nuclear-rocket engine with 75,000 pounds of thrust. The long-range application would have been for offensive missile applications, but initially Project Rover was a technology feasibility study aimed simply at exploring whether such an engine was possible.

At the same time, another program, code-named Orion, theorized the use of a succession of nuclear explosions to create shock waves that would propel a vehicle through outer space. The obvious downside of such an approach would be that it would leave vast and expanding clouds of radioactive particles and debris in its wake.

In 1958, in response to the sudden Space Race between the United States and the Soviet Union, Congress moved to create the National Aeronautics & Space Administration (NASA), the single federal agency that would serve as the umbrella for all—or at least most—American space activities. Among the programs that NASA inherited was Project Rover.

A high priority for NASA was the development of large rockets for human space-flight activities. Initially, off-the-shelf military rockets were adapted. The U.S. Army Redstone and U.S. Air Force Atlas were adapted for the Project Mercury manned space flights in 1961–1963, and the larger U.S. Air Force Titan was adapted for the subsequent Project Gemini flights in 1965 and 1966. Even as these programs were ongoing, NASA was working on the massive Saturn launch vehicle that would ultimately take Apollo astronauts to the moon. Standing 363 feet tall and powered by engines delivering 7.7 million pounds of thrust at launch, the Saturn V used in the Apollo lunar missions was the largest and most powerful rocket in history.

While Saturn was heavily publicized throughout the 1960s, few people knew that NASA was also working on nuclear propulsion, with an eye to eventually using this huge vehicle for a mission to Mars.

The Nuclear Engine for Rocket Vehicle Application (NERVA) program was officially begun in 1960 as a direct offshoot of Project Rover, which had conducted the first experimental low-power test firing of a nuclear rocket engine, designated as Kiwi A, in July 1959. NERVA was to be managed by the newly created Space Nuclear Propulsion Office, a joint venture of NASA and the AEC. The industrial team of Aerojet General Corporation and Westinghouse Electric had the responsibility to develop the actual hardware. The tests of the hardware were to be conducted at the Nuclear Rocket Development Station at Jackass Flats, Nevada, sharing some of the Project Pluto infrastructure.

A second test, designated as Kiwi A-Prime, was conducted at full power in July 1960. The first of a series of Kiwi B tests was conducted in December 1961. This was followed by an unfolding series of reactor and engine experiments with such colorful code names as Phoebus, Peewee, and Nuclear Furnace. Meanwhile, the parallel Reactor In Flight Test (RIFT) program was also intertwined with NERVA.

Nearly two dozen reactor and rocket engine tests were conducted at the Nuclear Rocket Development Station through 1971, with some engines operating for as long as an hour and a half. These achieved thermal power output up to 4,500 megawatts and thrust up to 250,000 pounds. The latter was significantly less than the thrust of the Saturn V's five engines, but not bad for the test program of a new technology engine.

Meanwhile, in early 1969, NASA officially unveiled its plan to send a six-man crew to the Martian surface. As described in official 1969 NASA documents, six astronauts would rendezvous with the NERVA-powered Mars vehicle in Earth orbit and depart for Mars on November 12, 1981.

They would arrive at Mars on August 9, 1982, and leave the NERVA ship in orbit while they descended to the Martian surface for a 10-week visit. The astronauts would then depart Mars on October 28, 1982; conduct a close flyby of Venus on February 28, 1983; and return to Earth on August 14, 1983.

However, in August 1969, shortly after Apollo 11 first landed on the moon, the Nixon administration quietly canceled the 1981–1983 Mars mission. NERVA continued until 1973, when it, too, was officially canceled.

Timberwind

More than a decade after the cancellation of the NERVA program, the nuclear thermal-propulsion concept for space flight resurfaced as Project Timberwind. Babcock and Wilcox built a subscale reactor for the Brookhaven National Laboratory in approximately 1985 under Project Pipe, and this seems to have been the basis for Timberwind, a "black" project not known outside the Strategic Defense Initiative Organization until April 1991.

It has subsequently been learned that the Timberwind program was initiated in November 1987 by Lieutenant General James Abrahamson, Director of the Strategic Defense Initiative Organization and that it was managed by the Air Force Phillips Laboratory at Kirtland AFB in New Mexico.

The object of Timberwind was to develop a 40 megawatt particle bed reactor (PBR) for space-launch activities. The earlier Project Pipe derived its name from the acronym for Pulsed Irradiation of PBR Fuel Element. Project Pipe had tested a subscale PBR model at the Sandia National Laboratory Annular Core Research Reactor (ACRR) located at Kirtland AFB. These tests investigated the complex thermomechanical PBR fuel element system. Pipe 1, a test conducted in October 1988, achieved a peak output of 1,900 kilowatts. Pipe 2, in July 1989, experienced anomalies not seen earlier and was shut down less than half a minute into the experiment.

Timberwind would use Nuclear Thermal Rockets (NTR) in which rocket fuel, such as hydrogen, flows through a reactor and is heated before flowing through the nozzle. Although the heat is no greater than a typical hydrogen/oxygen chemical rocket, there would be a higher specific impulse because hydrogen has a lower molecular weight than hydrogen plus oxygen.

In the fall of 1990, concepts were delivered to the Strategic Defense Initiative Organization outlining conversion of General Dynamics Atlas or Martin Marietta Titan launch vehicles to Timberwind test beds that would use eight NTRs, each with 250,000 pounds of thrust. This could put up to 70 tons of payload into low-Earth orbit.

Initially, Timberwind was to be the Strategic Defense Initiative Organization's means of launching large numbers of the Brilliant Pebbles interceptors discussed in chapter 16 of this volume. Eventually, other applications were also seriously considered. In July 1991, Stanley Browski at NASA's Nuclear Propulsion Systems Office told the International Conference on Emerging Nuclear Energy Systems that "If you want to initiate major lunar activity where significant amounts of cargo and people are sent to the moon routinely, Nuclear Thermal Rockets can do it more efficiently and cost effectively than chemical rockets."

This was, as the Strategic Defense Initiative Organization would have pointed out, certainly true of Earth orbit, but Browski added the tantalizing promise of Timberwind NRVs doing what NERVA NRVs might have done a decade earlier—send humans on a fast trip to the planet Mars.

Regardless of the potential of NTRs, Timberwind would not long survive the end of the Cold War. On October 18, 1991, the Department of Defense officially approved the termination of the Timberwind program. Apparently, it was a slow death, though. On January 15, 1992, the Air Force Space Technology Test Center at Kirtland AFB formally proposed using Timberwind as a system to make a six-month Mars mission a reality early in the twenty-first century.

CHAPTER 16

Star Wars

THE PHRASE ITSELF IS MISLEADING, AND THE HISTORY OF the technology that it includes predates the term by three decades. Nevertheless, when it was coined in 1983, the buzzwords *Star Wars* would quickly enter the popular lexicon as a synonym for the concept of antiballistic missile (ABM) systems.

The basic premise is rudimentary. It takes no stretch of imagination to perceive intercontinental ballistic missiles armed with thermonuclear bombs as the most terrible weapons of the Cold War. It also is not taxing to the imagination to suppose that the potential victims of an attack by such weapons would want to defend themselves.

In this chapter, we will consider the history of antiballistic missile systems during the Cold War. Essentially, there were two phases to this story. The first culminated in the Anti-Ballistic Missile Treaty of 1972, and the second began in 1983.

During the first period, the United States antiballistic missile programs, specifically Project Sentinel and Project Safeguard, were headed by the U.S. Army and a direct extension of the Army's responsibility for ground-based air defense. During the post-1983 phase, the antiballistic missile program, known as the Strategic Defense Initiative (SDI), would be managed by the Strategic Defense Initiative Organization (SDIO) at the Department of Defense and would involve input from all of the armed services.

The Antiballistic Missile Treaty, properly known as "the Treaty on the Limitation of Antiballistic Missile Systems," was signed in Moscow on May 26, 1972; ratified by the United States Senate on August 3, 1972; and entered into force on October 3, 1972. Under the treaty, the United States and the Soviet Union agreed to restrict their antiballistic missile development so that neither side would have nationwide defensive coverage. The idea was that if one side felt invulnerable, it might decide to attack the other with nuclear weapons. The treaty permitted research, but restricted deployment. Under a protocol to the Treaty, each side was allowed a single antiballistic missile site. The United States Project Safeguard site in North Dakota (discussed below) was deactivated in 1975. The Soviet site complex designed to defend Moscow remained active and on alert past the end of the twentieth century.

Also under the Antiballistic Missile Treaty, early warning radar designed to detect incoming ICBMs was to be located on each nation's periphery and oriented outward to prevent it from being used to aid an offensive strike. By 1983, the Soviet Union was building such radar near Krasnoyarsk, 500 miles from the nearest border. This, combined with other weapons development then known to be occurring inside the Soviet Union, led the United States to reconsider an antiballistic missile system. Though the development, and even testing, of such a system was permissible under the Antiballistic Missile Treaty, the United States had virtually ignored the technology since 1975.

By 1983, the United States was essentially defenseless against a Soviet ICBM attack, while the Soviet Union had a relatively sophisticated, albeit partial, missile-defense system in place. The only defense that the United States had was the threat of retaliation under the old doctrine of Mutual Assured Destruction (MAD).

In his famous address to the nation on March 23, 1983, President Ronald Reagan proposed superseding MAD with a defensive system. In his speech, Reagan decried "deterrence of aggression through the promise of retaliation" and asked rhetorically whether it might be "better to save lives than to avenge them? Are we not capable of demonstrating our peaceful intentions by applying all our abilities and our ingenuity to achieving a truly lasting stability?"

He then went on to outline a proposal to undertake the Strategic Defense Initiative and to build the space-based system to defend the United States from an ICBM attack.

"I know this is a formidable, technical task," Reagan acknowledged. "Yet, current technology has attained a level of sophistication where it's reasonable for us to begin this effort. It will take years, probably decades of effort on many fronts. There will be failures and setbacks, just as there will be successes and breakthroughs."

In his remarks, Reagan said, "I call upon the scientific community in our country, those who gave us nuclear weapons, to turn their great talents now to the cause of mankind and world peace, to give us the means of rendering these nuclear weapons impotent and obsolete."

With this, Reagan directed a comprehensive and intensive effort to define a long-term research-and-development program to begin to achieve the ultimate goal of eliminating the threat posed by strategic nuclear missiles. The Defense Department established the SDIO, a multiservice, joint activity that was initially under the command of Lieutenant General James Abrahamson of the U.S. Air Force. In September 1987, the president authorized the first phase of a Strategic Defense System that would begin to explore a variety of technical approaches to the SDI mission.

Whereas the pre-1975 programs such as Project Sentinel and Project Safeguard had relied on antiballistic missiles using nuclear weapons, the SDIO would focus on a wide variety of nonnuclear systems. These would range from lasers and particle beams to Kinetic Kill Vehicles (KKV) that destroy targets through the use of nonexplosive projectiles moving at very high speeds. Some of these projectiles incorporated homing sensors and onboard rockets to improve accuracy, while others would follow a preset trajectory, much like a shell launched from a gun or cannon. The projectiles could be launched from a rocket, a conventional gun or a rail gun.

The reaction to the SDI concept in the United States and elsewhere in the West found people grouped generally into three categories. There were those who embraced the concept, those who felt that it was technically impossible or too expensive to warrant trying, and those who did not want the United States to have the ability to defend against Soviet ICBMs.

Much of America's mass media, who generally fell in the middle category, lampooned the president, labelling the SDI as "Star Wars" and deriding it as a preposterous boondoggle.

The term was derived from the 1983 release of the George Lucas movie *The Return of the Jedi*, the third in his extremely popular Star Wars trilogy of science-fiction films. So renowned were these films and the phrase *Star Wars* that the media swiftly snatched it. The term implied that the Reagan administration intended to fight wars in outer space, which was incorrect. In fact, much of the hardware that would be tested by the SDIO was not even space based. For the media, however, the term was just too good not to use.

The critics also ignored the fact that the Soviet antiballistic missile system that had been in service since the 1970s was nuclear armed, and that the United States had no system at all since 1975. Also ignored would be that the systems developed by the SDIO after 1983 would not have relied on nuclear weapons, while the Soviet systems did.

The Soviet Union initially objected to the SDI even though development and testing of antiballistic missile systems were permitted. Their interpretation was that only fixed, land-based systems and their components were permitted. This restriction was not literally true, although back in 1972 when the treaty was written, all that had existed were fixed, land-based systems.

The Soviets would complain, but it would later be learned that the Soviet Union had space-based antisatellite systems in orbit since the early 1970s, and their Polyus Skif "battle star" was in the works before Reagan had called for SDI.

As outlined in October 1995 by President Reagan's National Security Adviser, Robert McFarlane, the SDI did not contravene the Antiballistic Missile Treaty. He said that the United States interpretation was that all development and testing was allowed, which was the letter of the treaty.

In order to be accommodating, the Reagan administration even went so far as to propose an "open laboratories" arrangement under which both sides would be furnished with information on the other's strategic defense research programs and visits to associated laboratories would be arranged. The Soviet Union declined. They wanted Polyus Skif to remain secret.

Ultimately, even though they were never operationally deployed, the weapons of the SDI were more significant than anyone could have imagined in 1983. Merely the scientific breakthroughs achieved by the SDIO presented such a technological challenge to the Soviet war machine that they are now credited with being among the most important weapons in winning the Cold War.

Indeed, they may well have been the ultimate secret weapons. When the Soviet leadership came to realize that the SDI was insurmountable, they chose simply to close down the Soviet Union rather than engage in a futile attempt to perpetuate the Cold War.

On the eve of the collapse of the Soviet Union, the SDIO was planning for an initial deployment of the system between 1994 and 2000, but these plans would be overtaken by other events. As the hammer and sickle came down from the Kremlin for the last time in 1991, it seemed to be time for the SDI to be placed on the dusty shelves of weapons system history.

However, the postscript was yet to be written.

In March 1990, a few months after the Berlin Wall came

down, Ambassador Henry Cooper, the chief United States negotiator at the Defense and Space Talks in Geneva, had suggested that a new ballistic missile threat existed in the world. Cooper predicted that soon intermediate range ballistic missiles would be in the hands of rogue nations and terrorist groups. He suggested that the SDI turn its attention to this threat. Many people basking in the glow of the end of the Cold War would call him an alarmist, but within a year, Saddam Hussein was lobbing Scud missiles into Israel and Saudi Arabia. Within a decade, North Korea's playboy potentate, Kim Jong Il, would be working on missiles with which he could strike portions of the United States.

In 1991, President George H. W. Bush ordered that the United States Department of Defense begin working on technology designed to achieve a worldwide defensive capability against attacks of limited scope. This new doctrine would be known as Global Protection Against Limited Strikes (GPALS). In 1993, the SDIO was officially redesignated as the Ballistic Missile Defense Organization (BMDO). Just as SDIO had picked up the technical thread that had been pursued in the 1960s and 1970s, so too did the BMDO use the work that had originated during the Cold War to develop technology to meet the challenges of the twenty-first century.

Nike

Since the advent of ballistic missiles of intermediate and intercontinental range, there has been an ongoing effort to develop an effective means of countering them. During World War II, air attacks on cities and industry had become commonplace. So, too, did efforts to counter these attacks through the use of antiaircraft artillery and interceptor aircraft. After the war, air defense remained a high priority as the Cold War gathered momentum. A similar defense against incoming missiles was a natural and seamless evolution from the doctrine of air defense.

The Douglas Aircraft Company of Southern California was among the first American firms tasked with constructing a missile to intercept and shoot down enemy aircraft, and the company would lead the way to creating a similar weapon to counter ICBMs.

In the late 1940s, Douglas began to work on what would become the Nike family of antiaircraft missiles. Meanwhile, the U.S. Army had contracted with Bell Telephone Laboratories of Western Electric (later Lucent Technologies) to develop the guidance system for an antiaircraft missile system to protect American cities from enemy bombers. Bell Labs, in turn, contracted with Douglas to produce the missile portion of the system. The result was the SAM-A-7 (later MIM-3) Nike Ajax, the world's first operational surface-to-air guided missile. These were built by Douglas at the Army Ordnance facility at Charlotte, North Carolina. The first Nike Ajax battery became operational near Washington, D.C., in December 1953. By the end of the decade, Nike sites were in place near every major metropolitan area in the United States. The U.S. Army had forty Nike battalions, each controlling four sites with between nine and twelve launchers each.

The successor to the Nike Ajax would be the SAM-N-25 (later MIM-14) Nike Hercules, which had a range of 87 miles and which began replacing the Ajax at existing sites in January 1958. The Nike sites in the United States would remain on alert until they were deactivated in February 1974.

With the Nike antiaircraft missiles widely deployed at the end of the 1950s, the idea of a similar system to intercept missiles came to the fore behind the closed doors at the Pentagon. The idea was to develop an exoatmospheric interceptor, a missile that could intercept another missile outside the Earth's atmosphere. This was defined as at least 60 miles above the Earth's surface.

Because of Nike's successful deployment, it was natural that the United States Department of Defense would consider Nike technology as the basis for an antiballistic missile. In 1958, the Department of Defense placed an initial order for the experimental XLIM-49 Nike Zeus, which had a range of 250 miles. First tested in December 1959, the Nike Zeus weapon successfully intercepted an Atlas ICBM in a test in 1960.

In 1961, the Kennedy administration canceled Nike Zeus for budgetary reasons, and ordered further research that would incorporate emerging technologies, such as phased array, electronically guided radar. This new program, which was known as Nike Experimental, or Nike X, was essentially a hardware research-and-evaluation program. During the Nike X program in the early 1960s, Nike Zeus missiles launched from Kwajalein succeeded in intercepting a number of ICBMs launched from Vandenberg AFB in California. In 1963, a Nike Zeus even intercepted a satellite in orbit.

While at least one Nike Zeus is said to have been on alert at Kwajalein for a possible interceptor mission against a Soviet warhead, it would not be until 1967 that the Department of Defense would be ready to seriously undertake deployment of a fully operational antiballistic missile system in the United States.

Project Sentinel

During the 1960s, as the United States was studying antiballistic missile technology, the Soviet Union was fielding ICBMs in greater numbers than might have been imagined. The People's Republic of China, too, was developing ICBMs that could be used to target the United States.

Against this gloomy backdrop, Nike X, and antiballistic missile systems in general, were rethought a number of times. This thinking flowed from the same premise that would dog the Strategic Defense Initiative a generation later. That is, that a 100 percent–effective antiballistic missile "shield" was theoretically impossible because of the sheer number of ICBMs and the high level of precision required in the interception of both missiles and Fractional Orbit Bombardment System (FOBS) warheads discussed in chapter 2. The technical problems were, of course, accompanied by the staggering price tag projected for the effort to reach as close as possible to the impossible goal of 100 percent reliability.

In 1967, the Johnson administration authorized Project Sentinel, an antiballistic missile program that would confront only the highest priorities—defined as those that were most easily accomplished and those which were too important to ignore.

The Soviet ICBM threat could not be dealt with totally, but the Chinese threat could be, so Sentinel envisioned a total-defense goal for Chinese ICBMs. That which could not be ignored would include a defense against attacks on major cities and United States ICBM fields, so guarding these and defending against Chinese missiles became the objectives of Project Sentinel.

The two missiles whose development would come into focus under Project Sentinel would be Spartan, a direct outgrowth of the Nike X studies, and Sprint, a high-acceleration missile developed by the Martin Marietta company.

System A (A35 or ABM-1)

The Soviet general staff reportedly first presented the idea of an antiballistic missile system to the Central Committee of the Soviet Union in 1953. After three years of preliminary design work, the Central Committee secretly authorized full-scale development of a prototype, designated simply as System A, in August 1956. Initially, the use of a high-explosive fragmentation warhead was envisioned, but nuclear-weapons tests conducted at Semipalatinsk in 1956 paved the way for a nuclear warhead for System A.

The overall design and development of the Soviet Union's first antiballistic missile system was under the direction of Grigory Vasilyevich Kusinko at the SKB30 design bureau. His team handled such specifics as missile command and control, as well as radar guidance. Kusinko also coordinated the design of the missile itself. Testing was done in the barren Betpak Dala desert, west of Lake Balkhash in what is now Kazakhstan. It took its name from

the nearest railway station, the lakeside village of Sary Shagan. Over the years, Sary Shagan would be well known to
Western intelligence services as one of the most secret and
most important of the top-secret Soviet weapons centers.

Kusinko's mandate at Sary Shagan was simple. His
team was to design, develop and test an antiballistic missile
that would be capable of intercepting and neutralizing the
United States Titan ICBMs that might threaten Moscow.

Initially, the prototype of the system was designated as
A35 by the Soviets. The United States Department of Defense and CIA would refer to the system as ABM-1. The
CIA would use this prefix to designate later Soviet systems
as they were discovered by the American agency. The first
operational missiles utilized within the system would be
those code-named Galosh by Western analysts. As
planned, the ABM-1 was to have consisted of eight launch
complexes in the Moscow area, each containing sixteen
launch sites. It is believed that only four of these complexes were actually completed.

The radar systems incorporated into the ABM-1 con-
sisted of two phased array systems and one fixed array.
They are perhaps best remembered by students of Cold
War culture for the colorful code names given to them by
NATO analysts. The two phased array systems were the
Dog House, which was a target-acquisition radar similar to
that used by the United States Safeguard system, while the
Cat House radar had a similar function, but was aimed toward China. The Hen House fixed array radar provided
early warning, but no weapons guidance capability. At
least one Hen House was located at Sary Shagan.

ABM-1 is said to have become operational in 1972,
three years ahead of the United States Safeguard antiballistic missile facility in North Dakota.

V1000 Griffon

The first antiballistic missile weapon tested by the Soviet
Union at Sary Shagan under System A (A35) was the
V1000, which would be code-named Griffon by NATO. It

was tested and placed into service ahead of the United States Nike Zeus, but its performance is not believed to have matched that of the American missile. The first V1000 test, which occurred in March 1961, involved intercepting an R-12 ballistic missile with a mock warhead. In this test, the Griffon was armed with a high-explosive warhead. The radar at Sary Shagan was reported to have locked onto the R-12 at a range of 900 miles.

By the time that the Griffon was first paraded in a Red Square display in Moscow in 1963, it was already being operationally deployed to a top-secret site known as RZ25. This antiballistic missile facility was located near Tallinn, the capital of Soviet-occupied Estonia. This site, located near the Baltic Sea, was on a line of trajectory from England, where the United States was then basing its SM-75 Thor ballistic missiles.

The interim Tallinn site was deactivated after a short time as the Soviet Union proceeded with the larger and more capable Galosh.

UR-96/A350 Galosh

The Soviet equivalent to the United States Nike Zeus antiballistic missile weapon was the UR-96/A350, given the NATO code name Galosh. First displayed in Moscow in 1964, it was paraded through Red Square in its launch container, so it was not actually seen. Though the Galosh would remain largely mysterious even after the end of the Cold War, it is known to have been a solid-fuel, exoatmospheric-interceptor rocket that was about 65 feet long as originally delivered, although later versions were closer to 70 feet in length. It had a range in excess of 200 miles and a nuclear warhead.

The Galosh was deployed within the ABM-1 system near Moscow, which consisted of four launch complexes constructed during the late 1960s. As noted above, this system had launchers to accommodate an estimated 64 Galosh antiballistic missile weapons.

During the 1970s, part of the Galosh arsenal is believed to

have been upgraded with a restartable liquid-fuel third stage for enhanced postlaunch retargeting. Some sources say that the Galosh had been retired by the early 1980s, while others state that Galosh test firings occurred as late as 1999.

ABM-2

The Soviet antiballistic missile system designated by United States analysts as ABM-2 was a complement to the contemporary ABM-1 system. While ABM-1 was constructed near Moscow to protect the Soviet capital, ABM-2 was to be situated farther north to defend against ICBMs coming over the North Pole. Unlike ABM-1 with its fixed launch complexes, ABM-2 was to have been road mobile.

One notable aspect of Soviet Cold War missile philosophy was a much greater use of mobile launchers for heavy missiles than was in the West. The Soviet Union deployed mobile ICBMs. The United States considered mobile Minutemen and mobile Peacekeeper, but deployed neither. Nor did the United States consider a mobile antiballistic missile system.

The mobile S225 intercept missiles of ABM-2 were centered near Murmansk, the big Soviet Arctic Ocean naval base on the Kola Peninsula, and at Riga, the capital of Soviet-occupied Latvia on the Baltic Sea. They were controlled and directed through radar and command-and-control facilities which NATO code-named Flat Twin and Pawn Shop. Work apparently began in 1965, and ABM-2 remained operational until 1978—five years after the Antiballistic Missile Treaty was signed. ABM-2 was supersecret at the time, but even after the end of the Cold War, few details have been made public.

Project Safeguard

Early in 1969, the incoming Nixon administration canceled Project Sentinel, but replaced it a few weeks later with a new antiballistic missile program called Project Safeguard. The new program would inherit, and eventually deploy, both the Spartan and Sprint missiles.

Officially undertaken in March 1969, Project Safeguard envisioned a dozen missile sites containing Spartans and/or Sprints. There was stiff congressional opposition to the proposal because of the cost, but the bill under which Project Safeguard would be initiated squeaked by in August 1969. The first two stages in the plan to build the Safeguard antiballistic missile system involved protecting United States Minuteman ICBM sites, the third was to construct a site that would defend Washington, D.C.

Protecting the ability to retaliate in the case of a Soviet first strike was seen as being of paramount importance. The Strategic Air Command Minuteman fields centered at Grand Forks AFB in North Dakota and Malmstrom AFB in Montana would be protected by the first two Safeguard installations. SAC missile fields surrounding Whiteman AFB in Missouri and Francis E. Warren AFB in Wyoming would be covered in round two. Only then would a Safeguard for Washington be incorporated into the program.

When the Antiballistic Missile Treaty between the United States and the Soviet Union was signed in 1972, only the Grand Forks and Malmstrom locations were under construction. The treaty permitted each side to keep a single antiballistic missile site. The Soviet Union chose to keep one protecting Moscow. Because the Grand Forks site was the nearest to completion at the time, the United States decided to finish it and mothball the Malmstrom Safeguard site.

The North Dakota facility was officially named for Lieutenant General Stanley R. Mickelson, who had commanded the U.S. Army Air Defense Command in the 1950s when the antiballistic missile concept was evolving. Designed by the Ralph Parsons Company, the complex consisted of six clusters of launch sites located 100 miles from Grand Forks near Nekoma in Cavalier County. Built by the Morrison-Knudsen construction firm, the thirty Spartan missile silos were completed by early 1973. In addition, seventy launch sites for Sprint missiles were also installed. Each silo was 9 feet square and 72 feet deep. Unlike ICBM silos, which were vertical, the Spartan silos were inclined toward the Soviet Union by 5 degrees.

The Mickelson Safeguard Complex achieved its initial operational capability in April 1975, with 28 Sprint and eight Spartan missiles in place. The full complement of 100 missiles was on alert by October. However, the United States Congress abruptly took the unexpected step of ordering the Ford administration to deactivate the site almost as soon as it became fully operational. All of the missiles and launch hardware were gone within a year and the site was officially closed. The U.S. Air Force would continue to operate some of the radar installations that had been built here.

Spartan

The XLIM-49A Spartan program evolved directly from the XLIM-49 Nike Zeus by way of the Nike X program, and it was originally known as Nike Zeus B. With the advent of the Sentinel program, it was renamed as Spartan. Genealogically, Spartan was a fourth-generation Nike.

As with Nike Zeus, Spartan was to be an exoatmospheric interceptor antiballistic missile. First test fired in 1968, the XLIM-49A was 48 feet 4 inches long, 4 feet longer than the Nike Zeus. The operational Spartan, LIM-49A was 55 feet 2 inches long, with its longest fins spanning nearly 10 feet. It weighed more than 14 tons, compared with 5.5 tons in the Nike Zeus. It had a top speed of Mach 4 and an operational altitude of 350 miles.

When Project Sentinel was superseded by Project Safeguard in 1969, Spartan became one of the cornerstones of the new program. The first successful interception of a dummy Minuteman reentry vehicle by a Kwajalein-based Spartan came in August of 1970.

Like the Nike Zeus, the Spartan was a remarkably accurate weapon. By the 1980s, however, what little that had leaked out regarding the Nike/Spartan program successes had been generally forgotten. Because Spartan was not common knowledge, the anti-SDI lobby was able to claim publicly that what Nike and Spartan had already accomplished was impossible.

Sprint

The Martin Marietta Sprint antiballistic missile complemented the Spartan. Whereas the Spartan was an exoatmospheric weapon, the Sprint was designed to operate within the atmosphere. Spartan was designed to knock down high-flying ICBMs at the midpoint of their trajectory and before the reentry vehicle carrying their nuclear weapons had reentered the Earth's atmosphere. The Sprint was described as a quick-shot, fast-reaction antiballistic missile. It was a last-minute weapon to be used to intercept submarine-launched missiles traveling in a shallow trajectory.

The first Sprint test launch occurred in 1965 at the U.S. Army facility at White Sands in New Mexico. In contrast to the silo-launched Spartan, the Sprint was designed for immediate surface launching and fast acceleration. It is said to have been capable of reaching speeds of ten times that of sound in a few seconds. It was also smaller than the Spartan, being just 27 feet long.

After a test series at White Sands, the program moved to Kwajalein at the end of 1970. Here, the first test against a Minuteman fired from Vandenberg AFB was successful. In May 1971, it successfully intercepted a Polaris SLBM that was launched from the USS *Observation Island*. More than forty tests were conducted from Kwajalein with only a handful being written off as failures.

Later in 1971, Martin Marietta received a contract to develop a more maneuverable Sprint II antiballistic missile. This project is still classified, but it is not believed to have reached the flight-test stage.

Like the Spartan, the Sprint became operational in 1975, but both were withdrawn from service before the end of the year for political reasons.

Despite their demonstrated speed and accuracy, neither the Sprint nor Spartan programs would be revived among the projects undertaken during the Strategic Defense Initiative (SDI) in the 1980s. The reason cited was that both systems used nuclear weapons to destroy incoming ICBMs. Under the SDI, conventional weapons would be used to intercept ICBMs.

Nevertheless, the total technical-knowledge base represented by these earlier systems was too good to ignore completely. Certain SDI projects, such as Homing Intercept Technology (HIT) and the Kinetic Kill Vehicle Integrated Technology Experiments (KITE), would adapt aspects of Sprint and/or Spartan technology for future conventional weapons.

A135 (ABM-3)

The successor to the Soviet A35 antiballistic missile system near Moscow was the A135 system, code-named ABM-3 by Western intelligence services. The new project was undertaken after the signing of the 1972 Antiballistic Missile Treaty and prior to the deactivation of the United States Safeguard complex in 1975.

The ABM-3 system would consist of five all-new launch complexes, plus a pair of converted ABM-1/Galosh complexes. Like the United States Safeguard paradigm, ABM-3 would consist of a mix of both exoatmospheric interceptor missiles and fast-reaction endoatmospheric missiles. There would be up to thirty-six 51T6 (SH-11) Gorgon exoatmospheric interceptors, which are analogous to the United States Spartan, and up to sixty-eight of the 53T6 (SH-8) Gazelle, which are like the American Sprint endoatmospheric interceptor. One major difference between Safeguard and ABM-3 would be in basing. In Safeguard, only the Spartan was silo launched. In ABM-3, both missile types were based in silos.

The system ABM-3 would be controlled through the Don-2NP radar system that Western analysts code-named Pill Box, and which supplemented the existing Dog House and Cat House systems. The existing Hen House sites, located as far afield as Sary Shagan and the Kamchatka Peninsula, would be augmented by phased array, early warning radar known as Pechora. ABM-3 is said to have been fully operational for the defense of Moscow by 1989.

After the end of the Cold War and the collapse of the Soviet Union, Russia maintained the ABM-3 and kept it in service. Though the system was apparently taken offline in 1997 for upgrades, Colonel General Vladimir Yakovlev, the commander of Russian Strategic Rocket Forces, commented that the "nuclear umbrella" over Moscow was in place. This fact probably accounts for Russian Premier Vladimir Putin's noticably muted, perfunctory response to President George W. Bush's December 2001 announcement that the United States was considering withdrawal from the Antiballistic Missile Treaty in order to shield itself from nuclear attacks by "rogue" states.

53T6 Gazelle

Given the NATO code name Gazelle, the nuclear-armed Soviet 53T6 endoatmospheric antiballistic missile interceptor was identified during the Cold War by the United States Department of Defense as SH-8. Analogous in function to the American Sprint interceptor, the Gazelle was a two-stage missile with a range of about 50 miles developed by the Toporkov design bureau.

Because it is silo based, its reaction time is thought to be considerably longer than the Sprint would have been. It made its first test flight in the early 1980s and was incorporated into the ABM-3 antiballistic missile system, where it remained on alert past the turn of the century.

51T6 Gorgon

First flown in the early 1980s, the 51T6 is an exoatmospheric antiballistic missile interceptor that complements the 53T6 in the Soviet antiballistic missile arsenal. It was code-named Gorgon by NATO and identified internally at the United States Department of Defense as SH-11. Created by the Grushin design bureau, it is a three-stage, liquid-fuel missile with a range of more than 200 miles. It is seen as a direct successor to the Galosh missile, although it is somewhat smaller. Part of the silo-based ABM-3 system defending Moscow, the nuclear-armed Gorgon remains on alert in the twenty-first century.

HiBEX Defender

A United States fast-reaction antiballistic missile similar to the Sprint missile, the High-G Boost Experiment (HiBEX) weapon is lesser known than the Sprint. Just 17 feet long, the HiBEX was built by Boeing for the DARPA Defender program. Designed to reach targets up to 20,000 feet within two seconds of launch, it was first test-launched at the U.S. Army's White Sands facility in February 1965. Though HiBEX never became operational, it is said to have provided data that were useful in the Sprint program.

Antisatellite Weapons

The early evolution of antiballistic missile systems is inextricably intertwined with much of the antisatellite technology that was unfolding at roughly the same time. Indeed, much of the antiballistic missile work done in the United States during the 1960s was geared toward countering the Soviet Fractional Orbital Bombardment System (FOBS), which was technically an orbital system. Parenthetically, both the Nike Zeus antiballistic missile and the Squanto Terror antisatellite system were operational at Kwajalein at the same time with generally simililar missions.

Both the United States and the Soviet Union invested a great deal of time and energy in antisatellite weapons. Originally, both sides imagined that the other was going to place nuclear weapons in orbit, and the idea was to develop systems to destroy these—using antisatellites with nuclear warheads.

In the minds of some, the "final frontier" could also now be seen as the "ultimate battlefield." Doomsayers could imagine galaxies of nuclear weapons drifting through space, ready to pounce on people on the Earth. It was written, for example, that the Soviet Union would be able to place nuclear weapons into geocentric orbit over the United States for the purpose of nuclear blackmail.

In fact, contrary to media myth implied by the term *Star Wars*, neither side truly wanted to invest in having to fight on an outer-space battlefield, and there were calls from both sides to ban weapons from this new theater.

The first series of nuclear tests in space conducted by the United States Department of Defense and Atomic Energy Commission (AEC) was Project Argus, which began with a detonation in August 1958. A follow-on to Argus was Project Fishbowl, which involved a series of tests in space during 1962. Within Fishbowl, the Bluegill Triple Prime detonation occurred in low Earth orbit on October 25, 1962, at the height of the Cuban Missile Crisis.

Meanwhile, between 1959 and 1962, a number of proposals were made to bar the use of outer space for military purposes. In September 1960, President Dwight Eisenhower proposed that the principles of the Antarctic Treaty be applied to outer space and that it be reserved for peaceful uses. The Soviet Union saw this as a bargaining chip to goad the United States into upsetting the balance of power on Earth, and the two sides wrangled for three years before the Soviet Union finally agreed to a ban on orbiting objects carrying nuclear weapons or placing them on the moon. A treaty to this effect was signed in Washington and Moscow in January 1967, and it entered into force on October 10 of that year.

The elimination of nuclear weapons from space did not, however, mark an end to studies of antisatellite weapons by either side. For example, between 1958 and 1962, the U.S. Air Force's Air Research and Development Command, the Defense Advanced Research Projects Agency (DARPA) and other agencies conducted numerous studies of both antisatellite weapons and defenses against them.

Bold Orion, High Virgo and Alpha Draco
In January 1984, in a tactical exercise that was generally well publicized within the aerospace community, a U.S.

Air Force F-15 interceptor aircraft first test-fired the Air Launched Miniature Vehicle (ALMV) antisatellite weapon into space. Hardly a secret weapon, the ALMV was a key element in the Air Force's program to provide the United States with an interim defensive system until the more technically exotic systems planned by the Strategic Defense Initiative Organization could be made available. A force of 100 ALMV-equipped F-15s was originally planned but the program was scaled back and eventually deleted from the Department of Defense budget in 1988.

While ALMV was no secret, few people realized that the notion of an antisatellite weapon being air launched from a high-flying U.S. Air Force aircraft had been studied and tested three decades earlier.

In 1957, the Strategic Air Command undertook the top-secret Weapons System 199A project, which evolved into three specific air-launched antisatellite weapons. These would be designated with a series of "199" designators. All were based on the Sperry MGM-29 Sergeant, an artillery missile then being produced for the U.S. Army. The weapons were test-fired from a B-47 Stratojet strategic bomber, but the intended launch platform would have been the B-58 Hustler supersonic bomber.

The 37-foot Martin WS-199B Bold Orion was test-fired a dozen times in 1958 and 1959. In the last such firing, in June 1959, the Bold Orion targeted the orbiting Explorer 4 satellite, coming within 4 miles of it at an altitude of 156 miles.

The 30-foot Lockheed WS-199C High Virgo was test-fired four times through September 1959, achieving speeds up to Mach 6. These flights included another attempted near miss of Explorer 4. The cause was found to be a failed communications link, and the High Virgo weapon was then grounded.

The 46-foot McDonnell WS-199D Alpha Draco was the subject of three tests in 1959, but little more is known. The whole top-secret Weapons System 199 program appears to have been terminated at the end of that year without evolving into an operational system.

SAINT

Between 1958 and 1962, the U.S. Air Force's Air Research and Development Command (ARDC), the Defense Advanced Research Projects Agency and other agencies conducted numerous studies of both antisatellite weapons and defenses against them.

In addition to WS-199, the Satellite Inspector for Space Defence is of special note. It was developed by the Air Force Ballistic Missile Division with the improbable acronym SAINT. Though it was canceled in December 1962, the technical ground that it covered made SAINT the grandfather of United States antisatellite systems for the foreseeable future.

Istrebitel Sputnik

The Soviet answer to SAINT was the Istrebitel Sputnik (interceptor spacecraft) program, which was undertaken in 1962. The idea was fairly simple and straightforward. Soviet guidance and tracking had not yet reached the "hitting a bullet with a bullet" level of precision that would be demanded of the American projects such as Squanto Terror, so the Soviets literally adopted a shotgun approach. A shotgun is used in hunting birds because birds are small and fast moving; hence, hard to hit with a bullet. A shotgun fires not a single bullet but a cloud of smaller projectiles, any of which can do the job. The Istrebitel Sputnik was designed to shower its target with a cloud of shrapnel, any fragment of which would be adequate to disable a fragile satellite or reentry vehicle.

The first experimental Istrebitel Sputnik, designated as Polyot, was launched toward the end of 1963 and was followed by a second Polyot test launch in the spring of 1964. The launch vehicle for the operational Istrebitel Sputniks was to be the Tsyklon 2 (Cyclone 2), a booster rocket based on the R-36 ICBM that was already being groomed for service with the dreaded Fractional Orbital Bombardment System (FOBS) discussed in chapter 2.

The Istrebitel Sputnik test program continued past the

end of the decade, with each launch covered by a Kosmos code name. The first successful live intercept of another spacecraft by a Polyot interceptor is said to have occurred in a test involving Kosmos 252 in November 1968. In a test in August 1970, an Istrebitel Sputnik is believed to have successfully destroyed a target spacecraft for the first time.

It is thought that a fully operational Istrebitel Sputnik system—involving a galaxy of killer spacecraft parked in orbit—was actually operational by 1979. Live practice firings continued into the 1980s, but are thought to have concluded with the Kosmos 1379 test in June 1983.

Even after the end of the Cold War, few details of the Istrebitel Sputnik program are known, although it has been suggested that it was phased out in anticipation of the much more ambitious Polyus Skif.

Squanto Terror (Program 437)

With its particularly fearsome code name, Squanto Terror was the test program for Air Force Program 437, which was the first practical antisatellite capability deployed operationally by the United States. The system involved Thor-launched spacecraft carrying a nuclear weapon that could knock out Soviet spacecraft by electromagnetic pulse.

AFP-437 was loosely based on SAINT technology and on nuclear tests that the United States Department of Defense had conducted under Project Argus and Project Fishbowl between 1958 and 1962. The Fishbowl detonation in July 1962 that was code-named Starfish had literally fried the electronics of several observer satellites with high-energy particles that were driven at high speed by the nuclear explosion. This was the catalyst for the idea of an antisatellite weapon that used radiation, rather than a direct hit.

General Bernard Schreiver of the Air Force Ballistic Missile Division proposed the idea and received approval from Secretary of Defense Robert McNamara before the end of the year to develop the concept. There was a great deal of urgency because of Soviet Premier Nikita Khrushchev's threats to orbit nuclear weapons under an ambiguous program now known to have been the R-36-O FOBS discussed in chapter 2. With this, AFP-437 was initiated and given the highest priority among Air Force development projects.

Beginning in February 1964, the Squanto Terror test firings involved antisatellite weapons launched by Thor boosters from Johnson Island in the Pacific to intercept missiles launched from Vandenberg AFB in California. The first tests went so well that the third interception, in April 1964, was conducted by personnel of the Air (later Aerospace) Defense Command's 10th Aerospace Defense Squadron, the same people who would have used the antisatellite operationally.

The tests were successful, with dummy warheads coming within a mile of their targets, and Squanto Terror became an operational system in June 1964. Two nuclear antisatellites went on alert at Johnson Island, ready for an actual launch against live Soviet targets. The reason that this location in the South Pacific was chosen was that the FOBS would have involved ICBMs launched south from the Soviet Union, traveling across the South Pole and approaching the United States from the south.

The existence of the United States antisatellite weapon was revealed by President Lyndon Johnson in September 1964 during his reelection campaign against hawkish Senator Barry Goldwater, either by accident or as a ploy to counter Goldwater's strong and popular anti-Soviet position. In any case, the President let slip no specific details about the weapon or where it was based.

In the meantime, the Air Force had developed a parallel to the basic AFP-437, which was designated as AFP-437AP for "Advanced Payload." The idea was to use the AFP-437 bus to carry a camera similar to that of the Corona photo-reconnaissance satellite program. The AFP-437AP could be launched on a moment's notice, whenever a quick picture was needed of a subject.

After the 1967 treaty banning nuclear weapons in

space, the 10th Aerospace Defense Squadron remained on alert for either AFP-437 or AFP-437AP launches, under the assumption they would not launch into space unless the Soviet Union put a nuclear weapon there first. In 1969, the nuclear warheads were put into storage at Johnson Island. The system was still operational, but no longer on high-alert status.

In 1972, after weather-related maintenance issues and after tropical storm Celeste had damaged the AFP-437 facilities on Johnson Island, the program was deactivated and its equipment shipped to the United States. It was not officially terminated, however, until 1975.

HIT, FLAGE and ERINT

The Homing Intercept Technology (HIT) program was an early project undertaken by the Strategic Defense Initiative Organization in 1983. The idea was to adapt the Spartan antiballistic missile as an interim exoatmosphere interceptor. Equipped with multiple, optically guided nonnuclear warheads, the proven technology of the Spartan system seemed a good choice, but the project was terminated after a number of tests due to the fear that the missile might run against the spirit of the SALT agreements.

The HIT project and its technology evolved into a number of successful, albeit little-known, research programs that would field test "hit-to-kill" Kinetic Kill Vehicles (KKV). These projects included the Maneuver Propulsion Assembly (MPA) and the Short Range Homing Intercept Technology (SRHIT) that was later known as the Flight-weight Agile Guided Experiment (FLAGE). In June 1986, a FLAGE test vehicle intercepted a target that was flying faster than 2,100 mph. Eleven months later, a FLAGE intercepted and destroyed a short-range, surface-to-surface MGM-52 Lance missile at 16,000 feet.

During the later 1980s, FLAGE technology was adapted for the Extended Range Intercept Technology (ERINT), which entered its flight-test stage in 1989. In November

1993 and February 1994 tests, ERINT scored a series of successive direct hits on targets up to 32,000 feet. ERINT technology was, in turn, incorporated into the PAC-3 (Patriot Advanced Capability) antimissile missile that became operational in the 1990s. A theater defensive system rather than a strategic system, the PAC-3 would have its baptism of fire during Gulf War II in 2003. Unfortunately, that baptism included deadly friendly-fire incidents. These were attributable to operator error rather than hardware failures.

Homing Overlay Experiment (HOE)

By the time of President Reagan's address to the nation on March 23, 1983, that initiated the Strategic Defense Initiative (SDI), the United States had not had an active missile-defense research effort for about a decade. In going back to pick up where Safeguard had left off, one of the first technical issues was the nature of the business end of any new defensive system.

Under the Safeguard era systems, a nuclear warhead would have been used in an effort to destroy everything within a given blast radius. As noted in the introduction to this chapter, the SDI paradigm would be to combine a conventional warhead with a better guidance system to "hit a bullet with a bullet."

One of the first of the new-generation systems to be tested was the Homing Overlay Experiment (HOE). Designed and built by the Lockheed Missiles & Space Company, HOE was a kinetic-energy weapon funded jointly by the Strategic Defense Initiative Organization (SDIO) and the U.S. Army's Ballistic Missile Defense Systems Command. It was designed to use a unique system of unfurlable fan blades to increase its ability to hit a target.

For test purposes, the HOE homing and killer module was attached as the upper stage of a Minuteman ICBM. It included long wavelength, infrared detection and homing techniques for in-flight guidance to the target. Prior to contact with the target, the interceptor would unfurl the "fan"—a metal, ribbed array structure with a diameter of about 13 feet. Because of the closure speed of the two objects, there was no need for an explosive device on the interceptor. Just the collision would be lethal to the target.

There were four tests of the HOE system, all launched from the Kwajalein missile range. In each, a Minuteman target missile was launched from Vandenberg AFB in California on a flight path which closely resembled the trajectory of an intercontinental ballistic missile. The course of the missile took it west over the Pacific. For reference, Kwajalein is in the Marshall Island chain, over 4,000 miles away from the launch site in California. While the unarmed ICBM was on its trajectory, the interceptor was launched, and it accelerated to a speed of more than 10,000 mph. When the radar at Kwajalein acquired the target, the interceptor was directed toward it and given final automatic control of the intercept.

The first three tests, between February and December 1983, involved successful launches but interceptor failures due to software and sensor glitches. On June 10, 1984, an HOE successfully intercepted a target ICBM. When the two missiles made contact at an altitude of about 90 miles above the Pacific, they had a combined closure speed of about 5.5 miles per second (almost 20,000 mph), and the force of the impact destroyed both missiles. Telemetry data showed that the intercept was nose to nose.

Of the test, U.S. Army Deputy Assistant Secretary Amoretta Hoeber said, "We tried to hit a bullet with a bullet and it worked."

The intercept of the ICBM by the HOE was quite significant for defense-system planners. It showed that the technology was available to kill offensive threats in the late boost through midcourse phases of a ballistic missile trajectory. The precision of the event was particularly impressive. The apparent success of the HOE won Lockheed the 1986 Strategic Defense Technical Achievement Award.

However, a 1993 report in the *New York Times* insinuated that the successful test nine years earlier had actually been faked in order to fool the Soviet Union, the United States Congress or both. It was said that the target missile was equipped with a transponder on which the HOE interceptor could have "homed." In fact, such gear is a standard safety precaution, and a device capable of homing on the transponder would have been too large for the HOE to have carried. The successful test was almost certainly not faked.

Exoatmospheric Reentry Vehicle Interceptor System (ERIS)

Using the technical knowledge base developed during the Homing Overlay Experiment, the Lockheed Missiles & Space Company undertook work on the Exoatmospheric Reentry Vehicle Interceptor System (ERIS), also developed for the U.S. Army as well as the SDIO. The ERIS system was similar to HOE, but it utilized more advanced technology and a much lighter kill vehicle. Like the High Endoatmospheric Defense Interceptor (HEDI), ERIS used a thrust vector system for altitude control during boost phase. The interstage at the forward end of the booster contained a separation motor to ensure the kill vehicle's separation. The guidance system utilized data from midcourse sensors to allow ERIS to hit its target.

Early testing began in 1989, and the first publicly acknowledged successful intercept of a dummy warhead by ERIS occurred in January 1991, as the Cold War was coming to a close.

Polyus Skif

Little or nothing was known publicly until recently about the Soviet Union's Polyus Skif "death star." Envisioned as the Soviet answer to the United States Strategic Defense Initiative (SDI), the Skif was one of the largest uncrewed payloads ever launched into outer space.

The Polyus science and research institute was created in 1962 by the Soviet government to develop laser technology for weapons. By the 1980s, the long-standing Soviet interest in antisatellite weapons was wed with laser-weapons technology. In the United States, the SDI was gearing up, and it became clear that lasers had the potential of becoming an ideal antisatellite weapon. Being relatively fragile machines, satellites could be destroyed—or at least disabled—by a high-intensity laser beam. The United States was working toward the notion of space-based antiballistic missile weapons, and the Soviet Union saw lasers as the weapon of choice for shooting down these orbiting battle stations. The press had called it Star Wars, and the Polyus Skif would place weapons on both sides.

The Skif was a product of the Salyut design bureau, which was developing the first Soviet space stations, and the Khrunichev design bureau, with whom Vladimir Chelomei had developed the Rakatoplan spaceplane in the 1960s. The designer for the Skif program was reportedly Yuri Kornilov.

Initiated as a project early in the 1980s, Skif was to be the ultimate orbital death star, with both offensive weapons and defensive weapons to defend itself against American anti-satellite weapons. It was a massive machine, larger even than the United States Skylab Space Station, the largest object yet placed into orbit. It was 122 feet long, with a diameter of 13 feet 5 inches. Skif reportedly weighed between 194,000 and 220,000 pounds although there are discrepancies between sources.

To camouflage it, the Skif was reportedly painted black to absorb radar and to make it all but invisible visually. Offensively, Skif was designed with both radar and optical target-acquisition systems. The latter would be important because radar could be detected and optical sighting cannot. The epitome of a secret weapon, the first prototype Skif was even designed to be tested with ground-based lasers so that radio transmissions would not be detected.

Between 1982 and 1985, Yuri Andropov ruled the Soviet Union for 15 months and was succeeded for 13 months by Konstantin Chernenko. Each man called publicly for the demilitarization of space, but each eagerly, albeit secretly, encouraged the development of the death star, anxiously desiring its capability in the Soviet arsenal.

When Mikhail Gorbachev came to power in March

1985, he authorized work to continue to the flight-test phase, but he is reported to have insisted that it not be tested with offensive weapons installed.

The giant Energia launch vehicle that was then in development to launch the Buran spaceplane was earmarked for use in launching the massive Skif. Because of the aerodynamic stress to which Skif would be subjected during launch, it was decided to orient the craft upside down, with its own internal engines on the top. This meant that once it was in outer space, it would have to be turned completely around in order to be fired into its operational orbit. This would be Skif's undoing.

The first launch of the Polyus Skif on May 15, 1987, was successful, but once in space, the complex maneuver required to upend it failed. It fell out of orbit and crashed into the Pacific Ocean.

It is believed that the United States was aware of the existence of the Skif project, but no public comment was made. There may even have been an effort to recover the vehicle from the ocean floor.

Those involved in the Skif program were reported to have lost their jobs, and the project is thought to have been terminated. The Polyus science and research institute survived the collapse of the Soviet Union and was still active in laser research after the turn of the century.

KITE and HEDI

During the 1980s, the Strategic Defense Initiative Organization undertook a range of Kinetic Kill Vehicle Integrated Technology Experiments (KITE). In general, the KITE vehicles were rail launched in the manner of the earlier Sprint antiballistic missiles.

The first KITE was launched in January 1990 to determine whether an infrared homing seeker could intercept ICBM warheads entering the atmosphere while surviving the heat of high closing velocities. The test experienced premature warhead separation, but the test objectives were listed as 95 percent accomplished. There were two known subsequent tests, a September 1991 launch failure and a successful flight in August 1992.

The McDonnell Douglas High Endoatmosphere Defense Interceptor (HEDI) missile was to have been the operational-weapons system that evolved from KITE. However, with the end of the Cold War, the Department of Defense chose to cancel the HEDI portion of the project.

Lightweight Exoatmospheric Projectile (LEAP)

While Kinetic Kill Vehicle (KKV) systems such as the High Endoatmosphere Defense Interceptor (HEDI) missile were designed for use within the atmosphere, the Lightweight Exoatmospheric Projectile (LEAP) program was designed to be based in space. It was developed primarily by Boeing Aerospace, the space-systems component located at Kent, about an hour south of Seattle. The primary subcontractor was the Hughes Missile Systems Group, located in southern California. The engines would be aquired from Utah-based Morton Thiokol.

Prior to the existence of LEAP, only liquid-fuel systems were believed small enough to fit in a lightweight weapon and at the same time remain accurate during rapid pulsing required to intercept and destroy a target. In November 1991, a thirteen-pound LEAP demonstrator vehicle was tested at the Thiokol facility at Elkton, Maryland. At a simulated altitude of 100,000 feet, it fired 4,000-degree gases from ten thrusters at a rate of fire of 200 times per second for 37 seconds.

In January 1992, LEAP program manager Richard Matlock announced that the system "now enables solid propellants to be used for applications where we are providing precise control for a projectile to maneuver to hit a target."

By now, the Cold War was over, and the interest had shifted from strategic defense to the new doctrine of Global Protection Against Limited Strikes (GPALS). Because of the successful LEAP tests, there were discussions of a LEAP-based theater-defense weapon, and the Navy's Lockheed Trident missile was suggested as a launch vehicle. It is interesting to note that the huge Trident had a 13-to-1 thrust-to-weight ratio, while LEAP demonstrated a 120-to-1 thrust-to-weight ratio.

Spektr, Elas and Octava

In June 1995, three-and-a-half years after the demise of the Soviet Union, the Spektr scientific module was launched into space and successfully docked with the formerly Soviet—now Russian—space station Mir. The fifth module to be incorporated into Mir, it carried such hardware as spectrometers and radiometers, as well as the Taurus-Grif gamma ray and x-ray detection system. Few people watching this well-publicized event realized that Spektr had been developed more than a decade before as a component in the Soviet mirror of the Strategic Defense Initiative.

The huge 20-ton Spektr was based on the "bus" of the earlier Salyut series space stations, and it was designed to carry systems for tracking and killing both ICBMs and United States satellites. The tracking hardware included the Buton radar and the Lira optical-tracker system. Offensive hardware included the still-mysterious Elas high-energy system, as well as the Oktava interceptor rockets. Oktava would have been capable of targeting and destroying multiple targets in orbit.

By 1992, however, technical problems had delayed the program, the offensive mission was terminated and Spektr was rebuilt as a "civilian scientific" platform. Ironically, it would be visited by several American astronauts who crewed Mir in the late twentieth century. With Mir, Spektr crashed into the Pacific Ocean in 2000.

Kinetic Energy Antisatellite (KE-ASAT)

When images of the Kinetic Energy Antisatellite (KE-ASAT) weapon were first released during the final years of the Cold War, we saw a piece of hardware that lived up to our expectations of what a "central casting" antisatellite weapon should look like. It had the size and appearance of a very large television picture tube, wrapped in coils of colored cables and spewing jets of what look like blue flame from apertures in its midsection. In fact, the blue jets were the control system that would maneuver the KE-ASAT in outer space. The main part of the KE-ASAT system was a Kinetic Kill Vehicle (KKV) that was all business, designed to strike and neutralize enemy reconnaisance satellites, as well as enemy antisatellite weapons.

The program is officially acknowledged to have been undertaken by the U.S. Army Space & Missile Defense Command (USASMDC) in 1989 as an effort to develop a low-cost, space-based KKV. In 1990, the program's demonstration and validation contract was awarded to the Rocketdyne Division of Rockwell International (a Boeing Company component since 1996) in Canoga Park, California. The idea behind the program was to use proven technology so as to keep costs down and development time short.

Operationally, the KE-ASATs would be based a specific launch site in the western United States or in the Pacific Ocean area and launched on the order of the president to take out the target satellite or satellites. For example, if a photo-reconnaissance satellite belonging to the Soviet Union or another opposing power was able to monitor United States forces in time of war, the KE-ASAT would be launched by a Minuteman-class booster to take care of it. The KE-ASAT would use a visible light–optical seeker to acquire and track its target.

As with many of the weapons under development by the Strategic Defense Initiative Organization, the KE-ASAT was in limbo at the end of the Cold War. However, during the 1990s, there would be a perceived increase in the potential threat of rogue nations developing systems that might endanger United States assets. In 1996, a follow-on development contract was awarded to Boeing to finalize development of the on-board processor and seeker, and to build and flight-test three KE-ASAT units.

The first successful KE-ASAT hover test was conducted

in August 1997 by USASMDC at the Air Force Systems Command's Phillips Laboratory at Edwards AFB. The 94-pound device is reported to have leaped into the air as its sensor acquired and locked onto a simulated moving target (a distant light source). It maintained a precise position while hovering in the air, demonstrating that it could maintain stability and exercise control and guidance, while simultaneously acquiring and tracking a target.

Rail Gun Systems

One of the most inventive of the ICBM interceptor concepts under development in the latter years of the Cold War and beyond were rail guns. Utilizing a system of electromagnets to launch projectiles, these guns would have very high muzzle velocities, thereby reducing the lead angle required to shoot down fast-moving objects. If the guns were fired in the atmosphere, this fast-muzzle velocity would flatten trajectories.

A hypervelocity rail gun works very much like a nuclear particle accelerator. A metal pellet (the projectile) is attracted down a guide (the rail) of magnetic fields and accelerated by the rapid on-off switching of the various fields. The hypersonic speeds attained by these small projectiles are dazzling.

Hypervelocity rail guns were, at least conceptually, seen as an attractive alternative for a space-based defense system. This is because of their envisioned ability to quickly "shoot" many projectiles at many targets. Unlike larger kinetic weapons such as missiles, the system would be cheaper to operate. As with a conventional gun, only a relatively inexpensive projectile is expended.

In the 1960s, the Soviet Union developed an experimental gun that could shoot streams of particles of heavy metals, such as tungsten or molybdenum, at speeds of nearly 15 miles per second in air and over 36 miles per second in a vacuum. In one experiment conducted by the Strategic Defense Initiative Organization (SDIO) during the 1980s, a small particle was accelerated to a velocity of more than 24 miles per second. (At that speed, the projectile could circle the Earth at the equator in something less than 20 minutes.)

The Compact High Energy Capacitor Module Advanced Technology Experiment (CHECMATE), managed by the SDIO, was prepared during the mid-1980s to conduct an extensive rail gun test program.

One of the major technical challenges faced in operating a rail gun system is the rapid firing of the gun. The challenge has to do with the rails. In order to rapidly accelerate the pellet, the rail must rapidly switch its magnetic fields on and off. This extremely fast switching requires a tremendous current of electricity (almost a half-million amps) to pass through the rails every time the gun is fired. In some experiments, the rails had to be replaced after each firing.

Another challenge with the rail gun is the acceleration of the projectile. At the speeds mentioned above, the acceleration stresses the pellet to pressures in excess of 100,000 times the normal force of gravity. In more popular terms, the acceleration of the pellet can be expressed in terms of 100,000 Gs. A "G" is the acceleration of an object which is acted upon by gravity. If we drop a rock from a bridge, for instance, that rock will pick up speed at the rate of 1 G. As a passenger of a modern jetliner, you are pushed into your seat at takeoff by 2 Gs of acceleration, and 6 to 9 Gs are felt by fighter pilots in top-performance aircraft. On the average, humans tend to black out at about 10 Gs.

Even with this limited view of G forces, it is easy to understand that the jolt of explosive acceleration in a rail gun could easily tear the projectile apart. In order to be effective, the "bullet" must be able to withstand the initial acceleration in order to get to the target.

A further issue was the desire to install a sensor or homing device in larger rail gun projectiles. Such a projectile would need to be hardened to keep its shape, and the electronics inside it would need to be able to function after being stressed by the initial acceleration.

As the Cold War ended, rail guns were still only a step away from this side of science fiction, but in the twenty-first century, they have the potential to become an integral part of the high-technology defensive arsenal.

MIRACL and Sealite

The process of light amplification by stimulated emission of radar, better known as laser technology, was first achieved in a laboratory in 1957, although it had been theorized by Albert Einstein four decades earlier. In the meantime, malevolent villains were wielding destructive "death rays" in the pulp science fiction of the 1930s. As practical lasers began to be developed for various applications in the 1960s and 1970s, it was only natural that those who dream of secret weapons would begin to dream of making death rays a reality.

Both the United States Strategic Defense Initiative (SDI) and the Soviet Khrunichev design bureau investigated various laser technologies with the notion of using a death ray to shoot down incoming ICBMs. A laser beam, which travels at the speed of light, would be 5,166 times faster from launch to target than the fastest rail gun projectile, and this was an important property.

Even before the SDI, however, Thompson Ramo Woolridge (TRW) and Hughes Aircraft had developed the Mid-Infrared Advanced Chemical Laser (MIRACL) as an experimental system funded by the United States Department of Defense. First demonstrated in 1980, MIRACL was the highest power laser ever built in the Western world. A deuterium fluoride chemical laser, it was the first megawatt-class, continuous-wave laser in the United States.

MIRACL was designed to operate like a rocket engine, with ethylene fuel burned with a nitrogen trifluoride oxidizer. In turn, deuterium and helium were injected into the exhaust. The deuterium would combine with fluorine to produce deuterium fluoride molecules, while the helium stabilized the reaction and controlled the temperature. The laser's output power can be varied over a wide range by altering the fuel flow rates. Wrapped around the exhaust gas, mirrors extract optical energy, which is focused into a 5-inch laser beam that could be directed to a target.

In the early 1980s, MIRACL was incorporated into the U.S. Navy Sealite program, which was designed to demonstrate whether a lethal laser could be adapted as a defense system for ships. The Sealite Beam Director—a prototype of a shipboard laser turret—consisted of a large gimbaled telescope with a 6-foot aperture and optics to be used to point the MIRACL beam onto a target. The 9-ton turret proved to be exceptionally nimble and able to rotate at high speed. Infrared sensors atop the Sealite turret would have been used to track the target. The telescope was capable of focusing the laser beam from a minimum range of 1,300 feet to infinity.

Sealite tests showed that MIRACL could successfully engage targets—including Northrop BQM-34 target drones as well as supersonic missiles—at significantly long range.

In 1983, with the advent of SDI, the Department of Defense terminated the Sealite program and moved MIRACL to the High Energy Laser Systems Test Facility (HELSTF) at the U.S. Army's White Sands Missile Range in New Mexico. In its new home, MIRACL became operational in September 1985, when the U.S. Air Force conducted the first Lethality & Target Hardening (LTH) program test for the Strategic Defense Initiative Organization.

As with other SDI programs, the MIRACL test program went into hibernation as the Cold War came to a close, only to be quietly revived a few years later. MIRACL reemerged as part of a new program known as Tactical High Energy Laser/Advanced Concept Technology Demonstrator (THEL/ACTD). In June 1996, under this program, MIRACL reportedly became the first laser to successfully shoot down a missile with a death ray.

This test, conducted at White Sands, involved TRW (part of Northrop Grumman after 2002) and the U.S. Army as well as Israel's Ministry of Defense. The latter was the catalyst for the test, as Israel was looking to develop a defense against the Katyusha surface-to-surface rockets that are frequently fired into Israeli territory from Lebanon and Syria. Similar tests involving MIRACL and Israel continued past the turn of the century.

In October 1997, MIRACL was used for the first time against an orbiting satellite in a test designed to examine the potential vulnerability of satellites to high-energy lasers.

Chemical Oxygen Iodine Laser (COIL)

From the American MIRACL to the Soviet Polyus Skif, lasers were seen by many as the "magic bullet" of ballistic missile defense. Though it was destined to be a twenty-first century weapon, another laser system is important to mention here because its technology evolved from SDI studies. The high-energy Chemical Oxygen Iodine Laser (COIL) was first envisioned by the SDIO during the Cold War as a laser weapon that could be based in an airplane. Known simply as the Airborne Laser (ABL), the operational COIL program was initiated by the U.S. Air Force in 1996.

A series of development contracts were issued to the industrial firms that would be known as Team ABL. This team would design an ABL demonstration system that was to perform a successful boost-phase shootdown of a theater ballistic missile a decade later. Within this team, TRW (part of Northrop Grumman after 2002) would build the COIL itself, while Boeing would provide overall program management and systems integration, and modify an aircraft to fly with the laser. Lockheed Martin would develop and produce the ABL target acquisition, as well as the beam-control and fire-control systems.

The COIL carrier aircraft, designated as YAL-1A, was based on a 747-400F transport and built by Boeing at Everett, Washington, near Seattle. It was flown to Boeing's factory at Wichita, Kansas, in January 2000 to be fitted with a controllable nose turret for directing the laser beam. With this installed, flight testing began in July 2002. Meanwhile, Northrop Grumman built and ground tested the

COIL in Southern California and delivered it to Edwards
AFB in February 2003 for installation in the YAL-1A aircraft. Now fully configured, the YAL-1A would serve as
the prototype for a family of weapons to defend against the
threat of rogue missile attacks in the twenty-first century.

Particle Beam Weapons

Like lasers, particle beams conjure up notions of early
twentieth-century pulp science fiction "death rays." As a
laser uses amplified light, a neutral particle beam could use
accelerated negative ions as a disruptive energy force.
These weapons differ from Kinetic Kill Vehicles (KKV) in
that they use energy beams rather than tangible projectiles.

By definition, particle beam weapons are systems that
rely on the technology of particle accelerators to emit beams
of charged or neutral subatomic particles that travel at nearly
the speed of light. Such a beam could theoretically destroy a
target by several means, including electronic disruption,
softening of metal and explosive destruction.

Much of the knowledge base involving neutral particle
beam weapons came from experiments conducted within
the Soviet Union, where scientists had been studying this
area of science since the 1960s. Indeed, their research lit-
erature included extensive discussions about their research
efforts that were conducted well before the American
Strategic Defense Initiative. Apparently they became aware
of the potential weapons applications of the research in the
early 1970s, when they suddenly stopped reporting on this
sensitive subject in international scientific journals.

After the Cold War, a conspiracy theory was in circulation stating that the loss of the submarine USS *Thresher* in
the Atlantic in 1963 was the result of Soviet hostile action
involving a neutral particle beam weapon.

The neutral particle beam weapons that were being envisioned in the 1980s would have been configured much
like the space-based lasers. A series of these weapons
could have been placed in an orbital network, where they

could have been capable of engaging ballistic missile boosters and post-boost rockets as their launch trajectories lifted them out of the atmosphere.

A particle beam weapon could disable a missile without actually destroying it. The beam of charged particles would not burn a hole in the skin of a missile as would a laser beam. Instead, the particle beam would easily pass through the skin of a vehicle and disrupt the electronic devices on board.

Neutral particle beams are theoretically effective at altitudes of about 90 miles. More importantly, neutral particle beams offer the promise of efficient boost-phase destructive force. SDI planners were interested in the fact that particle beam weapons have an unlimited stream of energy. Because of this (and the fact the beams penetrate through the target), these weapons do not need to dwell on targets as lasers do.

Particle beam technology could also provide the same destructive punch as lasers. Depending upon what sort of particles are used (there are many choices: electrons, protons or hydrogen atoms), the beam can strike a physical blow as well as an electronic impact. The physical force would be quite destructive because of the near-light-speed velocity of the beam. It could be that the particle beams of the future will have the capability of either physically destroying a target or disabling it by way of electronic disruption.

Particle beam weapons would use an accelerator to speed up a stream of negative ions to a velocity near the speed of light. As with the accelerators used for rail guns, these particles are driven down the length of the accelerator by using electromagnetic fields. The negative ions are drawn even faster by the speed of on-off switching of the electromagnetic fields. Near the end of the accelerator, a final series of magnets "point" the particle beam at the target. Prior to leaving the weapon, though, one final step is required: The ions are stripped of their negative charges. This is a key step in the process. If the negative charges are not taken away, the negative ions in the beam will repel one another, and the beam will become diffused. Furthermore, negative ions in the beam could be attracted to the Earth's magnetic field and, as a result, be deflected from their intended target.

Although designed as a weapons system, the space-based particle beam stations could also provide a sensor function for the defense system during the post-boost and midcourse phases of a missile trajectory. It appears that when an object is "hit" by a particle beam, it emits gamma rays and neutrons. The gamma rays and neutrons released seem to be in proportion to the size and mass of the object. With this in mind, these emissions could be used to discriminate between lightweight decoys and heavier reentry vehicles.

In the late 1980s, SDIO scientists developed and successfully tested the radio-frequency quadruple "preaccelerator," which accelerates a charged beam. This development is considered a major improvement in particle beam technology. Experiments also produced an ion beam with qualities superior to SDI design goals.

Meanwhile, scientists demonstrated a method for precision aiming of a neutral beam. Indeed, the technology had demonstrated such promise that the SDIO funded a dedicated particle beam test bed at the Brookhaven National Laboratory.

In the final years of the Cold War, the Neutral Particle Beam (NPB) Technology Integration experiment investigated the technologies needed to perform midcourse discrimination or to detect nuclear material. This experiment was conducted in space at low power levels and used nearby co-orbital instrumented targets.

After the end of the Cold War, neutral particle beams remained of interest within the defense establishments of both Russia and the United States. Such a weapon was one of a vast array of leading edge weapons systems that were examined in a lengthy study commissioned by the chief of staff of the U.S. Air Force. Entitled *2025*, it was designed to examine the concepts, capabilities and technologies the United States would need to remain the world's dominant air and space force in the year 2025. Published in 1996, this report concluded that neutral particle beams are more difficult to control and point than lasers and more difficult and expensive to place in orbit.

The report noted that a neutral particle beam is "most useful against high-flying airborne or spaceborne targets. At relatively low powers, the penetrating beam can enter platforms and payloads, producing considerable heat and uncontrollable ionization. Thus, the neutral particle beam is useful at the low end of the spectrum of force, producing circuit disruption without necessarily permanently damaging the target system. At higher powers, the neutral particle beam most easily damages and destroys sensitive electronics, although it is fully capable of melting solid metals and igniting fuel and explosives."

However, the report concluded that "Precision is excellent in theory, but questionable in use due to earth's magnetic field and countermeasures. Since the beam is strongly affected by passage through the atmosphere, ground- or sea-based targets probably could not be targeted. Finally, the reliability of such a complex, easily-affected weapon is moderate at best. The neutral particle beam weapon system does not appear to be practical in 2025."

Nevertheless, work would continue into the twenty-first century in an effort to address these issues.

Brilliant Pebbles

In the late 1980s, many specific kinetic energy, hit-to-kill projects being studied by the Strategic Defense Initiative Organization emerged from behind their veil of secrecy. One of the most promising was revealed to have been a system utilizing swarms of small, lightweight interceptor projectiles.

Code-named Brilliant Pebbles, this weapon envisioned about 4,600 small interceptors that would be deployed in orbit. Because there would have been so many, the Brilliant Pebbles "galaxy" would have been effectively invulnerable to any imaginable Soviet antisatellite weapon.

Each individual "Pebble," or weapons capsule, would carry a sensor and would have been capable of operating independently from other Pebbles or an external guidance or control system. It would be inert until activated, but when triggered by a human operator, each Pebble would be capable of tracking the infrared signature of a potential target at it most vulnerable boost phase, computing the trajectory, plotting an intercept course and destroying the incoming hostile warhead. Brilliant Pebbles was to have been supported by a system of fifty tracking sensor satellites developed under the appropriate code name Brilliant Eyes.

The Pebbles would have been relatively small, measuring about three feet on their longest dimension and weighing about 100 pounds. They were designed to orbit 288 miles above the Earth for a period of ten years. Because they were so small and not armed with nuclear weapons, their reentry into the Earth's atmosphere after their service life had expired would have presented no hazard.

The Lawrence Livermore National Laboratory was tasked with developing the Brilliant Pebbles concept. Ironically, one of the physicists on the project would be Edward Teller, the "father" of the United States hydrogen bomb.

By 1988, the development was far enough along that it was time to present a progress report to the top of the chain of command. During July and August 1988, Lawrence Livermore physicists, including Teller himself, briefed President Reagan personally.

In February 1990, the Strategic Defense Initiative Organization was ready to issue the contracts to actually start building Brilliant Pebbles. The prime contractor for Brilliant Pebbles was the Space Transportation Systems Division of Rockwell International (a component of the Boeing Company after 1996), then located at Downey in suburban Los Angeles. The second source contractor would have been the Martin Marietta campus in Denver, Colorado (now Lockheed Martin Strategic and Space Systems).

The program was seen as the technological breakthrough that had been hoped for since 1983, a reasonably low-cost missile defense system that could have been in place by the turn of the century. With an estimated price tag of $55.3 billion to develop and deploy, Brilliant Pebbles was actually inexpensive by comparison to the other programs then being considered.

Ball Aerospace was the principal contractor for early test flights of Brilliant Pebbles, providing design, integration and test support. The latter extended to a sensor payload for the Delta Star (Delta 183) test, which was launched in 1989 as part of a lengthy series of successful SDI experiments involving intercepts in space.

After these experiments, Martin Marietta and TRW were given pre–full-scale development contracts for Brilliant Pebbles and Brilliant Eyes in June 1991. They are recalled as having been the first SDI programs to officially make the transition from experimental projects to major defense-acquisition programs.

On the eve of the collapse of the Soviet Union, the Strategic Defense Initiative Organization was planning for an initial deployment of the Brilliant Pebbles system between 1994 and 1996, but this was put on ice with the end of the Cold War. Late in the decade, however, as the Ballistic Missile Defense Organization revisited national missile defense under the Global Protection Against Limited Strikes (GPALS) doctrine, Brilliant Pebbles was brought in from the cold. Brilliant Eyes was also revived, and at the turn of the century, it was under development by TRW (a part of Northrop Grumman after 2002) as the Space Based Infrared System (SBIRS).

Though it had not evolved as originally planned, nor was it likely to face the foe that was originally feared, Brilliant Pebbles was now destined to be one of those secret weapons developed during the Cold War that would find a useful and potentially vital application in the dangerous new world of the twenty-first century.

INDEX

About the Author

Bill Yenne is the San Francisco–based author of more than two dozen books on military, aviation and historical topics. He is also a member of the American Aviation Historical Society and the American Book Producers Association, as well as a graduate of the Stanford Professional Publishing Course. He is a regular contributor to the journal *World Air Power Review* and the U.S. correspondent for Britain's *Flightpath* magazine.

He is the author of *Secret Weapons of World War II*, a companion volume to this book. His other works include *Aces: True Stories of Victory and Valor in the Skies of World War II* and *SAC: A Primer of Strategic Air Power*. Of the latter, Major Michael Perini wrote in *Air Force Magazine*: "This book deserves a place on any airman's bookshelf and in the stacks of serious military libraries."

Jack Hilliard, curator of the U.S. Air Force Museum, has called Mr. Yenne's military weapons books "Not only visually attractive, but very useful in day to day museum work."

Mr. Yenne was also a contributor and aviation consultant to *The Simon & Schuster D-Day Encyclopedia*. He worked with the legendary U.S. Air Force commander, General Curtis E. LeMay, to produce *Superfortress: The B-29 and American Airpower in World War II*, which *Publishers Weekly* described as "An eloquent tribute."